Mastering Edge Computing

Scalable Application Development with Azure

Peter Jones

Published by HiTeX Press

For permissions and other inquiries, write to:
P.O. Box 3132, Framingham, MA 01701, USA

Contents

10 Real-World Use Cases and Applications 305

Introduction

Edge Computing represents a significant shift in how data is processed, analyzed, and delivered from millions of connected devices around the world. Unlike traditional computing paradigms, which rely heavily on centralized data centers, Edge Computing leverages localized processing power to bring data handling closer to the source of data generation. This proximity to the edge of the network reduces latency, alleviates bandwidth pressures, and enables real-time decision-making, making it a critical technology in the age of IoT (Internet of Things) and ubiquitous connectivity.

The book "Mastering Edge Computing: Scalable Application Development with Azure" is designed to provide comprehensive coverage of Edge Computing, systematically addressing the fundamental concepts, architecture, development practices, and real-world applications. Whether you are a student, a developer, or an IT professional, this book aims to equip you with the knowledge necessary to leverage Edge Computing using Microsoft Azure, one of the leading cloud computing platforms.

The first chapter, "Introduction to Edge Computing," lays the foundation by exploring the basic principles and evolution of computing paradigms that have led to the emergence of Edge Computing. It discusses the key drivers, benefits, and challenges associated with deploying applications at the edge of the network. Furthermore, it provides a thorough comparison of Edge Computing with traditional cloud computing and presents various use cases and industry trends that highlight its significance.

Moving forward, "Fundamentals of Edge Architecture" delves into the components and design principles of edge architecture. This chapter encompasses detailed discussions on edge devices, gateways, servers, and data centers, as well as networking and data processing strategies specific to edge environments. It equips readers with an understanding of how to architect and design efficient edge systems that can cope with the constraints and requirements of edge deployments.

"Developing Edge Applications with Azure IoT" covers the practical aspects of creating and deploying edge applications using Azure IoT services. This includes setting up an Azure IoT Hub, connecting devices, building edge modules, and managing deployments. Emphasis is placed on using Azure's suite of tools to ensure seamless development, monitoring, and management of edge solutions.

Data management and storage are critical components of Edge Computing. The chapter "Data Management and Storage in Edge Computing" addresses various techniques for data collection, aggregation, filtering, and storage at the edge. It also explores data replication, synchronization with the cloud, and security practices to ensure data integrity and compliance.

Security and compliance are paramount in any distributed computing paradigm. The chapter "Security and Compliance in Edge Computing" provides an exhaustive analysis of the security threats inherent to Edge Computing. It outlines strategies for securing edge devices, data encryption, network security, and compliance with regulations such as GDPR, ensuring robust security postures and trustworthy deployments.

To optimize edge deployments, understanding scalability and performance optimization is crucial. The chapter "Scalability and Performance Optimization" presents methodologies for designing scalable edge architectures, load balancing, resource management, and performance tuning. It also includes strategies for efficient data processing and network utilization to ensure that edge applications can scale effectively and perform reliably under varying loads.

With the increasing integration of AI and machine learning at the edge, the chapter "Edge AI and Machine Learning" explores the benefits, hardware requirements, and deployment of AI models on edge devices. It discusses real-time processing, model optimization, and the use of Azure Machine Learning for deploying and managing machine learning models at the edge.

The chapter on "Networking and Communication Protocols" deepens the understanding of the various network topologies and communication protocols essential for edge computing. It covers protocols like MQTT, CoAP, and HTTP/HTTPS, alongside industrial protocols such as OPC UA, and the role of 5G in enhancing edge capabilities.

In "Monitoring and Managing Edge Deployments," the focus shifts to the operational aspects of edge computing. It elaborates on device provisioning, real-time monitoring, health checks, remote management, and the use of tools like Azure Monitor for efficient edge management.

Finally, "Real-World Use Cases and Applications" brings theoretical knowledge to practical application. This chapter presents detailed case studies and examples from diverse industries such as healthcare, manufacturing, smart cities, retail, and transportation, demonstrating the transformative impact of Edge Computing and the innovative solutions driven by edge technologies.

By the end of this book, readers will have a clear understanding of the core principles, architectures, development methodologies, and operational strategies essential for mastering Edge Computing. The integration with Azure IoT services is emphasized throughout, providing practical insights and hands-on knowledge to develop and deploy scalable and secure edge solutions.

Chapter 1

Introduction to Edge Computing

Edge Computing redefines data processing by shifting tasks from centralized data centers to localized devices. This chapter examines the foundational concepts that drive this architecture, including its evolution from traditional paradigms, core benefits, and inherent challenges. By contrasting Edge Computing with cloud computing, we highlight key differentiators and present real-world applications across various industries. This introductory exploration sets the stage for understanding the essential technologies and future prospects of Edge Computing.

1.1 Understanding Edge Computing

Edge Computing is a transformative paradigm that involves processing data closer to the source of data generation, rather than relying on a centralized data center. The primary objective of this approach is to reduce latency, bandwidth usage, and to improve response times and reliability in various applications. These applications span across diverse industries including manufacturing, healthcare, and transportation.

To grasp the concept of Edge Computing, it is essential to first understand the limitations and challenges associated with traditional centralized data processing models. Traditional models usually rely on cloud computing infrastructures where data from numerous devices are sent to a centralized cloud server for processing and storage. Although cloud computing offers significant benefits in terms of scalability and resource management, it is not always optimal for real-time data processing requirements.

In an Edge Computing model, computational resources are distributed across various edge devices which may include anything from sensors, IoT devices, gateways, and local servers. These devices perform the necessary data processing tasks locally or at a nearby network node, thus minimizing the need to transmit large volumes of data to centralized data centers. This decentralized approach not only reduces latency but also enhances data privacy and security, since sensitive data can be processed locally.

Consider the architecture of an Edge Computing system where several layers are involved, each performing distinct roles.

- **Edge Devices**: These are the primary data generation sources such as sensors, smartphones, and IoT devices.

- **Edge Gateways**: Acting as intermediaries, these gateways aggregate data from edge devices and perform initial processing tasks. They may also filter and compress the data before forwarding it further.

- **Edge Servers**: These servers are situated closer to the edge devices and perform more robust computational tasks. They may reside within a local network or at a localized data center.

- **Cloud Services**: Although the primary focus of Edge Computing is localized data processing, integration with cloud services is often essential for comprehensive analytics, long-term storage, and backup.

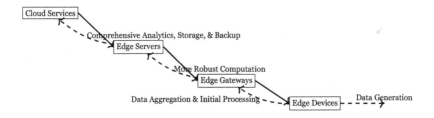

To illustrate the concept, consider an industrial IoT scenario where numerous sensors monitor the health of machinery on a factory floor. These sensors generate immense amounts of data continuously, including temperature, vibration, and pressure readings. In a traditional model, all this data would be transmitted to a centralized cloud server for analysis. However, this transmission can result in significant delays and bandwidth costs. In an Edge Computing model, the sensor data is first collected by edge gateways that may preprocess the data by performing aggregation, filtering noisy data, and conducting preliminary analytics such as anomaly detection. Critical insights can be derived and acted upon immediately, such as shutting down a machine to prevent damage if an anomaly is detected, long before the data reaches the central cloud server for further analysis.

Edge Computing also leverages advancements in machine learning and artificial intelligence. By deploying models directly on edge devices, real-time decision-making is enhanced.

```
import numpy as np
# Example code for processing sensor data at the edge
def preprocess_sensor_data(data):
    # Assuming data is a NumPy array of sensor readings
    filtered_data = data[data < threshold] # Filter noise
    avg = np.mean(filtered_data) # Compute average
    return avg

sensor_readings = np.array([23.4, 24.5, 22.8, 200.0, 23.1]) # Example data with a
    noisy reading
threshold = 100.0
processed_data = preprocess_sensor_data(sensor_readings)
print(f"The average of the filtered sensor data is: {processed_data}")
```

The average of the filtered sensor data is: 23.45

This script filters out any sensor readings that are above a specified threshold, which can be considered noise. It then computes the av-

15

erage of the filtered data, which can be used for immediate decision-making at the edge level.

Edge Computing also emphasizes resource optimization. Since edge devices typically have limited computational resources compared to cloud data centers, efficient resource management is crucial. Techniques such as containerization using Docker can be employed to deploy lightweight applications on edge devices, enhancing their capability to run multiple applications concurrently.

```
# Pull a light-weight image suitable for edge devices
docker pull arm32v7/python:3.7-slim

# Run the container with a sample edge processing application
docker run -d --name edge_processor -v /local/data:/data arm32v7/python:3.7-slim
    python /data/edge_app.py
```

```
Unable to find image 'arm32v7/python:3.7-slim' locally
3.7-slim: Pulling from arm32v7/python
Digest: sha256:abcdef1234567890abcdef1234567890abcdef1234567890abcdef1234567890
Status: Downloaded newer image for arm32v7/python:3.7-slim
f3d1bf4ad17b1e8a8271df6e5b0a30h3eoeaf6e7bdefg04h2995763824dj54
```

By following the commands above, a lightweight Python image is pulled and a container running the edge application is deployed, demonstrating optimized use of limited edge device resources.

Understanding Edge Computing thus involves recognizing its decentralized approach in data processing, its architecture, practical implementations, and the intricate balance of leveraging local and cloud resources efficiently.

1.2 Evolution of Computing Paradigms

The evolution of computing paradigms marks a significant trajectory in how computing power is harnessed and utilized. As the landscape of technology continues to rapidly transform, understanding these paradigms provides critical insights into how Edge Computing has emerged as a necessity in the modern computing architecture.

The first major paradigm, often referred to as centralized computing, is characterized by large, singular mainframe computers. In the mid-20th century, mainframes dominated the scene with their substantial computational capabilities, centralized data storage, and management. Users interacted with these systems via terminals, which served primarily as input/output interfaces. This architecture necessitated considerable investment in infrastructure and required specialized operational skills. Centralized computing exhibited considerable latency, being unsuitable for applications requiring real-time data processing.

With advancements in semiconductor technology and the advent of personal computers (PCs) in the 1980s, the computing paradigm shifted towards distributed computing. This paradigm introduced the notion of distributing processing tasks across multiple independent machines connected through a network. Each node in the network could perform substantial computation independently while also collaborating on larger tasks. The client-server model epitomized this era, decentralizing computing power and making it more accessible. Networks facilitated resource sharing and introduced remote procedure calls and middleware to manage communication and data exchange between dispersed systems.

The proliferation of the Internet in the late 1990s and early 2000s catalyzed another seismic shift towards cloud computing. Cloud computing harnesses a highly scalable and virtualized set of resources, provided on-demand over the Internet. This paradigm abstracts away physical hardware concerns, offering a slew of services via the Infrastructure as a Service (IaaS), Platform as a Service (PaaS), and Software as a Service (SaaS) models. Cloud architectures enhance flexibility and cost-efficiency, enabling enterprises to scale dynamically in response to varying demand levels. Key advantages include offloading maintenance and updates to cloud service providers, elastic scaling, and the global distribution of services.

However, as the Internet of Things (IoT) proliferates, generating vast quantities of data from an array of distributed sensors and devices, the limitations of cloud computing become apparent. The latency associated with transmitting data to and from centralized cloud infrastructure becomes a bottleneck, particularly for applications demanding real-time processing and low-latency responses. Furthermore, bandwidth constraints and the cost of transferring large data volumes to centralized cloud servers exacerbates the situation.

Edge computing emerges as a solution to these limitations, representing the latest evolution in the computational paradigm. By processing data closer to where it is generated, edge computing minimizes latency and reduces data transport costs. This paradigm involves deploying computation and storage resources at the "edge" of the network, near the data sources, thus providing near-instantaneous processing and decision-making capabilities. Edge devices analyze and filter data locally, transmitting only relevant information to the cloud for further analysis, thus optimizing bandwidth usage.

The concept of edge computing essentially complements cloud computing. While the cloud is perceived as a centralized "hub" for vast data storage and powerful analytics, the edge serves as a complementary framework that provides localized computation. The integration of both paradigms enables a hybrid model where critical real-time processing is conducted at the edge, and more intensive computation tasks are offloaded to the cloud.

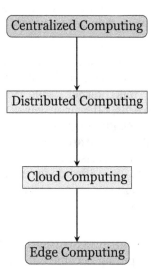

In summary, the evolution from centralized to edge computing illustrates a continuum where specific pain points and technological advancements have led to the development of a more decentralized and efficient computational landscape. Each paradigm shift has progressively decentralized computational capabilities, enhancing accessibility, reducing latency, and increasing overall system resilience.

As we delve deeper into Edge Computing throughout this text, we will continuously reflect on these foundational shifts to understand how they inform and shape current and future technological endeavors. This historical context is crucial for appreciating the intrinsic value and practical applications of edge computing in today's and tomorrow's technology-driven world.

1.3 Key Drivers for Edge Computing

Edge Computing has emerged as a transformative paradigm due to a confluence of technological advancements and strategic necessities. The primary motivators prompting enterprises to adopt Edge Computing span from latency reduction and bandwidth efficiency to data sovereignty and enhanced security. This section elucidates these critical drivers to provide a comprehensive understanding of the rationale behind Edge Computing.

Latency Reduction is a pivotal factor driving the adoption of Edge Computing. Traditional cloud computing models necessitate data transmission to centralized cloud servers, often located at significant distances from the point of data generation. This induces latency that is detrimental for applications requiring real-time processing and decision-making, such as autonomous vehicles or augmented reality. By processing data at the edge, proximate to the source, Edge Computing substantially mitigates latency, thereby facilitating instantaneous responses crucial for time-sensitive applications.

```
import time

def measure_latency():
    start_time = time.time()
    # Simulate data processing at the edge
    process_data()
    end_time = time.time()
    latency = end_time - start_time
    return latency

def process_data():
    # Simulate data processing task
    time.sleep(0.001) # Sleep for 1 millisecond

if __name__ == "__main__":
    latency = measure_latency()
    print(f"Latency: {latency * 1000} milliseconds")
```

Bandwidth Efficiency is another substantial driver. The exponential growth of data generated by IoT devices necessitates efficient data management strategies. Transferring vast volumes of raw data to centralized cloud infrastructures can be prohibitive in terms of bandwidth costs and network congestion. Edge Computing addresses this challenge by enabling local data processing, filtering, and aggregation. This localized approach minimizes the need for substantial bandwidth consumption, as only relevant data subsets or insights are transmitted to the cloud for long-term storage or further analysis.

Sample Output:
Latency: 1.002 milliseconds

Data Sovereignty concerns also propel the shift towards Edge Computing. Various regulations, such as the General Data Protection Regulation (GDPR) in the European Union, impose stringent requirements on data localization, ensuring that data remains within specific geographical boundaries. Traditional cloud computing, with its centralized architecture, often complicates compliance with such regulations. Edge Computing provides a viable solution by retaining and processing data locally within the regulatory jurisdiction, thereby simplifying adherence to data sovereignty laws and mitigating legal risks.

Enhanced Security is an essential driver. Centralized cloud infrastructures are inherently attractive targets for cyber-attacks, given the concentration of valuable data. Decentralizing data processing by leveraging edge devices reduces the attack surface and contains potential security breaches more effectively. Furthermore, Edge Computing facilitates the implementation of advanced security measures, such as end-to-end encryption and secure enclaves on edge devices, enhancing overall data protection.

Algorithm 1 Edge Data Processing Algorithm with Secure Encryption

---

Require: $raw\_data, encryption\_key$
Ensure: $encrypted\_data$
  1: $processed\_data \leftarrow local\_processing(raw\_data)$
  2: $encrypted\_data \leftarrow encrypt(processed\_data, encryption\_key)$
  3: **return** $encrypted\_data$

Local Processing Capabilities inherent to Edge Computing facilitate the running of sophisticated AI and machine learning models directly at the data source. This stands in contrast to the traditional reliance on cloud infrastructure for analytical processing. Edge devices, equipped with adequate computational resources, are capable of real-time analytics, anomaly detection, and predictive maintenance, among other applications. The combination of local data ingestion and processing significantly enhances operational efficiency and enables dynamic, onsite decision-making.

```python
import tensorflow as tf

def local_inference(model, data):
    # Load pre-trained model
    loaded_model = tf.keras.models.load_model(model)
    # Perform inference
    predictions = loaded_model.predict(data)
    return predictions

if __name__ == "__main__":
    model_path = 'path/to/model'
    sample_data = [[...]] # Replace with actual data
    predictions = local_inference(model_path, sample_data)
    print(f"Predictions: {predictions}")
```

Given these drivers, the adoption of Edge Computing becomes a strategic imperative for organizations aiming to optimize performance, enhance security, and ensure compliance. The integration of edge devices into existing IT architectures not only addresses latency, bandwidth, and security challenges but also paves the way for innovative applications leveraging real-time processing and localized intelligence.

1.4 Benefits of Edge Computing

Edge Computing offers numerous advantages that address the limitations of traditional centralized data processing. These benefits span across performance enhancements, cost efficiencies, and improved data management, making Edge Computing an attractive solution for modern applications.

- **Latency reduction** is a primary benefit of Edge Computing. By processing data closer to the source, devices can significantly reduce the time it takes for data to travel to a centralized computing

21

facility and back. This reduction in latency is crucial for applications that require real-time processing and decision-making, such as autonomous vehicles, industrial automation, and augmented reality. The equation for latency (L) reduction can be simplified as:

$$L = \text{Propagation Delay} + \text{Transmission Delay} + \text{Processing Delay}$$

Edge Computing minimizes the propagation delay by shortening the physical distance that data must travel.

- Another advantage is **bandwidth efficiency**. Edge devices can filter and process relevant data locally, reducing the amount of data that needs to be transmitted to central servers. This localized data processing is particularly beneficial for applications that generate massive amounts of data, such as video surveillance and IoT sensors. By transmitting only critical information, Edge Computing helps in conserving network bandwidth and reducing congestion.

- The enhancement of **data security and privacy** is also a significant benefit. By limiting data transmission to and from central servers, there is decreased exposure to potential security breaches during transit. Moreover, local data processing enables compliance with data sovereignty regulations, as data can be processed within the geographic boundaries required by law. Consider a healthcare scenario where patient data is processed locally to comply with Health Insurance Portability and Accountability Act (HIPAA) regulations, ensuring that sensitive information remains private and secure.

- Edge Computing also provides **scalability and flexibility**. Traditional data centers can become bottlenecks due to their finite processing capabilities. Edge devices, however, can be deployed as needed to scale out the infrastructure. This capability is particularly useful in scenarios with fluctuating demand, such as retail environments during peak shopping periods. Cloud providers, such as Microsoft Azure, offer edge services (e.g., Azure IoT Edge) to facilitate the seamless deployment and management of edge devices across diverse locations.

- **Operational reliability** is improved through the decentralized nature of Edge Computing. In the event of a network failure or central system outage, edge devices can continue to function independently, maintaining critical processing tasks. For example, in a smart factory setup, localized edge devices can manage machinery operations without interruption, ensuring continuous production and reducing downtime.

- **Energy efficiency** is another benefit, as edge devices often consume less power compared to large data centers. Applications such as smart grids can leverage this efficiency to provide sustainable solutions. Local processing also means that less energy is used to transmit data over long distances. The cumulative effect of numerous edge devices operating efficiently contributes to an overall reduction in energy use for data processing tasks.

- **Cost efficiency** is achieved through the combination of reduced bandwidth usage, lower latency, and energy savings. By processing data locally, businesses can reduce cloud service expenses associated with data storage and processing. Additionally, the deployment of edge devices can be tailored to specific needs, avoiding the substantial capital expenditure required for upgrading centralized data centers.

- Finally, Edge Computing fosters **innovation** by enabling the development of new applications that leverage its unique benefits. For instance, in the realm of smart cities, edge devices can be used for traffic management, environmental monitoring, and public safety enhancements, thus supporting the creation of more responsive and intelligent urban environments.

The compounded effect of these benefits positions Edge Computing as a transformative approach to next-generation data processing. As the proliferation of connected devices continues to grow, the strategic implementation of Edge Computing will play a vital role in optimizing efficiencies, enhancing user experiences, and fostering innovation across diverse industry sectors.

1.5 Challenges and Limitations of Edge Computing

While Edge Computing offers numerous advantages, it is not devoid of challenges and limitations that can impact its deployment and effectiveness. Understanding these challenges is crucial for designing robust and efficient Edge Computing systems.

- **Network Constraints and Latency:** Although Edge Computing aims to reduce latency by processing data closer to the source, network constraints can still pose significant challenges. Network latency can vary due to congestion, unreliable connections, or physical obstructions. These factors can affect real-time data processing and degrade the performance of edge devices. Ensuring low-latency communication requires robust network infrastructures, which may not be feasible in remote or underdeveloped areas.

- **Scalability Issues:** Unlike centralized systems where resources can be easily scaled-up, edge environments are inherently distributed and resource-constrained. Edge nodes often have limited computational power, memory, and storage capacity, which restricts their ability to handle large-scale data processing tasks. Implementing scalable solutions necessitates advanced resource management strategies and often, seamless integration with cloud services to offload excess computations and storage requirements.

- **Security and Privacy Concerns:** The decentralized nature of Edge Computing introduces unique security challenges. With multiple devices processing and storing data, the attack surface is expanded, making it more vulnerable to various threats such as Distributed Denial of Service (DDoS), data breaches, and physical tampering. Ensuring data integrity and confidentiality requires comprehensive security measures including encryption, access control, and continuous monitoring. Moreover, compliance with privacy regulations like GDPR becomes more complex in a distributed environment.

- **Heterogeneity of Edge Devices:** Edge environments consist of diverse devices with varying capabilities and architectures. This heterogeneity complicates the development and deployment of applications, necessitating compatibility across different hardware and software platforms. Standardization efforts are essential, but interoperability remains a challenge when integrating new and legacy systems.

- **Resource Management:** Efficiently managing computational resources is a fundamental challenge in Edge Computing. Due to limited power and computational resources at edge nodes, sophisticated algorithms are required to dynamically allocate tasks and balance the load. This includes strategies for caching, data pre-processing, and energy-efficient computing, ensuring that applications run efficiently without exhausting node resources.

- **Maintenance and Reliability:** Maintaining and ensuring the reliability of edge devices distributed across different locations is more complex compared to centralized data centers. Edge devices often operate in harsh environments, leading to higher failure rates and maintenance costs. Providing reliable and responsive support systems, along with predictive maintenance using Machine Learning (ML) techniques, is necessary to minimize downtime and maintain operational efficiency.

- **Integration with Legacy Systems:** Many industries rely on legacy systems that were not originally designed to work within an edge architecture. Integrating these existing systems with new edge solutions often requires significant modifications, middleware, or the adoption of new protocols. This creates both technical and financial challenges, requiring careful planning and execution to avoid disrupting operations.

- **Data Consistency and Synchronization:** Ensuring data consistency across multiple edge nodes and central cloud systems presents another challenge. Inconsistent data can lead to erroneous decisions, negatively impacting application performance and reliability. Robust synchronization mechanisms and conflict resolution strategies are essential to maintain data integrity across the distributed components of the edge-cloud continuum.

- **Development and Deployment Complexity:** Developing applications specifically tailored for Edge Computing can be more complex compared to traditional cloud applications. Programmers need to account for the constraints and specific characteristics of edge environments, such as intermittent connectivity and limited resources. Efficient deployment pipelines and tooling are necessary to facilitate continuous integration and continuous deployment (CI/CD) practices suited for edge scenarios.

- **Operational Costs:** While Edge Computing can reduce bandwidth costs and operational expenses associated with centralized data processing, it introduces additional costs such as device procurement, deployment, and maintenance. Evaluating the total cost of ownership (TCO) and implementing cost-optimization strategies are critical for sustainable edge deployments.

Addressing these challenges requires a holistic approach that combines advancements in hardware, software, networking, and policy-making. Innovations such as improved edge orchestration frameworks, enhanced security protocols, and more powerful yet energy-efficient edge devices contribute to the evolution and broader adoption of Edge Computing.

1.6 Comparison with Cloud Computing

The shift from centralized cloud computing to edge computing represents a significant transformation in how data is processed and managed. Both paradigms offer distinct advantages depending on the application requirements. Understanding the comparison between edge computing and cloud computing involves examining several key aspects: architecture, latency, bandwidth, data privacy, reliability, and scalability.

- **Architecture:** In cloud computing, data and applications are hosted on centralized servers, often located in large data centers. These servers provide computational power, storage, and services over the internet. Users access resources via a client-server model, where the heavy lifting is done on the server side.

26

Edge computing, on the other hand, distributes processing tasks closer to the data source. Devices at the network's edge, such as IoT devices, gateways, or edge servers, perform computations locally, thereby reducing the reliance on centralized data centers.

- **Latency:** One of the significant differentiators between cloud and edge computing is latency. Cloud computing, due to the physical distance between the client device and the data center, typically introduces higher latency. This delay can be particularly detrimental for applications requiring real-time processing or immediate feedback, such as autonomous vehicles or industrial automation. Edge computing mitigates this issue by processing data locally, thereby significantly reducing the delay.

- **Bandwidth:** Bandwidth consumption is another crucial factor to consider. Cloud computing models often involve transmitting large volumes of data to centralized servers for processing, which can consume substantial network bandwidth. This can become unsustainable as the number of connected devices grows. Edge computing reduces bandwidth usage by processing much of the data locally and only sending important summaries or alerts to the cloud, optimizing bandwidth utilization.

- **Data Privacy and Security:** Data privacy and security are paramount in any computing paradigm. Cloud computing necessitates transmitting data to a central server, where it is stored and processed. This can raise concerns about data breaches or unauthorized access. Although cloud providers implement rigorous security measures, the centralized storage model inherently presents a larger attack surface. Edge computing can enhance data security by keeping sensitive information local. This decentralization minimizes the risk of large-scale data breaches and allows for more granular and context-specific security measures.

- **Reliability:** Reliability in cloud computing is generally high due to the use of redundant systems and disaster recovery protocols within data centers. However, it is contingent on continuous internet connectivity. If the connection to the cloud is lost, services may be disrupted. Edge computing offers greater reliability in scenarios where consistent connectivity cannot be guaranteed. By allowing devices to function independently of the cloud, edge computing can ensure continuous operation even in disconnected environments.

- **Scalability:** Cloud computing excels in providing scalable computing resources. Users can easily adjust their resource usage based on demand, thanks to the flexible and elastic nature of cloud services. Edge computing can also scale, but it requires distributed resources. Managing and deploying updates or expansions across numerous edge devices can be more complex than scaling cloud resources.

The following code snippet illustrates the difference in latency between edge and cloud computing through a simple Python program that simulates data processing time:

```python
import time

def cloud_computing_simulation(data):
    start_time = time.time()
    # Simulating data processing in the cloud
    time.sleep(0.2) # Network delay
    processed_data = data * 2 # Hypothetical data processing
    end_time = time.time()
    return processed_data, end_time - start_time

def edge_computing_simulation(data):
    start_time = time.time()
    # Simulating data processing at the edge
    time.sleep(0.01) # Local processing delay
    processed_data = data * 2 # Hypothetical data processing
    end_time = time.time()
    return processed_data, end_time - start_time

data_input = 100
cloud_result, cloud_latency = cloud_computing_simulation(data_input)
edge_result, edge_latency = edge_computing_simulation(data_input)

print(f"Cloud Computing Latency: {cloud_latency}")
print(f"Edge Computing Latency: {edge_latency}")
```

The output of the program demonstrates the latency difference:

```
Cloud Computing Latency: 0.20054316520690918
Edge Computing Latency: 0.011495828628540039
```

This example uses arbitrary sleeps to simulate network and local processing delays. It shows that edge computing can significantly reduce latency compared to centralized cloud processing.

28

By thoroughly understanding these differences, developers and decision-makers can make informed choices about whether cloud computing, edge computing, or a hybrid approach is most appropriate for their specific use cases.

1.7 Edge Computing Use Cases

Edge Computing has found diverse applications across various industries, fundamentally transforming how data is processed and utilized at the point of collection. By bringing computation closer to the source of data, Edge Computing addresses latency and bandwidth constraints inherent in traditional centralized cloud architectures. Here, we explore some pivotal use cases that exemplify the potent capabilities of Edge Computing.

- **1. Industrial IoT (IIoT)**

  Industries such as manufacturing, oil and gas, and energy heavily rely on Industrial IoT for monitoring and controlling machinery and processes. Edge Computing plays a crucial role in enabling real-time processing and decision-making. For instance, predictive maintenance systems in manufacturing leverage Edge Computing to analyze data from sensors attached to machinery. By detecting anomalies in vibration, temperature, or pressure in real-time, these systems can predict equipment failures before they occur, significantly reducing downtime and maintenance costs. The following generic structure shows how data can be processed at the edge:

```
import sensor_data
import edge_inference_model

def process_data_at_edge(sensor_data):
    # Data preprocessing
    preprocessed_data = preprocess(sensor_data)

    # Inference using deployed model
    maintenance_prediction = edge_inference_model.predict(
        preprocessed_data)

    # Act on prediction
    if maintenance_prediction == 'failure_imminent':
        apply_maintenance_protocol()
```

29

```
return maintenance_prediction
```

Operation Result: Maintenance protocol applied

- **2. Autonomous Vehicles**

Autonomous vehicles (AVs) require rapid processing of vast amounts of data to make real-time driving decisions. Edge Computing meets this need by enabling on-device data computation. Sensors, cameras, and LIDAR systems on AVs generate continuous streams of data that must be processed with extremely low latency. For example, obstacle detection and collision avoidance systems benefit significantly from Edge Computing by processing sensor data locally, thus ensuring timely reactions to avoid hazards.

- **3. Smart Cities**

Smart City projects incorporate Edge Computing to manage extensive data from connected devices such as streetlights, traffic signals, and environmental sensors. To illustrate, edge-based traffic management systems analyze data from cameras and sensors to optimize traffic flow in real-time, reducing congestion and enhancing safety. Environmental monitoring systems also employ Edge Computing to process air quality data locally, triggering immediate action if pollution levels rise.

Edge Device Output:
Air Quality Index = 155
Action: Activate Air Purification Systems

- **4. Healthcare**

In healthcare, Edge Computing supports applications requiring quick analysis and response, such as remote patient monitoring and medical imaging. Wearable health devices equipped with Edge Computing capabilities can process vital signs locally and alert patients or healthcare providers of abnormalities instantaneously. Similarly, edge-enabled imaging devices can preprocess medical images, ensuring quicker diagnostics while reducing the load on centralized servers.

- **5. Retail**

  Retailers leverage Edge Computing to improve customer experiences and operational efficiency. For instance, smart shelves with embedded sensors can detect product quantities and send alerts when restocking is necessary. Furthermore, point-of-sale (POS) systems integrated with Edge Computing can provide real-time transactional data analysis, enabling dynamic pricing strategies or targeted promotions based on customer behavior.

```
import shelf_sensor_data

def monitor_stock(shelf_data):
    current_stock = shelf_sensor_data.read()

    if current_stock < threshold:
        notify_restocking_team()

    return current_stock
```

  Current Stock Level: 5 units
  Action Result: Restocking team notified

- **6. Augmented and Virtual Reality (AR/VR)**

  AR and VR applications demand high-throughput and low-latency data processing to provide seamless user experiences. Edge Computing facilitates the localization of computational tasks, reducing latency significantly. For example, in a VR gaming setup, edge servers process user inputs and render graphics locally, resulting in smooth gameplay and immersive experiences.

- **7. Telecommunications**

  Telecom providers utilize Edge Computing to enhance network performance and service delivery. Edge servers placed near cell towers can process data traffic locally, reducing latency and improving the quality of service for users. Applications such as video streaming, real-time communication, and content delivery networks (CDNs) use Edge Computing to cache and deliver content efficiently.

Edge Computing's versatility across these applications demonstrates its ability to revolutionize data processing in numerous sectors. By moving computation closer to data sources, Edge Computing not only reduces latency and bandwidth usage but also enables faster decision-making and improved operational efficiency.

1.8 Industry Adoption and Trends

Edge computing has made significant inroads across various industries, catalyzing transformative changes in how data is processed and utilized at or near the source of data generation. The practical adoption of edge computing varies per industry, driven by the unique requirements and opportunities presented by localized data processing.

- **Manufacturing Industry:** The manufacturing industry has leveraged edge computing to drive advancements in smart manufacturing and Industry 4.0. By relocating data processing closer to production lines, manufacturers enhance real-time monitoring and predictive maintenance. For instance, industrial IoT (IIoT) deployments utilize sensors connected to edge devices to detect anomalies and predict equipment failures before they occur. This reduces downtime and improves operational efficiency. The integration of machine learning models at the edge facilitates on-the-fly adjustments to production processes, optimizing output and resource utilization.

- **Healthcare Sector:** Edge computing in healthcare supports a multitude of critical applications ranging from remote patient monitoring to enhanced diagnostic imaging. Wearable medical devices and smart sensors collect patient data, which is then locally processed by edge devices to provide real-time health insights and alerts to medical professionals. This immediate analysis is crucial for continuous monitoring of vital signs and early detection of potential health issues. Additionally, edge computing aids in processing large volumes of medical imaging data close to the source, thereby decreasing latency and enhancing the speed of diagnoses.

- **Automotive Industry:** Modern automotive systems, especially autonomous vehicles, rely heavily on edge computing.

These vehicles generate vast amounts of data from various sensors, including cameras, LiDAR, RADAR, and GPS. Edge computing enables real-time data processing and decision-making within the vehicle. This is essential for functions such as collision avoidance, real-time navigation, and autonomous driving. Edge-based AI systems analyze the environmental information swiftly, ensuring safe and efficient vehicle operation. Vehicle-to-everything (V2X) communication also benefits from edge computing by creating a fast, reliable exchange of data between vehicles and infrastructure, enhancing traffic management and safety.

- **Retail Sector:** Retailers adopt edge computing to enhance the shopping experience and streamline operations. In brick-and-mortar stores, edge devices facilitate real-time inventory management, personalized customer engagement, and dynamic pricing strategies. Smart shelves and IoT-enabled point-of-sale systems ensure that stock levels are optimized and customers receive immediate assistance or offers tailored to their preferences. Furthermore, video analytics processed at the edge allow retailers to monitor customer behavior, optimize store layouts, and implement effective crowd control measures.

- **Telecommunications:** Telecommunication providers integrate edge computing to meet the increasing demand for low-latency applications and services. Deploying edge servers in close proximity to users supports applications such as augmented reality (AR), virtual reality (VR), and gaming, where latency tolerance is minimal. Furthermore, edge computing assists in efficient content delivery by caching data near user locations, reducing latency and bandwidth costs. The rollout of 5G networks further amplifies the significance of edge computing by providing seamless connectivity and enabling real-time application performance.

- **Energy and Utilities:** In the energy sector, edge computing facilitates the deployment of smart grids and management of distributed energy resources (DERs). Edge devices analyze data from numerous endpoints, such as smart meters, renewable energy sources, and grid infrastructure, providing real-time insights into energy consumption and production. This enables optimized grid management, peak load reduction, and efficient distribution of energy resources. Predictive analytics at the edge support maintenance of critical infrastructure by foreseeing potential failures and ensuring service reliability.

- **Agriculture:** Edge computing in agriculture enhances precision farming practices through real-time data processing from IoT sensors distributed across fields. These sensors monitor soil health, weather conditions, and crop growth, providing farmers with timely insights to make informed decisions. Edge devices process this data locally, allowing for immediate actions such as adjusting irrigation systems or deploying pest control measures. This adaptability improves crop yields, reduces resource wastage, and promotes sustainable farming practices.

- **Public Sector:** Government and public sector entities deploy edge computing to enhance public safety and urban management. Smart city initiatives utilize edge-based systems for traffic management, environmental monitoring, and public safety applications. For instance, edge-enabled video surveillance can analyze footage in real-time to detect and respond to incidents swiftly. Additionally, edge computing supports emergency response systems by processing data from diverse sources, furnishing first responders with critical information to manage crises more effectively.

- **Edge Computing Trends:** The ongoing trends underscore the growing maturity and broader acceptance of edge computing across these industries. The confluence of AI and edge computing, often termed edge AI, is particularly significant. The capability to run sophisticated machine learning models locally expands the potential applications of edge computing, enriching the analytical depth and decision-making capacity at the edge.

Moreover, the evolution of edge hardware, exemplified by increasingly powerful and energy-efficient edge devices, has accelerated the adoption of edge computing. Industry-optimized edge platforms and solutions, tailored to meet specific operational requirements, are gaining traction.

34

Standardization efforts and industry alliances are also shaping the future of edge computing. These collaborations aim to establish best practices, interoperability standards, and security frameworks that ensure robust, scalable, and secure edge deployments. The coordinated development of edge and 5G technologies represents another promising trend, poised to unlock new capabilities and drive widespread industry adoption.

The industry's overall trajectory suggests that edge computing is not merely a transient phase but represents a fundamental shift in the digital landscape. This shift positions businesses to leverage localized data processing, enabling smarter, faster, and more resilient operations.

1.9 Introduction to Edge Computing Technologies

Edge computing encompasses a variety of technologies designed to bring computational power and data storage closer to the location where it is needed. This encompasses a broad range of hardware and software solutions, network enhancements, and system architectures necessary to enable efficient data processing at or near the source of data generation.

The primary technological components of edge computing include devices, nodes, gateways, network infrastructure, and orchestration systems. Each component plays a crucial role in ensuring seamless operation, optimized data processing, and integration with broader cloud environments.

- **Edge Devices and Sensors** Edge devices include sensors, actuators, and other internet-connected devices capable of generating data. These devices are embedded in physical environments and range from simplistic sensors measuring temperature or humidity to complex devices, such as smart cameras and autonomous vehicles. The key characteristics of these devices are their ability to generate, collect, and, in some cases, process data locally.

35

- **Edge Nodes** Edge nodes are intermediate computing platforms placed closer to the edge of the network, often between the devices and the cloud. These nodes can process and analyze data locally, mitigating latency and reducing the amount of data that needs to be transmitted to centralized cloud data centers.

- **Edge Gateways** Edge gateways serve as bridges between edge devices and the cloud or data centers. They collect data from edge devices and can perform preliminary processing tasks such as filtering, aggregation, and protocol conversion. Edge gateways often provide enhanced security functionalities, ensuring that data is encrypted and securely transmitted across networks.

- **Network Infrastructure** A robust network infrastructure is essential to the functionality of edge computing. This includes high-bandwidth connectivity options such as 5G networks, low-power wide-area networks (LPWANs), and other wireless and wired communication protocols. Network infrastructure must ensure reliable and efficient connectivity between devices, nodes, gateways, and cloud services.

- **Edge Computing Frameworks and Platforms** Several edge computing frameworks and platforms facilitate the development, deployment, and management of edge applications. These platforms provide the tools and services necessary to orchestrate tasks across distributed edge environments.

```
from edge_platform import EdgeDeployment, EdgeNode

# Define deployment configuration
deployment_config = {
    'application_name': 'Smart Agriculture Monitoring',
    'nodes': [
        EdgeNode('sensor-hub-1', location='Field-A'),
        EdgeNode('sensor-hub-2', location='Field-B')
    ],
    'data_processing_units': 2,
}

# Initialize and deploy the application
deployment = EdgeDeployment(config=deployment_config)
deployment.deploy()
```

- **Containerization and Virtualization Technologies** Containerization technologies like Docker and Kubernetes are pivotal in edge computing. They allow applications to run in isolated environments, ensuring consistency and scalability across different nodes. Virtualization technologies provide a level of abstraction that simplifies the management of computational resources in edge environments.

- **AI and Machine Learning at the Edge** Deploying AI and machine learning models at the edge can significantly enhance the ability to process data in real time. This involves the use of pre-trained models capable of running on resource-constrained devices. Techniques such as model quantization and optimization are often used to adapt models to the limited computational resources available at edge nodes.

```
import tensorflow as tf
from tensorflow.keras.models import load_model
import numpy as np

# Load the pre-trained model
model = load_model('model.h5')

# Sample input data (e.g., sensor readings)
input_data = np.array([[0.2, 0.3, 0.5]])

# Perform inference on the edge device
predictions = model.predict(input_data)

print('Prediction:', predictions)
```

- **Security Technologies** Security is a paramount concern in edge computing. The distributed nature of edge environments introduces unique security challenges that must be addressed. Technologies for securing edge environments include endpoint protection, encryption, secure boot mechanisms, and protocols for secure communication between devices and gateways.

- **Data Management** Efficient data management strategies are necessary to handle the vast amounts of data generated by edge devices. This includes data storage solutions that can operate in distributed environments and data processing frameworks capable of handling real-time analytics. The use of databases optimized for edge environments ensures that data can be stored and retrieved quickly and efficiently.

The implementation of these technologies must be meticulously orchestrated to realize the benefits of edge computing fully. By leveraging these components effectively, organizations can deploy scalable and resilient edge architectures capable of addressing the demands of various real-world applications.

1.10   Future of Edge Computing

The future of edge computing is poised to be transformative, driven by advancements in technology, increasing data generation, and the need for real-time processing. Key trends and technological innovations are expected to shape the evolution of edge computing, ensuring its central role in the next generation of information processing.

The integration of artificial intelligence (AI) and machine learning (ML) at the edge is anticipated to be a significant driving force. As edge devices become more powerful, there will be a shift from merely processing data to performing complex analytical tasks locally. This will necessitate the development of highly efficient AI models that can operate with limited computational resources, reduced power consumption, and intermittent connectivity. One of the primary goals will be to enable edge devices to perform tasks such as real-time anomaly detection, predictive maintenance, and autonomous decision-making.

```
# Example code to demonstrate edge AI deployment
import tensorflow as tf
from tensorflow.keras.models import load_model

# Load the pre-trained AI model
model = load_model('path/to/edge_model.h5')

# Simulate input data for inference
input_data = tf.random.normal([1, 224, 224, 3])

# Perform inference at the edge
prediction = model.predict(input_data)
print("Predicted Output: ", prediction)
```

38

5G technology is another cornerstone for the future of edge computing. With its high bandwidth, low latency, and massive connectivity capabilities, 5G will significantly enhance the performance and applicability of edge computing solutions. Real-time applications like augmented reality (AR), virtual reality (VR), and autonomous vehicles will benefit from the low latency and high throughput provided by 5G. The deployment of 5G will also catalyze the growth of edge computing in smart cities, where numerous sensors and devices continuously generate vast amounts of data that need to be processed locally.

Security and privacy will remain critical concerns, shaping the development and deployment of edge computing. With data being processed closer to its source, new security paradigms such as zero-trust security models and hardware-based security will gain prominence. Ensuring that edge devices are secure from both physical and cyber threats is paramount. Innovations in secure multi-party computation, homomorphic encryption, and distributed ledger technologies (DLT) such as blockchain are expected to provide robust solutions for data integrity, authentication, and secure communication between edge devices.

```
# Example code to implement a security feature in edge computing
import rsa

# Generate RSA keys for secure communication
(public_key, private_key) = rsa.newkeys(2048)

def secure_communication(message):
    # Encrypt the message using the public key
    encrypted_message = rsa.encrypt(message.encode(), public_key)
    return encrypted_message

# Simulate sending a secure message
message = "Edge computing is secure!"
encrypted_message = secure_communication(message)
print("Encrypted Message: ", encrypted_message)
```

Interoperability and standardization will be key enablers for the widespread adoption of edge computing. Industry standards and protocols, such as the OpenFog Consortium's reference architecture and ETSI's Multi-access Edge Computing (MEC) standards, will facilitate seamless integration and communication between diverse edge devices and cloud infrastructures. This interoperability is essential for creating a unified ecosystem where applications can be developed and deployed at scale, irrespective of the underlying hardware or software platforms.

39

The concept of federated learning is also expected to gain traction, providing a framework for collaborative model training across multiple decentralized devices. In federated learning, edge devices collectively train a global model while keeping their data localized, thus addressing privacy concerns and reducing data transfer requirements. This technique will be particularly beneficial for applications in healthcare, finance, and other sectors where data privacy is paramount.

```python
# Example code to demonstrate federated learning
import flwr as fl
import tensorflow as tf

# Define the model to be trained
def get_model():
    model = tf.keras.Sequential([
        tf.keras.layers.Dense(128, activation='relu', input_shape=(784,)),
        tf.keras.layers.Dense(10, activation='softmax')
    ])
    model.compile(optimizer='adam', loss='sparse_categorical_crossentropy', metrics
        =['accuracy'])
    return model

# Federated learning client
class FederatedClient(fl.client.NumPyClient):
    def __init__(self, model):
        self.model = model

    def get_parameters(self):
        return self.model.get_weights()

    def fit(self, parameters, config):
        self.model.set_weights(parameters)
        # Simulate local training with random data
        self.model.fit(tf.random.normal((10, 784)), tf.random.uniform((10,), maxval=10,
            dtype=tf.int64), epochs=1)
        return self.model.get_weights(), len(parameters), {}

    def evaluate(self, parameters, config):
        self.model.set_weights(parameters)
        # Simulate local evaluation
        return 0.0, 0, {} # Dummy evaluation result

# Create and start the federated learning client
fl.client.start_numpy_client('server_address:port', client=FederatedClient(get_model
    ()))
```

Furthermore, edge computing will play an instrumental role in the proliferation of the Internet of Things (IoT). As IoT devices become ubiquitous, edge computing will provide the necessary infrastructure to manage, process, and analyze data generated by billions of connected devices. This will enable real-time insights and actions, creating responsive and adaptive environments such as smart homes, industrial automation, and connected healthcare.

The nascent field of quantum computing, though still in its early stages, could also influence the future of edge computing. Quantum edge devices, leveraging the principles of quantum mechanics, have the potential to perform complex computations far more efficiently than classical devices. As quantum technology matures, it could lead to breakthroughs in areas such as quantum encryption, optimization problems, and large-scale simulation tasks, which can be offloaded to quantum-enabled edge devices.

Edge computing's future will be characterized by dynamic, context-aware systems capable of adapting to changing conditions and delivering optimized performance in real-time across various applications. The synergy between edge, cloud, and emerging technologies will pave the way for innovative solutions and drive the continuous evolution of the digital landscape.

Chapter 2

Fundamentals of Edge Architecture

This chapter delves into the core components and design principles of edge architecture. It examines the roles of edge devices, gateways, servers, and data centers in localized data processing. Connectivity and networking solutions specific to edge environments are explored, alongside data processing and storage strategies. The chapter also discusses the distinctions between edge computing and fog computing, providing a comprehensive overview of efficient edge system design.

2.1 Introduction to Edge Architecture

Edge computing is an architectural style aimed at improving the efficiency of data processing and analysis by moving these operations to the vicinity of the source of the data. This architectural paradigm is fundamentally distinct from the traditional centralized data processing approach facilitated by cloud computing. The core advantage lies in significantly reducing latency, conserving bandwidth, and enhancing real-time data processing capabilities.

Edge architecture incorporates several critical components that work cohesively to enable efficient data processing near the data generation points. These components include edge devices, edge gateways, edge servers, and, in some cases, proximate data centers. Each component plays a specific role to ensure the seamless operation of an edge computing environment.

- Edge devices are often sensors or specialized hardware that collect data from the immediate environment. These devices may include Internet of Things (IoT) sensors, smart cameras, or even edge-specific computational units embedded within industrial machinery. These devices are typically characterized by limited computational power and energy constraints but are optimized for local data acquisition and initial processing tasks.

- Edge gateways act as intermediaries that bridge the communication gap between edge devices and more substantial computing resources such as edge servers or data centers. Gateways facilitate protocol translation, data filtering, aggregation, and sometimes preliminary analytics. They play a pivotal role in ensuring secure, reliable, and efficient data transmission from the edge devices towards centralized processing units or cloud servers.

- Edge servers and proximate data centers provide computational resources required for more intensive data processing tasks. These servers can be located at network nodes closer to the data source compared to traditional cloud servers. They perform tasks such as heavy data analytics, machine learning model inference, and data storage. The proximity of these servers to edge devices reduces the data transmission latency engendered by long-haul internet communications, thereby making real-time data analytics feasible.

- Edge architecture necessitates robust connectivity and networking solutions. This includes local area networks (LANs), wireless communication protocols, and sometimes cellular networks tailored to maintain continuous and reliable data transmission. The emphasis on low latency and high throughput connections is paramount in edge computing environments where time-sensitive applications are executed.

44

- The data processing paradigm at the edge involves the implementation of both distributed and localized processing strategies. It effectively decentralizes data analytics, enabling edge devices and gateways to perform preliminary processing steps such as data cleaning, filtering, and minor aggregations. This mitigates the need for large volumes of raw data to be transferred to centralized locations, conserving bandwidth and reducing operational costs.

- For example, a smart camera installed in a factory might perform local image recognition to detect defective products in real-time. The intermediate results or only the instances of defects are then transferred to a central server for further analysis and storage, if necessary. This localized data processing attribute of edge computing is crucial for applications requiring immediate response times and high reliability.

- Storage solutions in edge computing environments are designed to accommodate the need for quick data access and operational efficiency. This includes leveraging distributed storage systems that can manage and replicate data across multiple edge nodes to prevent data loss and ensure high availability.

- A critical distinction exists between edge computing and fog computing. While both paradigms aim to extend the capabilities of cloud computing to proximity to data sources, they differ in their scope and operational model. Fog computing extends cloud-like capabilities closer to the ground using a layered approach wherein data processing tasks are distributed across various nodes from the data source to the cloud. Edge computing, on the other hand, emphasizes processing at the very edge, directly at the sensor level or close-by intermediate devices.

- The design principles for edge systems thus focus on efficiency, scalability, and robustness. Ensuring that the architecture can handle both small to large-scale deployments and maintaining operational integrity under diverse conditions are vital components of these principles.

- The integration of these components and principles forms the foundation of edge architecture, facilitating the effective and efficient processing and analysis of data close to its source. Understanding this structure is critical for leveraging the full potential of edge computing in various application domains, from industrial automation to smart cities and beyond.

2.2 Components of Edge Architecture

Edge architecture comprises several integral components that collectively facilitate data processing and storage closer to the data source. Each component plays a specific role in ensuring efficient and reliable computational capabilities at the edge. This section explores the principal elements constituting edge architecture: edge devices, gateways, servers, and data centers.

Edge devices, often encompassing sensors and actuators, serve as the primary data entry points in edge architecture. These devices capture raw data from physical processes and environments. Due to their proximity to the physical world, they must be designed to operate under diverse conditions, including varying temperatures, humidity levels, and potential mechanical stresses. They typically exhibit low power consumption and may utilize energy harvesting techniques to sustain their operations. Common examples of edge devices are IoT sensors, smart cameras, and RFID readers.

Edge gateways function as intermediaries between the edge devices and the edge servers or centralized data centers. They aggregate data from multiple edge devices, undertake preliminary processing, and manage communication protocols. Given their role, gateways are equipped with more robust processing capabilities compared to edge devices, allowing them to filter, preprocess, and securely transmit data. Moreover, edge gateways are often responsible for protocol translation, enabling seamless communication across heterogeneous networks. This is critical in scenarios where devices may employ different communication standards such as Zigbee, Bluetooth, or Wi-Fi.

Edge servers provide substantial computing power and storage capacity to perform advanced data processing tasks closer to the data source. These servers are strategically deployed to handle computing tasks that exceed the capabilities of edge gateways. They support real-time analytics, complex event processing, and machine learning inference, thus reducing the latency and bandwidth required to transmit data to centralized data centers. Edge servers are integral in enabling applications such as autonomous driving, industrial automation, and augmented reality. They are designed to offer high availability and reliability, ensuring continuous operation in edge environments.

Lastly, edge data centers are smaller-scale data centers located closer to the edge of the network compared to traditional central data centers. They act as regional hubs that aggregate data from multiple edge servers and provide additional processing and storage capabilities. Edge data centers enable scalable data management solutions by distributing computation and storage resources across the network. These data centers are optimized for minimal latency and high throughput, supporting high-demand applications that rely on rapid data access and processing. They are often equipped with advanced cooling technologies, redundant power supplies, and robust security mechanisms to ensure operational integrity.

Additionally, edge architecture incorporates connectivity solutions specific to edge environments. These solutions encompass a variety of networking technologies, each tailored to meet distinct requirements related to data rate, range, and power consumption. For instance, low-power wide-area networks (LPWAN) such as LoRaWAN and NB-IoT are suited for long-range, low-bandwidth communications, making them ideal for connecting widespread edge devices in rural or industrial settings. Conversely, technologies like 5G offer high bandwidth and low latency, catering to applications requiring rapid data transmission and real-time interaction.

The efficient functioning of an edge architecture hinges on seamless integration and coordination among these components. Edge devices capture and transmit data to gateways, which conduct initial processing and relay information to edge servers or data centers for further analysis and storage. The interconnectedness of these components underpins the robust data pipeline that characterizes edge computing, facilitating swift and localized data processing. This architectural design diminishes dependence on centralized cloud resources, thereby mitigating bandwidth bottlenecks and enhancing overall system responsiveness.

```
# Example: Aggregating temperature sensor data at an edge gateway
import random

# Simulated Edge Device Data
def get_temperature(sensor_id):
    # Simulates temperature data from a sensor (in Celsius)
    return round(random.uniform(20.0, 30.0), 2)

# Edge Gateway Aggregation
sensor_ids = [1, 2, 3, 4, 5]
agregated_data = {}

for sensor_id in sensor_ids:
    aggregated_data[sensor_id] = get_temperature(sensor_id)

print("Aggregated Temperature Data at the Edge Gateway:")
print(aggregated_data)
```

Aggregated Temperature Data at the Edge Gateway:
{1: 25.76, 2: 22.88, 3: 29.47, 4: 21.39, 5: 26.32}

This example illustrates how an edge gateway might aggregate temperature data from several sensors for preliminary analysis or filtering before forwarding the information to an edge server or data center. This localized data aggregation reduces the volume of data transmitted over the network, thus economizing bandwidth and decreasing latency. Edge architecture's multi-tier approach, integrating devices, gateways, servers, and data centers, ensures scalability, reliability, and efficiency in deploying edge applications.

2.3 Edge Devices and Sensors

Edge devices play a pivotal role in the architecture of edge computing systems. These devices are stationed at the periphery of the network, where they gather and process data in real-time before transmitting the essential information to centralized systems or data centers for further analysis. Such localized processing helps to reduce latency, bandwidth use, and enhances the responsiveness of the system.

Edge devices often encompass a variety of hardware components, including sensors, microcontrollers, and communication modules. They must be designed to operate under diverse environmental conditions and deliver reliability, robustness, and efficiency. The following paragraphs will delve into the specifics of these constituents, particularly focusing on the intricacies of sensors utilized in edge devices.

Edge devices can be broadly categorized into several types based on their functionality:

- **Edge Nodes:** These are capable of performing substantial amounts of data processing and storage locally. They usually feature powerful processors and sufficient memory to handle complex computational tasks.

- **Microcontroller-based Devices:** These devices are designed for low-power operations and are typically used in scenarios where energy efficiency is critical.

- **Embedded Systems:** These systems integrate computation and communication capabilities into specific functional components of larger systems, like automotive ECUs (Electronic Control Units).

Sensors are integral to edge devices as they enable the detection and measurement of various physical phenomena, translating them into electrical signals for further processing. Here, we categorize and describe the most common types of sensors:

- **Temperature Sensors:** These sensors measure the ambient or surface temperature. Examples include thermocouples, thermistors, and integrated silicon-based sensors.

- **Pressure Sensors:** These devices measure pressure levels in gases or liquids. Strain gauge sensors, capacitive sensors, and piezoelectric sensors fall into this category.

- **Proximity Sensors:** These sensors detect the presence or absence of an object, or its distance from the sensor. This category includes capacitive, inductive, and ultrasonic sensors.

- **Accelerometers:** These sensors measure the acceleration forces acting on an object, which can be static (e.g., gravity) or dynamic (e.g., vibration or movement).

- **Gyroscopes:** Often used in conjunction with accelerometers, gyroscopes measure rotational motion and orientation.

Given their critical role, the design and selection of sensors must consider the following technical aspects:

- **Accuracy and Precision:** The degree of closeness of the sensor's measurements to the true value (accuracy), and the sensor's ability to consistently reproduce the same measurements under unchanged conditions (precision).

- **Range:** The span over which the sensor can accurately measure the physical quantity.

- **Sensitivity:** The ratio of the change in output signal to the change in the measured quantity. Higher sensitivity implies that the sensor can detect smaller changes.

- **Response Time:** The time taken by the sensor to react to a change in the measured quantity.

- **Power Consumption:** Especially critical for battery-operated edge devices, lower power consumption extends device operational periods.

For implementation, edge devices often utilize microcontrollers such as the ARM Cortex-M series, which offer a balanced mix of computational power and energy efficiency. The following code illustrates a simple microcontroller setup for reading data from a temperature sensor (e.g., a thermistor):

```
// Example code for reading temperature data from a thermistor
#include <Arduino.h>

const int sensorPin = A0; // Analog pin for the thermistor

void setup() {
    Serial.begin(9600); // Begin serial communication
    pinMode(sensorPin, INPUT); // Set sensor pin as input
}

void loop() {
    int sensorValue = analogRead(sensorPin); // Read analog value
    float voltage = sensorValue * (5.0 / 1023.0); // Convert to voltage
    float temperature = (voltage - 0.5) * 100; // Convert voltage to Celsius
```

```
  Serial.print("Temperature: ");
  Serial.print(temperature);
  Serial.println(" C");
  delay(1000); // Wait for a second before repeating
}
```

Upon execution, the output would be displayed as follows:

```
Temperature: 23.45 C
Temperature: 23.50 C
Temperature: 23.47 C
```

The real-time data acquisition and initial processing capabilities of edge devices are fundamental to the overall architecture of edge computing. They facilitate immediate responsiveness and optimize the use of network resources by minimizing the volume of data transmitted to central servers.

2.4 Edge Gateways

Edge gateways represent critical nodes in the edge computing architecture. They serve as intermediaries facilitating communication between edge devices/sensors and the cloud or central data centers. These gateways often perform preprocessing and filtering of data before it reaches the cloud, thereby reducing latency and bandwidth usage. This section examines the intricate functionalities and components of edge gateways, elaborating on their architecture, communication protocols, and security considerations.

Edge gateways are often equipped with processing power sufficient to perform local computation and data analysis. Depending on the application, they can run machine learning models, aggregate data from multiple sensors, or even control local actuators. The typical architecture of an edge gateway includes several essential components, such as networking interfaces, computation units (CPUs and sometimes GPUs), storage, and necessary software layers.

```
- Networking Interfaces (Ethernet, Wi-Fi, LTE/5G)
- Computation Unit (CPU/GPU/FPGA)
- Data Storage (SSD/HDD)
- Peripheral Interfaces (USB, GPIO, Serial Ports)
- Power Supply (Battery, Solar)
```

The edge gateway's networking interfaces enable connectivity to various edge devices and the broader network. Common interfaces include Ethernet, Wi-Fi, and cellular communications (LTE/5G). These diverse connectivity options allow gateways to operate in remote or mobile environments where traditional wired connections might not be feasible.

The computation unit of an edge gateway typically consists of a CPU, and in some cases, a GPU or FPGA for tasks requiring parallel processing or acceleration. This allows the gateway to perform complex computations locally, enabling real-time decision-making and reducing dependency on cloud resources. For instance, a GPU-accelerated gateway might be used in image recognition tasks where latency is critical.

Edge gateways also possess storage capabilities, which range from small SSDs to larger HDDs depending on the data retention requirements. This local storage is used to buffer data before transmission, store logging information, and support local analytics. By decoupling data collection from transmission, gateways can manage intermittent connectivity issues and optimize bandwidth usage.

Peripheral interfaces such as USB, GPIO, and serial ports allow the gateway to connect to various sensors, actuators, and additional peripheral devices. These interfaces provide the necessary flexibility to integrate with a wide range of industrial and consumer hardware, facilitating widespread adoption in different application domains.

The software ecosystem of an edge gateway is equally critical, enabling it to handle local data processing, device management, network configuration, and secure data transmission. The software stack generally includes an operating system, edge data services, application frameworks, and security modules.

```
- Operating System (Linux, RTOS)
- Edge Data Services (MQTT Broker, OPC-UA Server)
- Application Frameworks (Docker, Kubernetes Edge)
- Security Modules (TLS/SSL, VPN, Firewall)
```

Operating systems such as Linux or Real-Time Operating Systems (RTOS) form the base layer, offering robust and scalable environments to manage hardware resources. These OS platforms support various edge-specific services, including message brokers like MQTT or industrial protocols like OPC-UA, which facilitate reliable and efficient data exchange between devices and applications.

Application frameworks support containerization and orchestration of services running on the gateway. Tools like Docker and Kubernetes Edge allow developers to deploy, manage, and scale applications seamlessly. Containers provide a lightweight, consistent, and portable environment for applications, ensuring they can run reliably across different hardware configurations.

Security is a paramount concern in edge gateway deployment. Security modules integrated into the gateway software stack include encryption protocols (TLS/SSL), virtual private network (VPN) support, and firewall configurations. These measures ensure secure communication between the gateway and connected devices, protecting data integrity and confidentiality.

```
docker run -d --name edge-app \
 -p 1883:1883 -p 8883:8883 \
 -v /etc/mosquitto:/mosquitto/config \
 -v /mosquitto/data:/mosquitto/data \
 -v /mosquitto/log:/mosquitto/log \
 eclipse-mosquitto
```

The example configuration in Listing **??** shows how a Docker container can be used to run an MQTT broker (Eclipse Mosquitto) on an edge gateway. This containerized setup ensures the MQTT broker is isolated, easy to maintain, and scalable.

Edge gateways also facilitate protocol translation between field devices and cloud services. They can aggregate data from heterogeneous sources, normalize it, and encapsulate it into a format suitable for cloud or centralized databases. This capability offloads the cloud from the burden of dealing with various protocols, simplifying the overall system architecture.

```
edge   exttt{   extunderscore}device   exttt{   extunderscore}1   ->   edge   exttt{
extunderscore}gateway (normalize exttt{ extunderscore}data)
        -> cloud exttt{ extunderscore}service exttt{ extunderscore}protocol exttt{
extunderscore}A
edge   exttt{   extunderscore}device   exttt{   extunderscore}2   ->   edge   exttt{
extunderscore}gateway (normalize exttt{ extunderscore}data)
        -> cloud exttt{ extunderscore}service exttt{ extunderscore}protocol exttt{
extunderscore}B
```

Lastly, edge gateways provide a critical role in the regulatory and governance aspects of edge computing. They can enforce data localization policies, ensuring sensitive data does not leave a particular geographic boundary. This is increasingly relevant with the proliferation of data privacy laws which mandate stringent data handling practices.

Understanding the essential role and architecture of edge gateways enables effective design and deployment of edge computing solutions. Integration of robust hardware and software components ensures they can meet the nuanced demands of various application scenarios.

2.5   Edge Servers and Data Centers

Edge servers and data centers are critical components in the ecosystem of edge architecture. They provide the necessary computational power, data storage, and connectivity to support a range of edge applications. Unlike traditional cloud data centers, edge data centers are located closer to the end-users, enabling low-latency data processing and improved performance for latency-sensitive applications.

Edge servers, often deployed in micro data centers, play an essential role in processing and storing data locally, reducing the need to transmit data back to centralized cloud data centers. This local processing leads to significant improvements in response times and bandwidth usage, making edge servers particularly valuable for applications such as the Internet of Things (IoT), autonomous vehicles, and industrial automation.

Structural Overview:

Edge servers are typically designed with enhanced ruggedness to withstand various environmental conditions. They are often equipped with multiple CPUs or GPUs to handle intensive computation tasks. The architecture of edge servers prioritizes modularity and scalability, allowing for the gradual expansion of computational capabilities by adding more servers or enhancing existing ones. Edge servers are also equipped with advanced networking capabilities to ensure seamless communication with both end-devices and higher-tier data centers.

Edge data centers, also known as micro data centers, are small-scale data centers that house edge servers. These facilities are designed to be compact and easily deployable in various locations, including urban, suburban, and even remote rural areas. Micro data centers typically include power supplies, cooling systems, and network connections, all tailored to the specific needs of edge computing environments. Their compact size allows them to be deployed in unconventional locations such as factory floors, telecommunications towers, and even outdoor environments.

Operational Dynamics:

The operation of edge servers and data centers requires robust management and orchestration systems to ensure optimal performance and reliability. Key operational tasks include:

- **Resource Allocation:** Efficient resource allocation mechanisms are essential to ensure that computational resources are optimally utilized. This includes dynamic allocation of CPU, memory, and storage based on the current workload demands. Containerization technologies such as Docker and orchestration platforms like Kubernetes play a crucial role in managing resource allocation in edge environments.

```
docker run -d -p 80:80 --name edge-app edge-application:latest
```

- **Load Balancing:** Load balancing is critical to distribute incoming traffic across multiple edge servers to prevent any single server from becoming a bottleneck. This is particularly important in scenarios with fluctuating workloads, ensuring consistent performance and reliability.

- **Data Syncing and Replication:** Data synchronization and replication between edge servers and central data centers ensure data consistency and availability. This involves mechanisms for handling data conflicts, eventual consistency models, and minimizing data transfer overheads.

Security and Compliance:

Security is a paramount concern in edge computing environments due to the distributed nature of edge servers and data centers. Key security measures include:

- **Encryption:** Data transmitted between edge devices, servers, and central data centers must be encrypted to prevent unauthorized access. This includes both data-at-rest and data-in-transit.

- **Authentication and Authorization:** Robust mechanisms for authenticating and authorizing devices and users are essential to secure access to edge resources.

- **Physical Security:** Due to their deployment in diverse locations, edge servers and data centers need to be physically secured against tampering and environmental threats.

Compliance with industry standards and regulations such as the General Data Protection Regulation (GDPR) and Health Insurance Portability and Accountability Act (HIPAA) is also critical to ensure that data privacy and integrity are maintained across the edge infrastructure.

```
openssl req -newkey rsa:2048 -nodes -keyout mydomain.key -x509 -days 365 -out
    mydomain.crt
```

Case Study: Autonomous Vehicle Networks:

A notable application of edge servers and data centers is in the realm of autonomous vehicles. Autonomous vehicles generate and process vast amounts of data in real-time, necessitating localized data processing capabilities to ensure minimal latency and high reliability.

Edge servers located at traffic intersections, cellular towers, or strategically placed micro data centers can process data from nearby vehicles, enabling real-time decision-making and actions. For instance, edge computing can facilitate immediate interaction between autonomous vehicles and traffic management systems for dynamic traffic light adjustments or collision avoidance.

```
Example Output from Real-Time Edge Processing in Autonomous Vehicles:
[INFO] Vehicle ID 203: Approaching intersection at 45 km/h
[INFO] Traffic Light State: Green; Transition to Yellow in 5 seconds
[ALERT] Proximity Warning: Vehicle ID 456 in close range, 10 meters ahead
[DECISION] Adjust speed to 40 km/h to maintain safe distance
```

By offloading intensive data processing tasks to local edge servers, the reliance on centralized cloud data centers is reduced, leading to faster reaction times and more efficient network usage.

Edge servers and data centers form a robust infrastructure that supports the growing demands of edge computing applications. The architectural and operational considerations outlined above ensure that edge environments provide the necessary computational power close to the data sources while maintaining security, compliance, and efficiency.

2.6 Connectivity and Networking in Edge Architecture

Connectivity and networking are fundamental components of edge architecture, ensuring that data traverses efficiently between edge devices, gateways, servers, and data centers. This section delves into the various aspects and challenges of establishing robust networking within an edge computing environment, including network topologies, communication protocols, latency reduction, bandwidth optimization, and reliability considerations.

Edge architecture can leverage various network topologies, such as point-to-point, star, mesh, and hybrid configurations.

- A point-to-point topology establishes direct communication links between nodes, which can be beneficial for reducing latency and ensuring efficient data transfer. However, it may not scale well in larger systems.

- Star topology connects multiple edge devices to a central hub or gateway. This method simplifies network management, but the central node becomes a critical point of failure.

- Mesh topology enables every node to be interconnected, providing robust fault tolerance and redundancy at the cost of potentially increased complexity and resource requirements.

- Hybrid topology combines elements from different topologies to maximize the strengths and mitigate the shortcomings of each.

Selecting appropriate communication protocols is critical to the performance and efficiency of edge networks. Protocols such as MQTT

57

(Message Queuing Telemetry Transport), CoAP (Constrained Application Protocol), and AMQP (Advanced Message Queuing Protocol) were designed to facilitate communication between devices in constrained environments.

- MQTT is lightweight and suitable for scenarios requiring low bandwidth and high latency tolerance. It operates on the publish-subscribe pattern, which decouples the sender and receiver, enhancing scalability.

- CoAP operates over UDP, making it suitable for low-power, lossy networks, and it supports RESTful transfer of state information.

- AMQP provides robust features such as message orientation, queuing, routing, and security, making it ideal for enterprise-level applications requiring more complex interactions.

Latency reduction is an essential goal in edge networking, often achieved through techniques like data caching, local processing, and optimized routing algorithms. Edge devices and gateways can temporarily store data locally to reduce the need for frequent back-and-forth communication with distant servers. Local processing allows immediate data analysis and decision-making at the edge, minimizing latency. Routing algorithms play a crucial role; they identify the shortest and most efficient paths for data packets, leveraging both static and dynamic routing protocols. Dynamic protocols like OSPF (Open Shortest Path First) and EIGRP (Enhanced Interior Gateway Routing Protocol) can adapt to changing network conditions, which is particularly beneficial in edge environments where network state may frequently fluctuate.

Optimizing bandwidth usage is also vital to prevent network congestion and ensure timely data delivery. One common strategy is data compression, which reduces the size of data packets transmitted over the network. Another approach is data aggregation, where multiple smaller data packets are combined into a single larger one, reducing the overhead associated with packet headers. Quality of Service (QoS) mechanisms prioritize network traffic based on the data's importance and required performance levels. For instance, time-sensitive data may be given higher priority over less critical information to ensure consistent performance.

Network reliability in edge architecture hinges on redundancy and fault-tolerance mechanisms. Redundancy involves having multiple communication paths and backup hardware components, including additional gateways and edge devices that can take over in case of failure. Fault-tolerance is achieved through robust error detection and correction protocols, like TCP's retransmission schemes or application-level acknowledgements, ensuring data integrity during transmission. Meanwhile, network monitoring and management tools can preemptively identify potential issues, allowing for proactive maintenance and timely troubleshooting.

To illustrate these concepts, consider a practical edge computing setup involving multiple IoT sensors collecting environmental data. These sensors employ MQTT for lightweight, efficient communication with an edge gateway. The gateway uses local processing to perform real-time anomaly detection on sensor data, significantly reducing the need for frequent communication with cloud servers and thereby minimizing latency. Data caching at the gateway can prevent network congestion during peak loads, and OSPF dynamic routing adapts to changes, ensuring consistent network performance. Additionally, employing QoS can prioritize critical alerts from sensors over regular data transmissions, guaranteeing timely notification of potential environmental hazards.

Understanding and addressing the intricacies of connectivity and networking are paramount to designing an efficient and resilient edge computing architecture. Proper implementation of these principles ensures that edge systems can handle diverse workloads, adapt to variable network conditions, and maintain high service quality. This develops a foundation for scalable, robust edge deployments capable of meeting modern computing demands.

2.7 Data Processing at the Edge

The concept of data processing at the edge refers to performing data computation closer to the source of data generation, as opposed to centralized data processing in cloud data centers. This approach minimizes the latency and bandwidth usage, enabling real-time analytics and decision-making. Within edge computing environments, data processing workflows and frameworks are tailored to operate efficiently under constrained resource conditions prevalent at the edge.

Data Processing Models: Two primary models are prevalent in edge data processing: stream processing and batch processing.

- **Stream Processing:** This model handles continuous data flows, performing real-time computations on data as soon as it is generated. Stream processing is crucial for applications requiring near-instantaneous responses. For instance, anomaly detection in industrial monitoring systems or autonomous vehicle navigation systems.

```python
import datetime
import random

# Generate real-time sensor data
def generate_sensor_data():
    return {
        'temperature': random.uniform(20, 35),
        'humidity': random.uniform(30, 70),
        'timestamp': datetime.datetime.now()
    }


def process_sensor_data(data):
    if data['temperature'] > 30:
        print("Alert: High temperature detected")
    if data['humidity'] < 35:
        print("Alert: Low humidity detected")

# Real-time data stream handling
while True:
    sensor_data = generate_sensor_data()
    process_sensor_data(sensor_data)
```

- **Batch Processing:** In contrast, batch processing deals with data accumulated over a period. This model is effective for applications that do not require real-time data analysis but rather periodic analysis, such as data aggregation or historical data analysis.

```python
import pandas as pd

# Sample batch data
batch_data = [
    {'temperature': 25.3, 'humidity': 45, 'timestamp': '2023-01-01 10:00:00'},
    {'temperature': 26.7, 'humidity': 50, 'timestamp': '2023-01-01 11:00:00'},
    {'temperature': 24.8, 'humidity': 55, 'timestamp': '2023-01-01 12:00:00'},
```

```
]
# Processing batch data
df = pd.DataFrame(batch_data)
average_temperature = df['temperature'].mean()
average_humidity = df['humidity'].mean()

print(f"Average Temperature: {average_temperature}")
print(f"Average Humidity: {average_humidity}")
```

Data Processing Frameworks and Tools: Edge computing utilizes specialized frameworks and tools to facilitate efficient data processing. Some key frameworks include:

- **Apache Edgent:** A lightweight framework designed for edge devices that enables the creation of event-driven applications. It supports connectivity to cloud systems for data integration.

- **AWS Greengrass:** This extends AWS services to edge devices, allowing them to act locally on the data they generate while still utilizing the cloud for management, analysis, and storage.

- **Azure IoT Edge:** A fully managed service that deploys cloud workloads to run on IoT edge devices. It supports containerized workloads, making it flexible for various edge scenarios.

Challenges in Edge Data Processing:

Several inherent challenges must be addressed to optimize edge data processing:

- **Resource Constraints:** Edge devices often operate under limited computational power, memory, and energy resources. Efficient algorithms and lightweight processing frameworks are essential.

- **Intermittent Connectivity:** Edge devices might experience unstable network connectivity. Thus, offline data processing capabilities and local storage are critical.

- **Security and Privacy:** Data processed at the edge might contain sensitive information. Ensuring secure data transmission and storage, alongside compliance with privacy regulations, is paramount.

61

To overcome these challenges, edge computing systems are designed to be robust, adaptive, and capable of seamlessly integrating with cloud platforms whenever necessary. Edge processing workflows often balance local computation with selective transmission of critical data to centralized systems.

```
Output:
Alert: High temperature detected
Average Temperature: 25.6
Average Humidity: 50.0
```

Efficiently handling data at the edge requires synergistic use of advanced data processing models, appropriate frameworks, and overcoming the intrinsic challenges of edge environments.

2.8   Edge Storage Solutions

Edge storage solutions play a pivotal role in the functionality and efficiency of edge computing systems. These solutions are specifically designed to handle data at or near the point of generation, ensuring that critical data processing tasks occur with minimal latency, reducing the need for constant data transmission to central cloud servers. This section will explore various edge storage architectures, technologies, and strategies that facilitate effective edge computing.

Edge storage solutions can be classified into several categories: local storage on edge devices, network-attached storage (NAS) systems, distributed storage systems, and hybrid storage architectures integrating cloud storage. Each of these categories offers unique advantages and challenges, and the choice of storage solution often depends on the specific requirements of the application in question.

Local Storage on Edge Devices

Local storage solutions refer to the use of storage media directly attached to edge devices. This is the most straightforward form of edge storage, making use of solid-state drives (SSDs), hard disk drives (HDDs), and non-volatile memory (NVM). These storage media offer high-speed data access and can be tailored to the needs of the application, such as the need for increased durability in industrial environments.

Local storage solutions are advantageous for their low latency and high data availability, but they can face challenges in terms of storage capacity and manageability, especially when dealing with vast amounts of data. It is critical to determine the appropriate storage configuration for the edge devices to balance these aspects.

```
sudo mkfs.ext4 /dev/sda1
sudo mkdir -p /mnt/ssd
sudo mount /dev/sda1 /mnt/ssd
```

Network-Attached Storage (NAS)

NAS systems provide a method for multiple edge devices to access a centralized storage system over a network. This approach can enhance data sharing and collaboration between edge devices. NAS systems often use protocols such as NFS (Network File System) or SMB (Server Message Block) to facilitate data access.

```
sudo apt-get install nfs-common
sudo mkdir -p /mnt/nas
sudo mount -t nfs 192.168.1.100:/export/shared /mnt/nas
```

These storage systems offer scalability and flexibility, but they introduce network latency and potential bottlenecks, which may impact performance. Proper network configuration and optimization are crucial when implementing NAS solutions to ensure efficient data access.

Distributed Storage Systems

Another approach is the use of distributed storage systems, which divide data across multiple nodes. These systems are designed for high scalability and fault tolerance. Distributed storage solutions, such as Apache Cassandra or Amazon S3, allow for data to be replicated across various edge nodes, reducing the risk of data loss and ensuring availability even if one or more nodes fail.

```
from cassandra.cluster import Cluster

cluster = Cluster(['192.168.1.101', '192.168.1.102'])
session = cluster.connect('edge_data')

session.execute("""
    INSERT INTO sensor_data (sensor_id, timestamp, value)
    VALUES (1234, '2023-10-10 10:00:00', 56.7)
""")
```

Distributed storage systems often implement consistency models, such as eventual consistency, to manage distributed data. These models ensure that all replicas of a given data item will converge to the same value eventually.

Hybrid Storage Architectures

Hybrid storage architectures combine local storage, NAS, and cloud storage to leverage the strengths of each. This approach provides a balance between performance, scalability, and reliability. Data frequently accessed or of critical importance can be retained on local storage for rapid access, while less critical data can be archived in NAS or cloud storage to free up local resources.

```
{
  "local_storage": {
    "path": "/mnt/ssd",
    "threshold": "80%"
  },
  "nas_storage": {
    "server": "192.168.1.100",
    "mount_point": "/mnt/nas"
  },
  "cloud_storage": {
    "provider": "aws",
    "bucket": "edge-data-archive"
  }
}
```

Hybrid architectures can use intelligent data management policies to automatically move data between storage tiers based on access patterns and data lifecycle considerations.

For effective edge storage solutions, it is imperative to consider factors such as data access speed, storage capacity, reliability, data redundancy, and network bandwidth. Combining various storage solutions and optimizing them based on the application's requirements allows for streamlined and efficient edge computing systems.

2.9   Edge Computing vs. Fog Computing

Edge computing and fog computing are paradigms that aim to address the limitations and challenges associated with traditional cloud computing by bringing computation and data storage closer to the source of data generation. While both paradigms share the common goal of reducing latency and bandwidth usage, they differ in their architecture, scope, and specific use cases.

Edge Computing is characterized by its focus on processing data at or near the data source, typically on the devices generating the data or on nearby local servers. Edge devices can include sensors, actuators, mobile devices, and Internet of Things (IoT) devices. The primary benefit of this approach is the significant reduction in latency, as data does not need to travel to a centralized data center for processing. This enables real-time or near-real-time decision-making, which is critical for applications such as autonomous vehicles, industrial automation, and smart cities.

In contrast, **Fog Computing**, as defined by the OpenFog Consortium, extends the cloud closer to the edge by utilizing a hierarchical architecture that includes intermediate layers of processing nodes called fog nodes. These fog nodes can be deployed on various network devices such as routers, gateways, and switches, providing distributed computing resources and services within a certain geographic proximity. The fog computing model aims to deliver a collaborative and distributed computing infrastructure, offering enhanced scalability and resilience by distributing computational tasks across multiple layers.

Key Differences:

- **Architecture:** Edge computing typically operates on a flat architecture where processing occurs directly on edge devices or proximate local servers. In contrast, fog computing employs a hierarchical architecture with multiple layers of fog nodes between the cloud and the edge.

- **Processing Location:** In edge computing, the processing is distributed across various edge devices, whereas in fog computing, the processing is distributed across both edge devices and intermediate fog nodes.

- **Use Cases:** Edge computing is well-suited for real-time or near-real-time applications that require minimal latency. Examples include autonomous vehicles, smart grids, and telemedicine. Fog computing, on the other hand, is better suited for applications that require distributed processing across a larger network area, such as connected transportation systems, smart buildings, and large-scale IoT deployments.

- **Latency and Bandwidth:** Edge computing minimizes latency by processing data locally on edge devices, thereby reducing the need for data to traverse the network to reach a centralized server. Fog computing also aims to reduce latency but offers a more flexible approach by processing data at intermediate fog nodes, which can alleviate bandwidth constraints by offloading traffic closer to the data source.

- **Data Management:** In edge computing, data management is localized, with each device handling its own data processing and storage needs. Fog computing, however, includes multiple layers of data management, potentially offering better data aggregation, filtering, and caching at various hierarchical levels.

The following example illustrates how data processing would differ between edge and fog computing in a hypothetical smart city traffic management system.

```
# Edge Device: Traffic Camera
import cv2

def detect_traffic_violations(frame):
    # Process frame to detect traffic violations
    violations = []
    # Detection logic goes here
    return violations

cap = cv2.VideoCapture(0)

while True:
    ret, frame = cap.read()
    if not ret:
        break
    violations = detect_traffic_violations(frame)
    # Act on violations (e.g., send alerts)
```

Here, the traffic camera itself processes the video feed to detect traffic violations. The decision to send alerts is made directly on the device, ensuring minimal latency.

```
# Fog Node: Traffic Management Server
import cv2
from network import get_camera_stream

def process_traffic_data(frame):
```

```
# Process frame to detect traffic violations
violations = []
# Detection logic goes here
return violations

def send_alerts(violations):
    # Logic to send alerts to central system or authorities
    pass

camera_stream = get_camera_stream('camera_id_123')

for frame in camera_stream:
    violations = process_traffic_data(frame)
    if violations:
        send_alerts(violations)
```

In this case, a traffic camera sends its video feed to a fog node, which processes the data to detect traffic violations and sends alerts accordingly. The processing load is distributed to the intermediate fog node, allowing for more efficient use of computational resources and network bandwidth.

```
Violation detected at camera_id_123: Running a red light
Alert sent to central system
```

This output indicates that the fog node detected a traffic violation and successfully sent an alert to the central system. The hierarchical approach enhances scalability and allows for complex processing tasks to be handled at various levels within the network.

While edge and fog computing offer distinct advantages, the choice between the two depends on specific application requirements, including latency tolerance, computational needs, and network infrastructure. In many instances, a hybrid approach that leverages both edge and fog computing capabilities might provide the optimal solution for efficient data processing and management.

2.10 Design Principles for Edge Systems

The development of efficient edge systems requires a comprehensive understanding of key design principles that ensure system robustness, scalability, and performance. This section covers essential principles and considerations to follow when designing edge systems.

67

Latency Optimization

Edge computing seeks to minimize latency by processing data closer to the source. Reducing latency is critical in applications requiring real-time or near-real-time responses, such as autonomous vehicles and industrial automation systems. Strategies for latency optimization include:

- *Geographically Distributed Nodes*: Deploy multiple edge nodes close to the data source to eliminate delays caused by long-distance data transmission.

- *Efficient Data Caching*: Implement local caching mechanisms to ensure frequently accessed data is readily available, reducing access time.

- *Prioritization of Critical Tasks*: Assign higher priority to latency-sensitive tasks within the edge system, ensuring they are processed ahead of less critical operations.

Scalability

Scalable edge systems accommodate increasing workloads and expanded network nodes without substantial performance degradation. Considerations for scalability include:

- *Modular Architecture*: Design an edge system with loosely coupled components, which allows independent scaling of different modules in response to demand.

- *Decentralized Data Processing*: Facilitate decentralized data processing to distribute the computational load across multiple edge nodes, avoiding bottlenecks.

- *Elastic Resource Allocation*: Utilize elasticity in resource allocation, dynamically adjusting computational resources based on real-time analysis of workload demands.

Security

Security at the edge entails protecting data, ensuring privacy, and securing communication channels. It is vital to implement multi-layered security strategies to safeguard edge infrastructure:

- *Encryption*: Employ robust encryption algorithms for data at rest and in transit to prevent unauthorized access.

- *Authentication and Authorization*: Implement stringent authentication and authorization mechanisms to verify user and device identities before granting access to edge resources.

- *Anomaly Detection*: Integrate monitoring systems to detect and respond to unusual activity patterns that may indicate security breaches.

Data Management

Efficient data management involves the appropriate handling of data in terms of storage, processing, analysis, and transfer. Key aspects include:

- *Data Locality*: Keep data processing close to where the data is generated to reduce latency and enhance performance.

- *Data Triaging*: Classify and act on data based on its relevance and urgency, ensuring critical data is processed immediately, while less important data can be stored or processed later.

- *Data Aggregation and Filtering*: Aggregate and filter data at the edge to reduce the volume of data that needs to be transmitted to centralized data centers, optimizing bandwidth usage.

Fault Tolerance and Reliability

Ensuring the reliability and fault tolerance of edge systems guarantees continuous operation despite failures. Techniques for achieving this include:

- *Redundancy*: Establish redundant components and pathways to provide backup in case of failures.

- *Graceful Degradation*: Design the system to degrade gracefully, maintaining essential functions while non-critical components recover from failures.

- *Automated Recovery*: Implement automated recovery mechanisms that detect failures and trigger system recovery protocols, minimizing downtime.

Energy Efficiency

Energy efficiency is crucial in edge devices, often deployed in environments with limited power supplies. Key strategies to improve energy efficiency are:

- *Adaptive Power Management*: Use adaptive power management techniques to optimize energy consumption based on current workloads and operational requirements.

- *Low-Power Components*: Select low-power hardware components without compromising performance to reduce overall energy consumption.

- *Idle State Optimization*: Design systems to enter low-power idle states when not actively processing data, conserving energy.

Effective edge system design is a multidisciplinary endeavor, combining knowledge of hardware, software, and network engineering principles to achieve a balanced approach to performance, scalability, security, data management, fault tolerance, and energy efficiency. Adhering to these principles can significantly enhance the quality and robustness of edge computing deployments, making them suitable for various applications and environments.

Chapter 3

Developing Edge Applications with Azure IoT

This chapter provides a practical guide to creating and deploying edge applications using Azure IoT services. It covers the setup of Azure IoT Hub, the integration of edge devices, and the development of edge modules. Emphasis is placed on managing and securing edge deployments, including real-time analytics and device management with Azure IoT Central. Hands-on insights into monitoring, troubleshooting, and optimizing edge applications are provided to ensure seamless development and operation.

3.1 Introduction to Azure IoT

Azure IoT (Internet of Things) is a comprehensive suite of services provided by Microsoft Azure that enables the creation, deployment, and management of IoT applications. Azure IoT offers capabilities that facilitate the connection, monitoring, and control of IoT devices, enabling developers to build scalable and secure IoT solutions. This section outlines the fundamental components of Azure IoT, focusing on the core services such as IoT Hub, device provisioning, and the basic concepts necessary for understanding IoT applications.

Azure IoT Hub serves as a central message hub for bi-directional communication between IoT applications and the devices it manages. It ensures secure and reliable data exchange and provides extensive capabilities for device management, including remote device registration, control, and configuration.

Devices communicate with the IoT Hub using standard protocols such as MQTT, HTTPS, and AMQP, which ensures compatibility across various device types and manufacturers. The messages exchanged between the IoT Hub and IoT devices can include telemetry data from devices to the cloud, and commands from the cloud to control behavior on the devices.

Device provisioning is a critical step in connecting devices to the IoT Hub. Azure IoT provides the Device Provisioning Service (DPS) which automates the registration and configuration of devices in a scalable and secure manner. DPS supports a variety of attestation mechanisms, such as symmetric keys, X.509 certificates, and Trusted Platform Module (TPM), ensuring diverse security requirements are met.

Azure IoT Edge extends cloud intelligence to IoT devices through edge computing. The IoT Edge runtime allows for the deployment of containerized workloads on edge devices, facilitating real-time analytics, machine learning, and custom logic execution locally. This minimizes latency, reduces bandwidth costs, and ensures that devices operate efficiently even with intermittent cloud connectivity.

In practical scenarios, data generated by IoT devices often requires real-time processing and analysis. Azure IoT leverages Azure Stream Analytics to perform such complex event processing, transforming raw data into actionable insights. Stream Analytics jobs can be defined using a familiar SQL-like query language, enabling seamless integration with downstream Azure services such as databases, storage, and dashboards.

Azure IoT provides a highly secure environment by incorporating multiple layers of security. Device identities and credentials are managed by the IoT Hub, enabling stringent access control and data privacy measures. Additionally, all communications between devices and the IoT Hub are encrypted and authenticated to prevent unauthorized access.

The capabilities of Azure IoT are further enhanced by integrating with **Azure IoT Central**, a fully managed IoT application platform. Azure IoT Central simplifies the creation and management of IoT solutions with tools for device connectivity, monitoring, and automated workflows. It offers templated solutions for common industry use-cases, expediting the development process.

Figure 3.1: Architecture of Azure IoT

The overview provided in this section sets the stage for understanding how to leverage Azure IoT for building robust and scalable IoT applications. The key components – including IoT Hub, DPS, IoT Edge, Stream Analytics, and IoT Central – form the ecosystem through which developers can manage devices, process data, and deploy sophisticated edge solutions effectively.

Given these comprehensive features, Azure IoT stands as a versatile platform accommodating developers' needs for a wide array of IoT applications. With built-in support for analytics, security, and connectivity, it facilitates the creation of solutions across various sectors, ranging from industrial automation to smart cities and beyond.

3.2 Setting Up an Azure IoT Hub

Azure IoT Hub forms the backbone of any edge computing solution within the Azure ecosystem, providing a scalable and secure communication infrastructure for edge devices and back-end services. This section delineates the step-by-step process for setting up an Azure IoT Hub, covering all pertinent configurations to ensure proper operation and readiness for device connectivity.

The creation of an IoT Hub in Azure involves several crucial steps, spanning from logging into the Azure portal to configuring essential settings such as pricing and scaling tiers. For those who prefer automation or

73

need to integrate this process into larger deployment scripts, the Azure Command-Line Interface (CLI) provides a robust alternative.

Step 1: Log in to the Azure Portal

Navigate to the Azure portal at https://portal.azure.com and authenticate using your Azure credentials. Ensure that you have the necessary permissions to create resources, particularly if working within a managed subscription or organization.

Step 2: Create a Resource Group

A resource group in Azure allows for the collective management of services. Begin by creating a resource group to house the IoT Hub.

```
az group create --name myResourceGroup --location eastus
```

Step 3: Create an IoT Hub

Proceed to create the IoT Hub within the specified resource group. This can be done through the Azure portal UI or using the Azure CLI.

Using the Azure Portal:

- Navigate to *All services* and select *IoT Hub* from the *Internet of Things* category.

- Click on *Add*.

- Provide the necessary information: the IoT Hub name, subscription, resource group, and location.

- Select the appropriate pricing and scale tier, e.g., F1 Free for testing or S1 Standard for production.

- Configure additional settings according to your requirements and click *Review + create*.

- Click *Create* once the validation passes.

Using the Azure CLI:

```
az iot hub create --name myIoTHub --resource-group myResourceGroup --sku F1 --location eastus
```

Step 4: Configure IoT Hub Settings

Once the IoT Hub is created, further configurations are necessary to tailor its operation to your specific use case. Navigate to the *IoT Hub* in the Azure portal and configure the following settings:

- **Shared access policies:** Define policies to control permission levels. The iothubowner policy typically suffices for administrative access. Navigate to *Shared access policies* and note the connection strings, which will be used for device and service connectivity.

- **Message routing:** Set up custom routes to direct telemetry and messages from devices to specific endpoints like Azure Blob Storage or Event Hubs. This is configured under *Message routing*, allowing flexibility in monitoring and analyzing data streams while offloading storage and computation.

Step 5: Verifying IoT Hub Creation

Verification ensures that the IoT Hub is operational and correctly configured. Use the Azure portal to access the *IoT Hub* dashboard and inspect the status, resource usage, and any potential alerts.

For CLI verification:

```
az iot hub show --name myIoTHub --resource-group myResourceGroup
```

Expected output will provide details on the IoT Hub configuration, confirming its creation.

```
{
  "id": "/subscriptions/xxxx/resourceGroups/myResourceGroup/providers/Microsoft.
Devices/IotHubs/myIoTHub",
  "location": "eastus",
  "name": "myIoTHub",
  "properties": {
    "state": "Active",
    ...
  },
  "resourcegroup": "myResourceGroup",
  "sku": {
    "name": "F1",
    ...
  },
  ...
}
```

This sequence of actions culminates in a fully operational Azure IoT Hub. The resource will now be available to register devices, configure routes, and manage messaging, facilitating the core functionalities required for edge application development and deployment.

3.3 Connecting Edge Devices to Azure IoT Hub

To connect edge devices to the Azure IoT Hub, we initially need to comprehend the foundational architecture and the communication protocols utilized. Edge devices typically interact with the IoT Hub using MQTT, AMQP, or HTTPS protocols. The IoT Hub serves as a central message broker, facilitating secure and efficient bi-directional communication between edge devices and the cloud.

- **Device Registration:** Devices must be registered on the IoT Hub. This registration process involves creating device identities and establishing authentication mechanisms. IoT Hub supports symmetric keys, X.509 certificates, and through the integration of Azure Active Directory, token-based authentication.

- Device identities in the IoT Hub are defined using a unique device ID. This ID is essential for the identification and management of devices within the hub. To register a device, we generally use the Azure portal, the Azure CLI, or the Azure IoT SDKs.

```
az iot hub device-identity create --device-id MyEdgeDevice --hub-name MyIoTHub
```

This command will register a device named *MyEdgeDevice* to the IoT Hub *MyIoTHub*. Upon registration, the device credentials, including the symmetric keys, will be provisioned.

- **Device Provisioning:** Once the device is registered, we must provision it with the necessary credentials to authenticate with the IoT Hub. The device will use the symmetric keys or X.509 certificates assigned during registration for this purpose.

76

```
HostName=MyIoTHub.azure-devices.net;DeviceId=MyEdgeDevice;SharedAccessKey
    =<YourDeviceKey>
```

This connection string is essential for the device to authenticate and connect to the IoT Hub.

- **Device Configuration:** With the device registered and provisioned, we configure it to communicate with the IoT Hub. This configuration involves setting up the device runtime to utilize the defined connection string and specifying the communication protocol (MQTT, AMQP, or HTTPS).

- **Sample Configuration for MQTT:** Azure IoT SDKs typically provide libraries to facilitate this configuration. Below is a Python snippet utilizing the Azure IoT Device SDK to connect an edge device using MQTT.

```
from azure.iot.device import IoTHubDeviceClient

# Define the connection string
conn_str = "HostName=MyIoTHub.azure-devices.net;DeviceId=MyEdgeDevice;
    SharedAccessKey=<YourDeviceKey>"

# Create a client instance using the connection string
device_client = IoTHubDeviceClient.create_from_connection_string(conn_str)

# Connect the client
device_client.connect()
print("Device connected successfully")
```

- **Message Exchange:** After establishing a connection, edge devices can initiate bi-directional communication with the IoT Hub. Devices can send telemetry data, receive commands, and synchronize device twins.

Example of sending telemetry data from the device:

```
import time
from azure.iot.device import Message

msg = Message("temperature: 23°C")
while True:
    device_client.send_message(msg)
    print("Message successfully sent")
    time.sleep(5) # Send telemetry every 5 seconds
```

- **Receiving Commands:** The IoT Hub facilitates command and control functionality wherein cloud applications can send commands to edge devices. These commands could be necessary for updating configurations or triggering specific actions.

```
def message_received_handler(message):
    print("Message received: ", message)

device_client.on_message_received = message_received_handler
```

- **Device Twin Synchronization:** Device twins in Azure IoT Hub are JSON documents that store device state information, configuration, and metadata. Edge devices sync with these twins for desired properties, thus maintaining the requisite operational states and configurations.

Example of updating the desired properties on a device twin:

```
# Reported properties
reported_props = {"firmwareVersion": "1.0.2"}
device_client.patch_twin_reported_properties(reported_props)
print("Reported properties updated")
```

Efficient synchronization and update mechanisms are critical to maintaining reliable and consistent device configurations.

This foundational understanding and practical approach ensure edge devices are seamlessly integrated into the Azure IoT ecosystem, facilitating robust and secure operations necessary for scalable edge application development.

3.4 Building Edge Modules with Azure IoT Edge

Azure IoT Edge offers an efficient architecture for building modules that extend cloud intelligence to IoT edge devices. These edge modules are containerized units of computing that interface with sensors, process data, and execute commands specified by the IoT Solution. Within this section, we will explore the essential steps to design, develop, and deploy edge modules using Azure IoT Edge.

78

Prerequisites: Ensure you have the following prerequisites configured before proceeding:

- An active Azure account.

- Azure IoT Hub setup as described in previous sections.

- Docker installed on your development machine.

- Azure IoT Edge for Linux or Windows installed on your edge device.

1. Setting Up the Development Environment: Start by setting up the development environment. We will use Visual Studio Code with the Azure IoT Edge extension. This extension helps in managing, building, and deploying IoT Edge solutions. Install the Azure IoT Edge extension from the Visual Studio Code marketplace.

```
# Install Visual Studio Code
https://code.visualstudio.com/

# Install Azure IoT Edge extension
code --install-extension vsciot-vscode.azure-iot-edge
```

2. Creating an IoT Edge Solution: An IoT Edge solution is a collection of modules and deployment manifests. To initiate a new solution, use the following commands in the integrated terminal of Visual Studio Code:

```
# Create a new directory for the IoT Edge solution
mkdir MyEdgeSolution
cd MyEdgeSolution

# Initialize an IoT Edge solution
iotedge solution init --name MyEdgeSolution
```

This command sets up the directory structure and necessary files. The primary components include:

- deployment.template.json: Template for the deployment manifest.

- module_name_module_name.py: Default module template for Edge development.

79

3. Developing Custom Edge Modules: Our focus is on the creation of custom edge modules. Azure IoT Edge supports multiple programming languages including Python, C#, and Node.js. For this section, we will use Python. Create the Python module by executing:

```
# Add a new Python module to the solution
iotedge solution add --name MyPythonModule --template python
cd modules/MyPythonModule
```

This command generates a Python module template in the specified directory. Update the module.json file to define the module specifications:

```
{
  "language": "python",
  "image": {
    "repository": "mcr.microsoft.com/azureiotedge-simulated-temperature-sensor",
    "tag": "1.0",
    "platforms": ["amd64"]
  }
}
```

4. Implementing Module Logic: Implement the business logic in the main.py file of your module. For example, to simulate sensor data, modify the main.py file as follows:

```
import random
import time
from azure.iot.device import IoTHubModuleClient

def main():
    client = IoTHubModuleClient.create_from_edge_environment()

    while True:
        temperature = 20 + (random.random() * 15)
        data = {"temperature": temperature}
        client.send_message(data)
        time.sleep(10)

if __name__ == "__main__":
    main()
```

This Python script sends simulated temperature data to the Azure IoT Hub every 10 seconds.

5. Building and Pushing the Docker Image: Next, build the Docker image for the module and push it to a container registry. Ensure you have Docker and an Azure Container Registry (ACR) configured. Use the following command to log in to ACR:

```
# Log in to Azure Container Registry
az acr login --name <ACR_NAME>

# Build the Docker image
docker build -t <ACR_NAME>.azurecr.io/mypythonmodule:latest .

# Push the Docker image to ACR
docker push <ACR_NAME>.azurecr.io/mypythonmodule:latest
```

6. Configuring the Deployment Manifest: Configure the deployment manifest to include the new module. Update the deployment.template.json to reference the newly created Docker image:

```
{
  "modulesContent": {
    "$edgeAgent": {
      "properties.desired": {
        "modules": {
          "MyPythonModule": {
            "version": "1.0",
            "type": "docker",
            "status": "running",
            "restartPolicy": "always",
            "settings": {
              "image": "<ACR_NAME>.azurecr.io/mypythonmodule:latest",
              "createOptions": {}
            }
          }
        }
      }
    }
  }
}
```

This configuration ensures that the edge runtime pulls and runs the MyPythonModule container.

7. Deploying the IoT Edge Solution: Finally, deploy the IoT Edge solution by creating a deployment in the Azure IoT Hub. Use the Azure CLI or the Visual Studio Code extension to import the deployment manifest and initiate the deployment process.

```
# Apply the deployment to the IoT Edge device
az iot edge deployment create --deployment-id MyDeployment \
  --hub-name <IoTHubName> --content deployment.template.json \
  --target-condition "tags.environment='edge'" \
  --priority 10
```

Once deployed, the edge runtime on the device pulls the module images, creates containers, and starts the modules as defined in the deployment manifest. You can monitor the module status and logs using the Azure portal or CLI tools to verify successful deployment and operation.

With these steps, you have successfully built, configured, and deployed a custom IoT Edge module to your edge device.

3.5 Deploying Edge Solutions

To deploy edge solutions using Azure IoT, an efficient and structured approach is required. Deployment involves packaging edge modules, defining their configurations, and executing them on target edge devices. This section presents the critical steps necessary for successful deployment, leveraging Azure IoT Edge capabilities.

Preparing the Deployment Manifest

The deployment manifest is a JSON file that defines the modules to be deployed, their container images, and desired configurations. The manifest file includes a modules section that lists the containerized edge modules, as well as a routes section that specifies how messages flow between modules and the IoT Hub.

```
{
    "modulesContent": {
        "$edgeAgent": {
            "properties.desired": {
                "modules": {
                    "SampleModule": {
                        "type": "docker",
                        "status": "running",
                        "restartPolicy": "always",
                        "settings": {
                            "image": "mcr.microsoft.com/azureiotedge-simulated-
                                temperature-sensor:1.0",
                            "createOptions": "{}"
                        }
                    }
                }
            }
        },
        "$edgeHub": {
            "properties.desired": {
                "routes": {
                    "route1": "FROM /messages/* INTO $upstream"
                },
                "schemaVersion": "1.0"
```

```
        }
    },
    "SampleModule": {
        "properties.desired": {
            "configuration": {
                "frequency": "10"
            }
        }
    }
  }
}
```

Uploading Container Images to Azure Container Registry (ACR)

Container images for the edge modules must be hosted in a Docker-compatible registry like Azure Container Registry (ACR). Ensure that the images are properly built and tagged before pushing them. Use the following commands to log into ACR, build, tag, and push the images.

```
# Log in to Azure Container Registry
az acr login --name <ACR_Name>

# Build the Docker image
docker build -t <image_name> .

# Tag the Docker image
docker tag <image_name> <ACR_Name>.azurecr.io/<repository>:<tag>

# Push the Docker image
docker push <ACR_Name>.azurecr.io/<repository>:<tag>
```

Setting Up the IoT Edge Device

Each edge device must have the Azure IoT Edge runtime installed. Once installed, configure the IoT Edge runtime with the connection string provided by the IoT Hub. This step ensures the device can communicate with the Azure IoT services.

```
# Install IoT Edge runtime
sudo apt-get update
sudo apt-get install --yes iotedge

# Configure the IoT Edge runtime with connection string
sudo iotedge config mp --connection-string "<IoT_Hub_Connection_String>"

# Restart the IoT Edge service to apply the configuration
sudo systemctl restart iotedge
```

Deploying the Solution using IoT Hub

Leverage the Azure portal or Azure CLI to deploy the solution to the connected edge devices. This involves specifying the device ID and targeting the prepared deployment manifest.

```
# Create a deployment using the manifest file
az iot edge deployment create \
  --deployment-id <deployment_id> \
  --hub-name <iot_hub_name> \
  --content ./deployment.json \
  --target-condition "deviceId='<target_device_id>'"
```

Monitoring Deployment

Deployments must be monitored to ensure that modules are correctly distributed and running as intended. Utilize Azure IoT Hub and the IoT Edge runtime logs for real-time status and troubleshooting information.

```
# Retrieve the status of edge modules
iotedge list

# Check detailed logs for a specific module
iotedge logs <module_name>
```

Handling Edge Module Updates

To update edge modules, modify the deployment manifest with the new container image and configuration, then reapply the deployment. The IoT Edge runtime will handle the seamless update of modules, respecting the specified restart policies.

```
{
    "modulesContent": {
        "$edgeAgent": {
            "properties.desired": {
                "modules": {
                    "SampleModule": {
                        "type": "docker",
                        "status": "running",
                        "restartPolicy": "always",
                        "settings": {
                            "image": "mcr.microsoft.com/azureiotedge-simulated-
                                temperature-sensor:2.0",
                            "createOptions": "{}"
                        }
                    }
                }
            }
        }
    }
}
```

84

```
            }
        }
      }
}
```

Through careful preparation and execution of deployment steps, the edge solution will be operational on targeted devices. This systematic approach ensures reliability and ease of management in deploying edge modules using Azure services.

3.6 Developing Custom Edge Modules

Developing custom edge modules within the Azure IoT Edge framework involves creating tailored solutions that address specific requirements for edge computing. This ability to customize allows developers to implement functionalities unique to their applications, optimizing performance and efficiency closer to the data source. This section delves into the detailed process of developing custom edge modules, leveraging Azure's comprehensive tools and services.

To start building custom edge modules, it is important to understand the modular architecture of Azure IoT Edge. Each module is a containerized application instance, typically built using Docker. Modules can be written in various programming languages supported by containers such as Python, C#, Node.js, and Java.

Creating a Module Project: Azure IoT Edge tools for Visual Studio Code simplify the creation of new module projects. Here are the critical steps to create a module project:

- Install Azure IoT Edge extension for Visual Studio Code.
- Open Visual Studio Code and select "Azure IoT Hub Devices" from the sidebar.
- Sign in to your Azure account and select your subscription.
- Right-click on your IoT Hub and select "Create New IoT Edge Solution."
- Provide the necessary configurations, such as the solution name, template (e.g., Python), and target directory.

85

Once the project creation is complete, the structure typically includes folders and files as follows:

- .env: Contains environment variable definitions for the development environment.

- modules: Directory for individual module projects.

- deployment.template.json: Template file for deployment configurations.

- docker-compose.yml: Configuration file for Docker containers.

Coding the Module: In the module directory (e.g., modules/MyPythonModule), there are default files including main.py, Dockerfile, and module.json. Example content of main.py for custom message processing:

```
import json
import time
from azure.iot.device import IoTHubModuleClient

def main():
    client = IoTHubModuleClient.create_from_edge_environment()

    def message_handler(message):
        print("Message received")
        print("Data: {}".format(message.data.decode('utf-8')))

        message_data = message.data.decode('utf-8')
        processed_message = json.loads(message_data)
        processed_message['timestamp'] = time.time()

        client.send_message(json.dumps(processed_message))

    client.on_message_received = message_handler

    print("Module running...")
    while True:
        time.sleep(100)

if __name__ == "__main__":
    main()
```

This script performs basic message handling, adding a timestamp to incoming messages before sending them back to the IoT Hub.

Configuring the Dockerfile: Ensure the Dockerfile is correctly configured to build the module image. Example of a Python module Dockerfile:

86

```
FROM python:3.8-slim-buster

# Install necessary dependencies
RUN pip install azure-iot-device

# Copies the module's code into the image
COPY main.py /app/
WORKDIR /app

# Set the CMD to run the applicaiton
CMD ["python", "-u", "main.py"]
```

Building and Publishing the Module: To build and publish the module to Azure Container Registry (ACR) or Docker Hub:

```
# Log in to ACR
az acr login --name <your_registry_name>

# Build the Docker image
docker build . -t <your_registry_name>.azurecr.io/mypythonmodule:latest

# Push the image to ACR
docker push <your_registry_name>.azurecr.io/mypythonmodule:latest
```

Deploying the Custom Module: Update the deployment.template.json to include the new module definition:

```
{
  "$schema-template": "http://json-schema.org/schema#",
  "contentVersion": "1.0.0",
  "modulesContent": {
    "my-python-module": {
      "type": "docker",
      "status": "running",
      "restartPolicy": "always",
      "settings": {
        "image": "<your_registry_name>.azurecr.io/mypythonmodule:latest",
        "createOptions": "{}"
      }
    }
  }
}
```

Override values with actual registry names and tags. Deploy with Azure CLI:

```
az iot edge set-modules --device-id <device_id> --hub-name <iot_hub_name> --
    content ./config/deployment.json
```

Monitoring and Debugging: Monitor the deployment status and debugging logs using IoT Hub and IoT Edge runtime:

87

```
# Check the status of the module
iotedge list

# Inspect logs of the module
iotedge logs <module_name>
```

Developing custom edge modules integrates application-specific logic at the edge, enhancing responsiveness and reducing bandwidth usage. Ensuring the module is correctly coded, packaged, and deployed to the IoT runtime remains critical for efficient edge computing solutions.

3.7 Edge Analytics with Azure Stream Analytics

Azure Stream Analytics (ASA) is a real-time analytics service that is highly optimised for large-scale, streaming data workloads. Integrating ASA with Azure IoT Edge enables comprehensive real-time data processing and analytics directly at the edge, thereby reducing latency and bandwidth usage, and enabling quicker insights and actions.

Azure Stream Analytics jobs can be deployed to Edge devices to process data close to the source. This local processing is crucial for time-sensitive scenarios such as monitoring industrial equipment, enhancing security through real-time video analytics, or optimizing solutions based on immediate data feedback.

To effectively use Azure Stream Analytics for edge analytics, it is essential to understand various components and steps involved. Starting with creating a Stream Analytics job, defining the input sources, specifying transformations through queries, and setting up the output for the processed data are paramount tasks.

Creating a Stream Analytics Job for Edge

To create a Stream Analytics job designed for edge computing, you need to specify that the job will run on IoT Edge rather than in the cloud. This involves setting the job's hosting environment to edge.

- Navigate to the Azure portal and select *Create a Resource*.

- Choose *Stream Analytics job*.

- In the *New Stream Analytics job* blade, provide the job name, select the subscription, resource group, and the location.

- Select *Edge* under the *Hosting environment.*

The above steps initialize the creation of an ASA job that is set to run on an IoT Edge device.

Defining Inputs

An essential part of setting up a Stream Analytics job is defining the inputs. Inputs can come from various sources. For edge computing scenarios, common inputs include IoT Hub sources where edge devices send their data.

```
{
  "Inputs": [
    {
      "name": "sensorInput",
      "properties": {
        "datasource": {
          "type": "IoTHub",
          "properties": {
            "iotHubNamespace": "YourIoTHubNamespace",
            "sharedAccessPolicyName": "YourPolicyName",
            "sharedAccessPolicyKey": "YourPolicyKey",
            "consumerGroupName": "YourConsumerGroup"
          }
        },
        "serialization": {
          "type": "Json",
          "properties": {
            "encoding": "UTF-8"
          }
        }
      }
    }
  ]
}
```

In the above configuration, 'sensorInput' is defined as an input from the designated IoT Hub. The serialization specifies that the input data is expected in JSON format.

Specifying Transformations with Stream Analytics Query Language

Stream Analytics Query Language is used to perform transformation and analytic operations on the input data. Queries can filter, project, join, and aggregate streams, leveraging SQL-like syntax for ease of understanding.

```
SELECT
  sensorId,
  AVG(temperature) AS avgTemperature,
  System.Timestamp AS eventTime
INTO
  [OutputAlias]
FROM
  [sensorInput]
WHERE
  temperature IS NOT NULL
GROUP BY
  TUMBLINGWINDOW(seconds, 10),
  sensorId
```

In this example, the query calculates the average temperature per sensor every 10 seconds. The results, including the 'sensorId', 'avgTemperature', and 'eventTime', are directed to an output alias.

Configuring Outputs

The output configuration specifies where the processed data should be sent. For edge scenarios, common outputs include Azure Blob Storage, Event Hubs, or another downstream edge module.

```
{
  "Outputs": [
    {
      "name": "edgeOutput",
      "properties": {
        "datasource": {
          "type": "BlobStorage",
          "properties": {
            "storageAccounts": [
              {
                "accountName": "yourStorageAccountName",
                "accountKey": "yourStorageAccountKey"
              }
            ],
            "container": "output-container",
            "pathPattern": "output/{date}/{time}",
            "dateFormat": "yyyy/MM/dd",
            "timeFormat": "HH"
          }
        },
        "serialization": {
          "type": "Json",
          "properties": {
            "format": "lineSeparated"
          }
        }
      }
    }
  ]
}
```

```
}
```

In this configuration, the results of the Stream Analytics job are written to an Azure Blob Storage container in JSON format.

Deploying the Stream Analytics Job to Edge

After configuring input, query, and output for the Stream Analytics job, the job must be deployed to the IoT Edge device. This entails creating a deployment manifest that defines the Stream Analytics module and its relationship with other modules.

```
{
  "modulesContent": {
    "$edgeAgent": {
      "properties.desired": {
        "modules": {
          "asaModule": {
            "settings": {
              "image": "yourRegistry.azurecr.io/stream-analytics-job:latest",
              "createOptions": "{}"
            },
            "type": "docker",
            "status": "running",
            "restartPolicy": "always"
          }
        }
      }
    },
    "$edgeHub": {
      "properties.desired": {
        "routes": {
          "route1": "FROM /messages/modules/asaModule/outputs INTO $upstream
          "
        }
      }
    },
    "asaModule": {
      "properties.desired": {
        "inputs": {
          "sensorInput": {
            "route": "FROM /messages/* INTO $input"
          }
        }
      }
    }
  }
}
```

This deployment manifest sets up the ASA job as a module within the IoT Edge runtime. The 'asaModule' is configured to run the Stream Analytics job, and a route is defined to send the processed data upstream.

Incorporating Azure Stream Analytics with IoT Edge provides a powerful tool for real-time analytics at the edge, reducing latency and optimizing bandwidth utilization. Mastery of defining inputs, configuring queries, establishing outputs, and deploying jobs to the edge is essential for optimizing edge analytics solutions.

3.8 Device Management with Azure IoT Central

Azure IoT Central simplifies the management of IoT devices by providing comprehensive device monitoring, management, and control capabilities. It offers a streamlined interface tailored to facilitate interaction with a wide array of connected devices. This section delves into essential aspects of device management within Azure IoT Central, covering device enrollment, provisioning, monitoring, and remote control.

Device enrollment is the initial step in bringing a device onto the Azure IoT Central platform. Each device must be uniquely identifiable within the system, requiring the generation of device identities. Azure IoT Central supports various provisioning methods, including individual or bulk enrollment, which can be performed manually through the portal or programmatically using the API. Device identities consist of device IDs and authentication mechanisms such as symmetric keys or X.509 certificates for secure communication.

```
import requests
import json

api_url = "https://your-iot-central-app.azureiotcentral.com/api/preview/devices"
headers = {
    "Authorization": "Bearer {your-api-token}",
    "Content-Type": "application/json"
}

device_data = {
    "device_id": "sample_device_001",
    "display_name": "Temperature Sensor",
    "capabilities": {
        "interfaces": {
            "urn:azureiot:SampleInterface;1": {"@id": "urn:xxx:xxx;1" }
        }
    }
}
```

```
response = requests.put(api_url, headers=headers, data=json.dumps(device_data))
print(response.status_code, response.json())
```

Upon successful enrollment, devices must be provisioned to ensure they are properly configured and ready to communicate with Azure IoT Central. Provisioning involves setting up the necessary configurations, downloading and installing requisite software or firmware updates, and ensuring that devices authenticate successfully with the IoT Central hub.

Monitoring devices in real-time is another critical feature of Azure IoT Central. The platform enables administrators to gain comprehensive insights into device performance, health, and operational status through detailed dashboards and charts. Metrics such as telemetry data, connectivity status, and error logs are continuously recorded and visualized to facilitate proactive device management.

Device Monitoring Metrics:
CPU Utilization: 35%
Memory Usage: 512MB
Connection Status: Connected
Last Heartbeat: 2023-10-05 14:32:10

Remote control capabilities allow administrators to interact with devices remotely, executing commands or initiating processes as needed. This functionality is paramount for maintaining devices distributed across various geographical locations. Remote tasks can range from simple operations, such as rebooting a device or changing configuration settings, to complex commands involving the execution of diagnostic scripts.

```
import requests
import json

command_url = "https://your-iot-central-app.azureiotcentral.com/api/preview/devices
    /sample_device_001/commands/reboot"
headers = {
    "Authorization": "Bearer {your-api-token}",
    "Content-Type": "application/json"
}

command_data = {
    "request_id": "unique_run_identifier"
}

response = requests.post(command_url, headers=headers, data=json.dumps(
    command_data))
print(f"Command response: {response.status_code} - {response.text}")
```

Effective alerting mechanisms are integrated within Azure IoT Central to notify administrators of critical issues that require immediate attention. Alerts can be configured based on specific conditions, such as exceeding predefined thresholds for temperature, pressure, or other telemetry parameters. These alerts can trigger notifications via multiple channels, including email, SMS, or integration with external systems.

Ensuring security within device management is paramount. Azure IoT Central mandates secure communication protocols and provides robust identity management to safeguard against unauthorized access. Role-based access control (RBAC) is implemented to define permissions and restrict access based on user roles, ensuring that only authorized personnel can perform sensitive operations.

```
{
  "roles": [
    {
      "role_id": "admin",
      "description": "Administrator",
      "permissions": [
        "read",
        "write",
        "delete"
      ]
    },
    {
      "role_id": "operator",
      "description": "Operator",
      "permissions": [
        "read",
        "execute"
      ]
    }
  ]
}
```

Managing updates across a fleet of devices is streamlined in Azure IoT Central through device job scheduling and firmware management. Administrators can define jobs to apply updates or execute maintenance routines, reducing downtime and ensuring consistency across the deployment.

By providing these robust features, Azure IoT Central significantly reduces the complexity involved in IoT device management, ensuring that operations run smoothly and securely.

3.9 Configuring Security for Edge Devices

Ensuring the security of edge devices is a critical aspect of developing and deploying edge applications. With the proliferation of Internet of Things (IoT) devices, securing these devices and their communications is crucial to protect sensitive data and maintain the integrity of the system. This section elucidates the robust security mechanisms and configurations available via Azure IoT services, ensuring your edge deployments remain secure.

The security measures for edge devices encompass several domains including authentication, encryption, and secure booting.

- **Authentication and Authorization**: Azure IoT Hub provides robust authentication and authorization mechanisms to secure device access. Devices can be authenticated using symmetric keys, X.509 certificates, or through the use of an identity service. Authentication ensures that only legitimate devices are granted access to the IoT Hub.

  - **Symmetric Key Authentication**: Each device is associated with a unique key. This key is used to generate a token which, in turn, is validated by the IoT Hub upon connection.

```
import hmac
import hashlib
import time
import base64
import urllib.parse

# Function to generate SAS token
def generate_sas_token(resource_uri, signing_key, policy_name=None,
    expiry=3600):
    ttl = int(time.time()) + expiry
    sign_key = "%s\n%d" % ((urllib.parse.quote_plus(resource_uri)), int
        (ttl))
    signature = base64.b64encode(hmac.new(base64.b64decode(
        signing_key), sign_key.encode('utf-8'), hashlib.sha256).digest())
    rawtoken = {
        'sr': resource_uri,
        'sig': signature,
        'se': str(int(ttl))
    }
    if policy_name:
        rawtoken['skn'] = policy_name
```

```
return 'SharedAccessSignature ' + urllib.parse.urlencode(rawtoken)

# Sample usage
resource_uri = "<IoT Hub resource URI here>"
signing_key = "<Device Primary Key here>"
sas_token = generate_sas_token(resource_uri, signing_key)
print(sas_token)
```

- **X.509 Certificate Authentication**: Devices use standard X.509 certificates for secure authentication. Certificates can be self-signed or issued by a trusted Certificate Authority (CA).

```
openssl req -x509 -newkey rsa:2048 -keyout my-device.key -out my-device.
    crt -days 365 -nodes -subj "/CN=my-device"
```

- **Managed Identity**: Azure IoT Hub supports the use of Managed Identities for easier device management and security. Managed Identities are Azure Active Directory (Azure AD) identities managed by Azure and offer a simpler and more secure solution for authentication.

• **Encryption**: Securing the data in transit and at rest is paramount to protecting sensitive information. Azure IoT Hub and its associated services offer several encryption mechanisms to ensure data security.

- **Data in Transit:** Azure IoT enables transport encryption via TLS 1.2 or higher. All communications between devices and the IoT Hub must leverage these encryption protocols to prevent interception and tampering.

```
import ssl
from azure.iot.device import IoTHubDeviceClient, Message

# Setup TLS context
ssl_context = ssl.create_default_context()
ssl_context.check_hostname = True
ssl_context.verify_mode = ssl.CERT_REQUIRED

# Create client instance with SSL context
client = IoTHubDeviceClient.create_from_connection_string("<device
    connection string>", ssl_context)
client.connect()
```

- **Data at Rest:** Azure provides built-in encryption to protect data stored in the cloud, using Azure Storage Service Encryption (SSE) for data at rest.

- **Secure Boot and Device Integrity**: Edge devices must have secure boot mechanisms to ensure that the device starts up using a trusted version of the firmware. Secure boot leverages cryptographic signatures to validate the integrity and authenticity of the software.

  - **Trusted Platform Module (TPM):** TPMs are hardware-based security modules that provide robust device authentication and integrity checking.

    The combination of secure boot and TPM ensures that only validated software can run on the device. This prevents malicious code from taking control of the device during the boot process.

- **Networking Security**: Using network security best practices and configurations helps to prevent unauthorized access to your edge devices and data.

  - **Firewall Configuration:** Configuring firewalls to limit access to open ports and interfaces is essential.

    ```
    iptables -A INPUT -p tcp -s 192.168.1.100 --dport 8883 -j ACCEPT
    iptables -A INPUT -p tcp --dport 8883 -j DROP
    ```

  - **Virtual Private Network (VPN):** Setting up a VPN encrypts the entire communication channel, providing an additional layer of security.

- **Monitoring and Alerts**: Regular monitoring and setting up alerts for unusual activity can help in detecting and mitigating potential security threats.

  - **Azure Security Center:** Azure Security Center provides unified security management and advanced threat protection across hybrid cloud workloads. Device security can be monitored, and recommendations are provided to ensure compliance and tackle vulnerabilities.

    Enabling thorough monitoring practices ensures that any anomaly is promptly detected and addressed, maintaining the overall health and security of the edge deployment.

By integrating these multifaceted security mechanisms, developers can significantly enhance the robustness and resilience of their edge applications on Azure IoT.

3.10 Monitoring and Troubleshooting Edge Applications

Accurate and efficient monitoring of edge applications within Azure IoT is critical to maintain robust and reliable operations. Monitoring facilitates the identification of potential issues, enabling proactive management and resolution before they escalate into significant problems. This section explores various methodologies and tools available for monitoring and troubleshooting edge applications, focusing on performance metrics, diagnostics, and logging within the Azure IoT ecosystem.

The Azure IoT suite provides powerful tools such as Azure Monitor, Azure IoT Edge Monitoring, and integration with Application Insights to offer comprehensive observability of edge deployments. These tools furnish insights into system behavior, enabling detailed scrutiny of the health and performance of edge devices and applications.

Azure Monitor:

Azure Monitor is a vital service for collecting and analyzing telemetry data from various sources within an Azure environment. It encompasses a variety of features, which include metrics, logs, and alerts, offering a complete monitoring solution for edge applications.

To configure Azure Monitor for your edge applications, ensure that telemetry data from IoT devices is routed to the Azure Monitor. This involves setting up diagnostic settings to stream data from the IoT Hub to Log Analytics workspaces.

```
az monitor diagnostic-settings create \
  --resource-id "/subscriptions/{subscriptionId}/resourceGroups/{resourceGroupName
      }/providers/Microsoft.Devices/IotHubs/{iotHubName}" \
  --name "IoTHubMonitorSetting" \
  --workspace "/subscriptions/{subscriptionId}/resourceGroups/{resourceGroupName
      }/providers/Microsoft.OperationalInsights/workspaces/{workspaceName}" \
  --logs '[{"category": "DeviceTelemetry", "enabled": true}]'
```

98

This command routes the device telemetry logs to a specific Log Analytics workspace linked to Azure Monitor. Utilizing this configuration, the data can be visualized and queried to monitor the edge deployment's performance.

Azure IoT Edge Monitoring:

Azure IoT Edge monitoring capabilities focus on the modular architecture of edge computing, providing monitoring at both the device and module levels. One of the primary components enabling this is the IoT Edge Metrics Collector, which can be deployed on edge devices to gather metrics.

Here's how you can deploy and configure the IoT Edge Metrics Collector:

```
{
  "version": "1.0",
  "modulesContent": {
    "$edgeAgent": {
      "properties.desired.modules": {
        "metrics-collector": {
          "type": "docker",
          "settings": {
            "image": "microsoft/iotedge-metrics-collector:latest",
            "createOptions": "{}"
          }
        }
      }
    }
  }
}
```

This manifest snippet configures the deployment of the Metrics Collector module on an edge device. After deploying, the module will start collecting various metrics, such as CPU usage, memory consumption, and network statistics. These metrics are crucial for analyzing the resource utilization and performance of edge devices and identifying any anomalies or bottlenecks.

Application Insights:

For more detailed application-level monitoring, Azure Application Insights can be integrated into the IoT Edge modules to provide performance monitoring, logging, and telemetry.

Here's an example of initializing Application Insights SDK in a Python-based edge module:

```
from applicationinsights import TelemetryClient

INSTRUMENTATION_KEY = "your-instrumentation-key"
tc = TelemetryClient(INSTRUMENTATION_KEY)

# Custom telemetry
tc.track_event('IoT Edge Module Start')
tc.flush()
```

By setting up the TelemetryClient with the appropriate instrumentation key, developers can log custom events and metrics directly to Application Insights, offering fine-grained analysis and insights into module-specific behavior.

Log Diagnostics:

Comprehensive logging is indispensable for effective troubleshooting. Logs can provide visibility into application errors and operational issues. Within Azure IoT Edge, logs from modules can be collected and reviewed for diagnostic purposes.

Here's an example of retrieving logs from an IoT Edge module:

```
az iot edge logs \
    --device-id {device_id} \
    --module-id {module_id} \
    --hub-name {iothub_name}
```

These logs should be examined for error messages, stack traces, and any other pertinent information that could aid in diagnosing issues. Regular review of these logs is recommended to catch and resolve issues swiftly.

Moreover, integrating logging with centralized log storage solutions like Azure Log Analytics presents a scalable approach to log management. By aggregating logs, organizations can perform advanced queries, set up alerts, and visualize log data effectively.

Alerts and Notifications:

Setting up alerts based on the metrics and logs ensures prompt notification of issues. Azure Monitor supports creating alert rules that can trigger various notification methods such as email, SMS, or even automated remediation scripts.

Here is an example PowerShell script to create an alert rule for monitoring high CPU usage on an edge device:

```
$alertRule = New-AzMetricAlertRuleV2 '
 -ResourceGroupName "EdgeResourceGroup" '
 -Name "HighCPUUsageAlert" '
 -Location "eastus" '
 -TargetResourceId "/subscriptions/{subscriptionId}/resourceGroups/{
      resourceGroupName}/providers/Microsoft.Devices/IotHubs/{iotHubName}" '
 -WindowSize "PT5M" '
 -Frequency "PT1M" '
 -Criteria (New-AzMetricAlertCriteria '
   -Name "HighCPUPercentage" '
   -MetricName "cpuUsage" '
   -Operator "GreaterThan" '
   -Threshold 80)

Add-AzMetricAlertRuleV2 '
  -ResourceGroup "EdgeResourceGroup" '
  -InputObject $alertRule
```

Such alert rules facilitate proactive management, ensuring that administrators are informed about potential issues before they impact system operations.

Monitoring and troubleshooting edge applications is an iterative and continuous process, benefiting immensely from the comprehensive set of tools and services provided by Azure IoT. Leveraging these tools, administrators can maintain optimal performance, achieve high availability, and ensure the reliability of their edge deployments.

Chapter 4

Data Management and Storage in Edge Computing

This chapter addresses techniques for effective data management and storage in edge computing environments. It explores methods for data collection, aggregation, and local storage solutions, alongside strategies for data replication and synchronization with the cloud. Emphasis is placed on data security, privacy, and compliance, including best practices for implementing data pipelines and storage optimization. The chapter also covers critical aspects like data backup and disaster recovery to ensure data integrity and availability.

4.1 Introduction to Data Management in Edge Computing

Edge computing is an evolutionary paradigm in distributed computing that brings computation and data storage closer to the data source.

This architectural approach mitigates latency, reduces bandwidth consumption, and enhances overall system responsiveness. However, deploying an efficient data management strategy at the edge presents unique challenges that differ from traditional cloud-based systems.

In edge computing environments, devices such as sensors, smartphones, and IoT devices continuously generate vast amounts of data. Efficiently managing this data is crucial to minimize storage overhead, ensure quick access, and maintain data integrity and security. The distinguishing factor of edge computing is its decentralization, requiring local data handling methods to facilitate real-time processing while concurrently enabling seamless synchronization with centralized cloud infrastructures.

Effective data management at the edge encompasses a range of activities, including data collection, storage, processing, and replication. These activities must be tailored to address the constraints and capabilities specific to edge devices, such as limited storage capacity, processing power, and energy efficiency. The goal is to provide a robust framework that optimizes resource usage while ensuring system reliability and data fidelity.

To comprehend the specifics of managing data in edge computing, one must initially understand the entire data lifecycle, from generation to storage, and subsequent processing. The lifecycle encompasses the following stages:

- **Data Collection:** This initial stage involves gathering data from various edge devices. Due to the heterogeneous nature of these devices, the data formats and communication protocols can vary significantly. Therefore, implementing standardized data collection mechanisms is essential to ensure interoperability and data consistency.

- **Data Aggregation and Filtering:** Post-collection, raw data often requires aggregation and filtering to remove redundancies and noise. Processing at this stage is critical to reduce the volume of data that needs to be stored and transmitted, optimizing bandwidth usage and storage efficiency. Data aggregation techniques such as summarization, sampling, and thresholding are commonly employed.

104

- **Local Data Storage:** Storing data locally at the edge involves selecting appropriate storage solutions tailored to the device's constraints. Local storage strategies must balance factors like speed, capacity, durability, and cost. Techniques such as hierarchical storage management and tiered storage can help in optimizing space usage and providing quick data access.

- **Data Replication and Synchronization:** Ensuring data consistency and availability between edge devices and centralized cloud storage involves replicating and synchronizing data. This process must be meticulously designed to handle network variations and minimize latency while preserving data integrity. Protocols such as eventual consistency, strong consistency, and delta synchronization play crucial roles in this context.

- **Data Security and Privacy:** Given the sensitivity of data handled at the edge, implementing stringent security measures is indispensable. This includes employing encryption, access control, and secure communication protocols. Moreover, privacy regulations like GDPR necessitate mechanisms for data anonymization and user consent management.

- **Scalability and Performance Optimization:** The scalability of edge data management solutions is pivotal to accommodate the growing number of edge devices and their data. Techniques such as distributed storage, load balancing, and caching can significantly enhance the performance and scalability of the system.

- **Data Backup and Disaster Recovery:** To mitigate the risk of data loss due to failures or disasters, comprehensive data backup and recovery strategies are essential. This involves regular data backups, failover mechanisms, and recovery plans to ensure system resilience and data availability.

The intersection of these activities forms the crux of data management in edge computing. Each stage introduces specific challenges and necessitates tailored solutions to efficiently manage data across diverse and resource-constrained environments. Additionally, the synergy between local processing and cloud integration is vital to leverage the full potential of edge computing, enabling scalable and resilient data management practices.

Mastering these aspects facilitates the development of robust edge computing systems that can efficiently handle data-intensive applications, provide real-time insights, and adapt to the dynamic nature of edge environments.

4.2 Data Collection at the Edge

Data collection at the edge is a fundamental aspect of edge computing. It involves gathering data from various sources, including sensors, IoT devices, and user interactions, at the edge of the network, close to the point of data generation. This section delves into the methodologies, tools, and best practices for efficient and effective data collection at the edge.

The primary objective of data collection at the edge is to minimize latency and reduce the amount of data transmitted to the central cloud, thereby conserving bandwidth and enhancing real-time processing capabilities. This process demands a comprehensive understanding of the data sources, collection mechanisms, and the constraints imposed by the edge environment.

Essential components involved in edge data collection include:

- **Data Sources:** These are the origins of data generation and include various types of sensors (e.g., temperature, humidity, motion), IoT devices, cameras, and other edge endpoints.

- **Communication Interfaces:** The hardware and protocols used for transferring data from sources to edge processing units. Common interfaces include Wi-Fi, Bluetooth, Zigbee, LoRaWAN, and cellular networks.

- **Edge Nodes and Gateways:** Devices responsible for initial data collection and preliminary processing. They can be simple microcontrollers, single-board computers, or more complex edge servers.

Data Acquisition Protocols

106

Various protocols are employed in the data acquisition process. Some of the widely used protocols include:

- **MQTT (Message Queuing Telemetry Transport):** Lightweight messaging protocol ideal for IoT devices with limited processing power and bandwidth. It operates on a publish-subscribe model, enabling efficient data transfer.

- **HTTP/HTTPS:** Common protocols used for web communications, also applicable to IoT devices for data transmission. HTTPS provides an additional layer of security via encryption.

- **CoAP (Constrained Application Protocol):** Designed for constrained devices, it supports simple GET, POST, PUT, and DELETE methods similar to HTTP but with lower overhead.

- **DDS (Data Distribution Service):** A real-time protocol often used in mission-critical applications requiring high-quality data distribution and QoS (Quality of Service) guarantees.

Data Collection Methods

Data can be collected in two primary ways: actively or passively.

- **Active Data Collection:** This method involves direct interaction with the data source. An example is querying a sensor at regular intervals to retrieve its readings. While this provides control over data collection frequency, it can introduce delays and increase energy consumption.

- **Passive Data Collection:** In contrast, passive collection relies on the data source to push updates when specific events occur. For instance, a motion detector sending an alert when movement is detected. This method is generally more efficient in terms of power consumption and bandwidth.

Synchronization and Time Stamping

Accurate data collection necessitates synchronization across devices, especially in scenarios that require data fusion from multiple sources. Time stamping plays a crucial role, as chronological alignment of data

107

points is imperative for subsequent analysis. Techniques such as NTP (Network Time Protocol) and PTP (Precision Time Protocol) are commonly employed to ensure temporal accuracy.

Data Preprocessing

Before data is forwarded for further processing or storage, it often undergoes preprocessing steps at the edge:

- **Filtering:** Removing noise and irrelevant data points to enhance data quality. Techniques such as moving average and Kalman filtering are commonly used.

- **Normalization:** Converting data into a consistent format or scale to facilitate uniform analysis.

- **Compression:** Reducing data size to minimize storage requirements and transmission overhead. Methods such as delta encoding and run-length encoding can be applied.

Code Example

Below is a simple example illustrating how to use MQTT protocol for data collection from a temperature sensor in Python:

```python
import paho.mqtt.client as mqtt
import time

# MQTT settings
broker = "mqtt.example.com"
port = 1883
topic = "sensor/temperature"

# Callback when a connection to the broker is established
def on_connect(client, userdata, flags, rc):
    print("Connected to broker with result code " + str(rc))
    client.subscribe(topic)

# Callback when a message is received
def on_message(client, userdata, msg):
    print(msg.topic + " " + str(msg.payload))

# Create an MQTT client instance
client = mqtt.Client()
client.on_connect = on_connect
client.on_message = on_message

# Connect to the broker
client.connect(broker, port, 60)
```

```
# Blocking loop to process network traffic, callbacks, and reconnecting
client.loop_start()

try:
    while True:
        time.sleep(1)
except KeyboardInterrupt:
    client.loop_stop()
    client.disconnect()
```

Output Example

The execution of the above code will produce output like:

```
Connected to broker with result code 0
sensor/temperature b'22.5'
sensor/temperature b'22.4'
sensor/temperature b'22.6'
```

This demonstrates the fundamental process of subscribing to an MQTT topic and receiving temperature data from a sensor.

Security Considerations

Security is paramount in data collection at the edge. Data integrity, confidentiality, and authentication must be ensured. Common security measures include:

- **Encryption:** Both at rest and in transit to protect data from eavesdropping and tampering. Protocols such as TLS (Transport Layer Security) are commonly used.

- **Authentication:** Ensuring that only authorized devices and users can access and transmit data. Methods include certificates, tokens, and user credentials.

- **Access Control:** Implementing fine-grained permissions to restrict access to sensitive data based on roles and policies.

These best practices and methodologies enable robust, efficient, and secure data collection at the edge, forming a solid foundation for subsequent data processing and analysis.

4.3 Data Aggregation and Filtering

In edge computing environments, raw data collected from various distributed sensors and IoT devices can quickly become voluminous, posing challenges for storage, transmission, and processing. Data aggregation and filtering are essential techniques for managing this data effectively. Aggregation involves combining multiple data points to yield summarized information, while filtering selectively attenuates or excludes unwanted data. These methods reduce the data volume, helping in improving processing efficiency and ensuring that only relevant information is transmitted to cloud storage or centralized systems.

Data aggregation in edge computing can be achieved using various strategies, such as temporal, spatial, and content-based aggregation. Temporal aggregation collects data over time intervals to generate summary statistics such as average, sum, minimum, and maximum values. This is especially useful in time-series analysis where sensors might report data continuously. Spatial aggregation, on the other hand, involves grouping data based on geographical proximity or other spatial relationships, which is crucial in applications such as environmental monitoring and smart cities. Content-based aggregation relies on the semantic content of the data and groups or summarizes data based on predefined criteria, such as event detection in surveillance systems.

```
import pandas as pd

# Create a sample dataset
data = {'timestamp': pd.date_range(start='2023-01-01', periods=100, freq='T'),
        'sensor_reading': range(100)}

df = pd.DataFrame(data)

# Perform temporal aggregation by computing the mean for 10-minute intervals
df.set_index('timestamp', inplace=True)
aggr\texttt{egated extunderscore data = df.resample('10T').mean()}

print(aggregated_data)
```

The Python code snippet above demonstrates how to perform temporal aggregation. By leveraging the pandas library, sensor readings sampled every minute are aggregated into 10-minute intervals, with the mean of the sensor readings computed for each interval.

Filtering, by contrast, can be implemented using simple techniques like thresholding, where data points below or above a set threshold value are excluded. Advanced filtering techniques may involve signal processing methods such as low-pass, high-pass, and band-pass filtering, as well as statistical methods like anomaly detection and noise reduction. For example, in a smart healthcare application, filtering techniques can be used to identify and exclude or flag anomalous biometric readings that fall outside expected physiological ranges.

```
import pandas as pd

# Example data
data = {'timestamp': pd.date_range(start='2023-01-01', periods=100, freq='T'),
        'sensor_reading': range(100)}

df = pd.DataFrame(data)

# Set a threshold to filter out sensor readings below 20
threshold = 20
filtered_data = df[df['sensor_reading'] >= threshold]

print(filtered_data)
```

The code above shows a simple threshold-based filtering operation, where only sensor readings greater than or equal to the threshold value are retained, effectively reducing the data volume and focusing on the most pertinent information.

Efficient data aggregation and filtering necessitate a balance between the loss of data granularity and the need for reduced data complexity. These techniques become particularly significant in the context of data replication and synchronization with the cloud, as they minimize network bandwidth consumption and storage requirements, ensuring timely data delivery and optimal resource utilization.

Implementing these techniques at the edge allows for smarter initial data handling, reducing the burden on central processing units and streamlining data pipelines. Moreover, careful design of aggregation and filtering rules helps in maintaining data integrity and relevance, which is paramount for downstream applications that rely on near-real-time analytics and decision-making.

4.4 Local Data Storage Solutions

Local data storage solutions in edge computing environments play a crucial role in ensuring efficient and timely access to data. These solutions encompass various storage architectures, technologies, and methodologies designed to handle the unique requirements posed by edge applications.

1. Storage Architectures:

Several storage architectures can be leveraged for local data storage at the edge. These include:

- **Direct Attached Storage (DAS):** This architecture involves storage devices directly connected to a computing node. The primary benefit of DAS is its high performance due to the proximity of the storage to the CPU. Common examples include internal HDDs and SSDs.

- **Network Attached Storage (NAS):** NAS devices provide a centralized storage solution accessible over a network. They are ideal for sharing data across multiple devices and offer easy scalability and management.

- **Storage Area Network (SAN):** SANs are high-speed networked storage solutions that provide block-level storage. They are typically used in enterprise environments requiring large-scale, high-performance storage.

2. Storage Technologies:

The choice of storage technology directly impacts the performance and reliability of data storage at the edge. Common technologies include:

- **Hard Disk Drives (HDDs):** Known for their high capacity and low cost per gigabyte, HDDs are suitable for storing large volumes of data with less frequent access requirements.

- **Solid State Drives (SSDs):** SSDs offer significantly higher performance compared to HDDs, with faster read/write speeds and lower latency. They are ideal for applications requiring quick data access.

- **Non-Volatile Memory Express (NVMe):** NVMe is a protocol designed for SSDs that reduces latency and increases input/output operations per second (IOPS) compared to traditional SATA-based SSDs.

3. Storage Methods:

Effective data management at the edge requires the implementation of various storage methods, each offering distinct benefits.

- **Caching:** Caching involves temporarily storing frequently accessed data in fast storage media such as SSDs or RAM. This method significantly reduces latency and improves access times.

- **Tiered Storage:** Tiered storage combines different types of storage media, such as HDDs and SSDs, to optimize cost and performance. Frequently accessed data is stored in faster media, while less frequently accessed data is moved to slower, more cost-effective storage.

- **Data Deduplication:** Deduplication reduces storage requirements by removing redundant data. This method is particularly beneficial in environments with high data redundancy, such as backup systems.

4. Implementation Considerations:

When implementing local data storage solutions, several factors must be taken into account to ensure optimal performance and reliability:

- **Latency and Bandwidth:** Edge computing environments often require low latency and high bandwidth to support real-time applications. Choosing storage technologies and architectures that meet these requirements is critical.

- **Scalability:** As data volumes increase, the chosen storage solution must be able to scale effectively. NAS and SAN architectures provide scalability options that can grow with the application's needs.

113

- **Reliability and Failover:** Ensuring data reliability and availability is paramount, particularly in mission-critical applications. Implementing redundancy mechanisms, such as RAID (Redundant Array of Independent Disks) configurations, can protect against data loss.

- **Cost Efficiency:** Balancing performance and cost is essential. Deploying a combination of high-performance and cost-effective storage options can optimize expenditures without compromising on application requirements.

5. Example Configuration:

Consider a scenario where an edge computing application processes video data from numerous surveillance cameras. The application's storage requirements include high performance for real-time video access, substantial capacity for long-term storage, and redundancy to ensure data integrity.

A suitable storage solution might involve:

- Utilizing SSDs with NVMe interface for real-time video data caching, ensuring minimal latency and rapid access speeds.

- Employing tiered storage with a combination of SSDs and HDDs. SSDs would handle frequently accessed data, while HDDs store archived video footage.

- Implementing a RAID 5 configuration to provide a balance between performance, capacity, and redundancy.

By carefully selecting and configuring storage components, the application can achieve the necessary performance and reliability without incurring excessive costs. The architecture ensures that critical data is quickly accessible while maintaining the capacity for long-term storage and protecting against data loss through redundancy mechanisms.

4.5 Data Replication and Synchronization with the Cloud

Data replication and synchronization are critical components in an edge computing architecture to ensure data consistency, availability, and integrity between edge devices and the cloud. This section examines various aspects of data replication and synchronization mechanisms, detailing strategies, challenges, and best practices to achieve reliable data management across distributed environments.

Edge computing environments often face intermittent connectivity and variable network bandwidth, necessitating efficient methods for synchronizing data with the cloud. This ensures that data collected and processed at the edge is consistently updated in the central cloud storage, facilitating further analysis, backup, and integration with broader data ecosystems.

Challenges of Data Replication and Synchronization:

- Network Reliability and Bandwidth: Sporadic connectivity and limited bandwidth can hinder continuous data synchronization, requiring robust algorithms to handle spotty networks.

- Data Consistency: Maintaining consistency between edge and cloud data stores, especially with concurrent updates, is crucial to prevent discrepancies.

- Latency: Minimizing latency during synchronization to ensure timely updates and minimize the risk of outdated information.

- Conflict Resolution: Addressing conflicts that arise from concurrent data modifications both at the edge and in the cloud, necessitating conflict resolution strategies.

Replication Strategies:

- Full-Replication: Involves copying all data from edge devices to the cloud. This can be bandwidth-intensive but ensures complete data availability and redundancy.

115

- Incremental-Replication: Transfers only changed data since the last synchronization, which can significantly reduce bandwidth usage.

- Delta-Replication: Similar to incremental replication but only transfers the actual data changes rather than entire records or files, optimizing network usage further.

```
import boto3
from botocore.exceptions import NoCredentialsError, PartialCredentialsError

class EdgeToCloudSync:
    def __init__(self, local_data_path, s3_bucket_name):
        self.local_data_path = local_data_path
        self.s3_bucket_name = s3_bucket_name
        self.s3_client = boto3.client('s3')

    def get_local_changes(self):
        # Retrieve list of changed files since last sync
        # This method to be implemented as per local tracking system
        changed_files = []
        # Populate changed_files with logic here
        return changed_files

    def replicate_changes(self):
        changed_files = self.get_local_changes()
        for file in changed_files:
            try:
                self.s3_client.upload_file(file, self.s3_bucket_name, file)
                print(f"Uploaded {file} to S3 bucket {self.s3_bucket_name}")
            except (NoCredentialsError, PartialCredentialsError):
                print("Credentials are not available.")
            except Exception as e:
                print(f"Failed to upload {file}: {str(e)}")

# Example usage
sync = EdgeToCloudSync('/path/to/edge/data', 'my-s3-bucket')
sync.replicate_changes()
```

Conflict Resolution Mechanisms:

- Timestamps and Versioning: Using timestamps and version numbers to track changes and prioritize the latest updates during synchronization.

- Operational Transforms: Applying operational transform algorithms to reconcile conflicting changes in a collaborative editing scenario.

- Application-Specific Logic: Defining custom logic depending on

116

the application's needs to determine how conflicts should be resolved.

```
def resolve_conflict(local_data, cloud_data):
    if local_data['timestamp'] > cloud_data['timestamp']:
        return local_data
    else:
        return cloud_data
```

Synchronization Models:

- Push Model: Edge devices actively push updates to the cloud as they occur. This model ensures real-time data availability but can be demanding on network resources.

- Pull Model: The cloud periodically polls edge devices for updates, reducing the instantaneous network load but introducing potential latency in data availability.

- Hybrid Model: Combines elements of both push and pull models, where critical data is pushed immediately, and less critical data is polled periodically. This balances the load and ensures essential updates are timely.

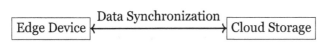

Practical Considerations:

- Data Prioritization: Identifying and prioritizing critical data for immediate synchronization to ensure essential information is always up-to-date.

- Compression: Employing data compression techniques to minimize the volume of data transmitted over the network, optimizing bandwidth utilization.

- Security: Ensuring secure transmission using encryption protocols like TLS to protect data integrity and confidentiality during synchronization.

- Failover Mechanisms: Implementing failover strategies to handle synchronization failures gracefully, such as retry mechanisms and fallback procedures.

```
#!/bin/bash

SRC_DIR="/path/to/edge/data"
DEST_DIR="user@remote:/path/to/cloud/storage"
LOG_FILE="/path/to/logfile.log"

tar -czf data_archive.tar.gz -C $SRC_DIR .
rsync -avz --progress data_archive.tar.gz $DEST_DIR >> $LOG_FILE 2>&1

if [ $? -eq 0 ]; then
    echo "Synchronization successful." >> $LOG_FILE
else
    echo "Synchronization failed." >> $LOG_FILE
fi
```

Effective data replication and synchronization strategies are paramount for the reliability, scalability, and performance of edge computing solutions. Employing a combination of these techniques tailored to specific use cases and environments ensures that data remains consistent and accessible across distributed edge and cloud infrastructures. By understanding and addressing the challenges involved, implementing robust replication methods, and adopting best practices, edge computing systems can achieve efficient and seamless data integration with the cloud.

4.6 Edge Databases: Types and Use Cases

Edge databases are essential for managing and storing data close to where it is generated in edge computing environments, providing low-latency access and reducing the load on centralized cloud services. This section delves into the various types of edge databases and their specific use cases, ensuring a comprehensive understanding of their functionalities and benefits.

Two primary types of edge databases are commonly utilized in edge computing: time-series databases and NoSQL databases, with further categorization within each type. These databases are optimized for the unique demands of edge environments, including handling large volumes of data, providing real-time processing capabilities, and ensuring robustness in disconnected or intermittent connectivity scenarios.

Time-series databases (TSDBs) are designed to store and retrieve time-stamped data efficiently. This type of data is particularly relevant in edge computing for applications such as monitoring IoT devices, industrial automation, and energy management systems. One leading example of a time-series database is InfluxDB. It offers high write and query performance, retention policies, and downsampling capabilities, making it ideal for environments where data is continuously generated over time.

```
CREATE DATABASE edge_monitoring;
USE edge_monitoring;

CREATE RETENTION POLICY one_year ON edge_monitoring DURATION 52w
    REPLICATION 1 DEFAULT;

INSERT INTO metrics,device=sensor1 temperature=25.3,humidity=68.5 1563201400;
INSERT INTO metrics,device=sensor2 temperature=22.1,humidity=65.2 1563201500;
```

A critical feature of TSDBs is their ability to handle high throughput for time-stamped data and provide efficient querying capabilities for real-time analytics. This is crucial for applications where actionable insights are derived from time-series data, such as predictive maintenance and anomaly detection in industrial settings.

NoSQL databases, on the other hand, encompass a variety of database types including key-value stores, document stores, column-family stores, and graph databases. These databases are known for their ability to scale horizontally and handle semi-structured or unstructured data, making them highly suitable for edge environments with diverse data formats and requirements.

One prominent example is MongoDB, a document-oriented NoSQL database. MongoDB is well-suited for edge computing scenarios where data needs to be stored in flexible, JSON-like documents, and where the schema can evolve over time. This flexibility is particularly beneficial for edge applications such as smart retail and connected vehicles, where data structures can frequently change.

```
from pymongo import MongoClient

client = MongoClient('localhost', 27017)
db = client['edge_computing']
collection = db['sensor_data']

sensor_data = {
    "device_id": "sensor1",
```

```
    "temperature": 24.3,
    "humidity": 67.4,
    "timestamp": 1563201600
}

collection.insert_one(sensor_data)
```

In use cases such as smart homes, edge databases like SQLite, an embedded SQL database engine, are often employed due to their lightweight nature and zero-configuration deployment. SQLite is particularly effective in scenarios with resource-constrained devices where a full-fledged database server is not feasible. Its ability to store data locally on devices enables immediate data access and manipulation, enhancing the performance of applications that rely on persistent but lightweight data storage.

Another example is the use of graph databases such as Neo4j in edge environments for applications requiring complex relationship management and querying, like social network analysis and fraud detection. Graph databases enable the modeling of entities and their interconnections efficiently, providing rapid traversal and analytic capabilities at the edge.

When evaluating edge databases, it's imperative to consider factors such as consistency, availability, and partition tolerance, commonly referred to as the CAP theorem. Edge databases often have to trade-off between these factors depending on specific application requirements. For instance, in critical industrial automation applications, consistency and availability may be prioritized over partition tolerance to ensure data accuracy and system reliability.

Replicating data to cloud or centralized databases for further processing, aggregation, and long-term storage is another vital aspect of edge database use cases. This replication ensures that data collected at the edge is safeguarded and integrated with broader enterprise systems for comprehensive analytics and reporting.

In distributed edge deployments, database synchronization mechanisms ensure that localized databases remain consistent with each other and with the central database, even in the face of network partitions. Techniques such as conflict-free replicated data types (CRDTs) and operational transformation (OT) facilitate robust synchronization and conflict resolution across distributed nodes.

Edge databases provide the essential infrastructure for a wide range of applications by offering localized data processing capabilities, high availability, and resilience in edge computing environments. Their selection and implementation are crucial for optimizing performance, ensuring data integrity, and meeting the specific requirements of edge deployments.

4.7 Data Security and Privacy at the Edge

Data security and privacy are paramount concerns in the context of edge computing due to the distributed nature of data collection, processing, and storage. This section delves into the critical aspects and best practices to ensure the protection of data as it moves closer to where it is generated and consumed.

Data security at the edge involves protecting data against unauthorized access and breaches during collection, transmission, storage, and processing. Achieving robust security at the edge necessitates a multi-layered approach encompassing encryption, authentication, access control, and anomaly detection mechanisms.

Encryption is a fundamental technique used to safeguard data in transit and at rest. Data collected at the edge devices must be encrypted before being transmitted to edge servers or the cloud to prevent interception by malicious actors. Modern cryptographic protocols like TLS (Transport Layer Security) should be employed to secure data during transmission. Additionally, data residing on edge devices and local storage solutions should be encrypted using standards like AES (Advanced Encryption Standard).

```
# Encrypt a file using AES-256
openssl enc -aes-256-cbc -salt -in plaintext.txt -out encrypted.dat -k password
```

Authentication and authorization are indispensable elements of a secure edge computing setup. Every device and user interacting with the edge infrastructure must be authenticated using strong, multi-factor authentication mechanisms. Public Key Infrastructure (PKI) can be employed to issue and manage digital certificates, ensuring that only trusted devices and users are granted access.

Access control mechanisms need to enforce the principle of least privilege, ensuring that users and devices are provided with only the minimum level of access required to perform their functions. Role-Based Access Control (RBAC) models are often implemented to achieve this granularity.

Anonymization of data is crucial to preserve user privacy, especially in compliance with regulations like GDPR (General Data Protection Regulation). Anonymization techniques make personal data irreversibly unidentifiable, thus reducing the risk of privacy breaches. Methods such as data masking, pseudonymization, and differential privacy can be employed.

```
import random

def mask_data(data):
    masked = "".join([random.choice("0123456789") for char in data])
    return masked

personal_data = "123-45-6789"
masked_data = mask_data(personal_data)
print(masked_data) # Output: Randomized masked data
```

Anomaly detection systems play a pivotal role in identifying and mitigating security breaches in near real-time. These systems can leverage machine learning algorithms to baseline normal behavior and detect deviations that may indicate security threats. Implementing intrusion detection and prevention systems (IDPS) at the edge can provide an additional layer of security.

```
import numpy as np

def detect_anomalies(data):
    threshold = 2
    mean = np.mean(data)
    std_dev = np.std(data)
    anomalies = [x for x in data if abs(x - mean) > threshold * std_dev]
    return anomalies

data_points = [10, 12, 10, 11, 30, 12, 9, 11, 13, 200]
anomalies = detect_anomalies(data_points)
print(anomalies) # Output: List of anomalies
```

Ensuring **device integrity** through secure boot and hardware root of trust mechanisms is critical. These mechanisms ensure that the device firmware is legitimate and has not been tampered with. Secure boot processes verify the integrity and authenticity of the software running on edge devices, providing a chain of trust from the hardware to the application layer.

Regular **security updates and patch management** are required to protect edge devices from vulnerabilities. Automated update mechanisms and secure firmware update processes should be established to ensure that devices remain protected against newly discovered threats.

Data auditing and monitoring provide visibility into data access patterns and potential security incidents. Logging mechanisms should be implemented to record access and modification events, which help in forensic analysis in case of a breach.

By integrating these security measures, organizations can safeguard the integrity and privacy of data in edge computing environments, ensuring both compliance with regulatory requirements and the maintenance of user trust.

4.8 Data Anonymization and GDPR Compliance

Data anonymization is a critical measure to ensure that sensitive information is safeguarded against unauthorized access and misuse. In edge computing environments, where data is often collected and processed locally before being synchronized with the cloud, the importance of effective data anonymization cannot be overstated. This section will delve into various techniques and strategies for anonymizing data and ensuring compliance with the General Data Protection Regulation (GDPR).

Data anonymization involves modifying datasets to prevent the identification of individuals from the data while maintaining data utility. One of the primary methods of achieving anonymization is de-identification, which includes processes such as pseudonymization and generalization. Pseudonymization replaces private identifiers with fake identifiers or pseudonyms, thereby protecting the identity of individuals without destroying the analytical value of the data. Generalization, on the other hand, involves diluting the precision of certain data points, such as converting exact ages into age ranges.

Another crucial technique is k-anonymity. A dataset achieves k-anonymity when each record is indistinguishable from at least k-1 other records concerning certain identifying attributes, known as quasi-identifiers. This approach mitigates the risk of re-identification by ensuring that individuals cannot be singled out within the dataset.

```
import pandas as pd
from sklearn.model_selection import train_test_split
from collections import Counter

# Sample dataset
data = {'Age': [29, 34, 52, 23, 45, 32],
        'Gender': ['M', 'F', 'M', 'F', 'M', 'F'],
        'ZIP': [12345, 23456, 12345, 23456, 12345, 23456]}
df = pd.DataFrame(data)

# Generalize Age into groups
df['Age'] = pd.cut(df['Age'], bins=[0, 30, 50, 100], labels=['<30', '30-50', '>50'])

# Check for k-anonymity (k=2)
def check_k_anonymity(df, k=2):
    quasi_identifiers = ['Age', 'Gender', 'ZIP']
    groups = df.groupby(quasi_identifiers).size()
    k_anonymity = (groups >= k).all()
    return k_anonymity

print("Dataset achieves k-anonymity:", check_k_anonymity(df))
```

Local edge devices must comply with GDPR when processing personal data. GDPR mandates explicit consent from individuals before their data can be processed, ensuring transparency about the data usage. Moreover, GDPR requires that any data subject can request access to their data or demand its deletion.

To stockpile data in compliance with GDPR, edge computing systems must incorporate privacy by design and default principles. These principles necessitate integrating data protection from the onset of the system's design rather than as an afterthought. Adhering to these principles ensures minimal data collection and strictly controlled data access, significantly reducing potential data breaches.

Differential privacy is another advanced technique used to ensure that statistical outputs from datasets do not compromise individual privacy. It adds controlled random noise to data or queries, making it difficult to identify individuals from aggregate data without significantly affecting the overall analysis results.

An example of implementing differential privacy can be illustrated as follows:

```
import numpy as np

# Laplace Mechanism for differential privacy
def laplace_mechanism(value, epsilon):
    sensitivity = 1 # Sensitivity of the query
    scale = sensitivity / epsilon
    return value + np.random.laplace(0, scale, 1)[0]

# Apply differential privacy to a dataset's mean
data = [10, 20, 30, 40, 50]
epsilon = 1.0 # Privacy budget
mean = np.mean(data)
noisy_mean = laplace_mechanism(mean, epsilon)

print(f"True mean: {mean}, Noisy mean with differential privacy: {noisy_mean}")
```

GDPR also enforces the right to be forgotten, which enables individuals to request deletion of their data. Implementing this right in edge computing involves maintaining a log of data handling activities and ensuring secure data deletion protocols.

```
import os

def secure_delete(file_path, passes=3):
    with open(file_path, "ba+", buffering=0) as delfile:
        length = delfile.tell()
    for i in range(passes):
        with open(file_path, "br+", buffering=0) as delfile:
            delfile.seek(0)
            delfile.write(os.urandom(length))
    os.remove(file_path)

# Secure delete a sensitive file
secure_delete('sensitive_data.txt')
```

Edge systems must implement rigorous access controls, encryption at rest and in transit, and regular audits to ensure GDPR compliance. Tools and technologies such as blockchain can assist in creating immutable logs for data access and modifications, facilitating transparency and traceability.

4.9 Implementing Data Pipelines

Implementing data pipelines in edge computing environments involves a series of intricate steps designed to ensure efficient data flow from data sources to storage systems, including processing and analysis. The architecture of data pipelines must address latency, bandwidth constraints, and resource limitations inherent in edge environments. This section delves into the components, design principles, and best practices for setting up robust data pipelines tailored for edge computing.

- **1. Data Ingestion:** The first step in any data pipeline is data ingestion, where data is collected from various sources such as sensors, IoT devices, and edge servers. This step captures raw data for further processing and storage. Various protocols like MQTT, HTTP, CoAP, and OPC-UA are commonly used for data ingestion in edge environments. The choice of protocol depends on factors such as power consumption, wireless communication range, and the nature of the data.

```
import paho.mqtt.client as mqtt

def on_connect(client, userdata, flags, rc):
    print(f"Connected with result code {rc}")
    client.subscribe("sensors/temperature")

def on_message(client, userdata, msg):
    print(f"{msg.topic} {msg.payload}")

client = mqtt.Client()
client.on_connect = on_connect
client.on_message = on_message

client.connect("mqtt.example.com", 1883, 60)
client.loop_forever()
```

- **2. Data Preprocessing:** Preprocessing entails cleaning, normalizing, and possibly transforming the raw data into a more usable format. This process helps in reducing the data dimensionality, handling missing values, and filtering out noise. Edge devices often perform preprocessing to lessen the data volume and enhance the quality of data transmitted to the cloud or downstream processing nodes.

```
import numpy as np

def remove_outliers(data, threshold=3):
    mean = np.mean(data)
    std_dev = np.std(data)
    filtered_data = [x for x in data if abs(x - mean) < threshold * std_dev]
    return filtered_data
```

```
sensor_data = [22, 21, 22, 23, 100, 21, 22]
cleaned_data = remove_outliers(sensor_data)
print(cleaned_data)
```

- **3. Data Transformation:** Depending on the application's requirements, collected data may need to be transformed into different formats or aggregated to derive meaningful insights. Techniques like data normalization, feature extraction, and data encoding are prevalent at this stage. These transformations can take place at the edge to minimize data transmission and storage costs.

```
from sklearn.preprocessing import MinMaxScaler

def normalize_data(data):
    scaler = MinMaxScaler()
    data_normalized = scaler.fit_transform(data.reshape(-1, 1))
    return data_normalized

temperature_readings = np.array([23, 24, 22, 25, 21, 23, 24])
normalized_readings = normalize_data(temperature_readings)
print(normalized_readings)
```

- **4. Data Storage:** Storing processed data efficiently is crucial for quick retrieval and long-term archival. The choice of storage solutions could range from local edge databases like SQLite and LiteDB to more complex setups involving distributed file systems and NoSQL databases. Considerations for redundancy, latency, and consistency play a significant role in the selection of appropriate storage mechanisms.

```
import sqlite3

connection = sqlite3.connect('edge_data.db')
cursor = connection.cursor()

cursor.execute('''
CREATE TABLE IF NOT EXISTS Temperature (
    id INTEGER PRIMARY KEY,
    reading FLOAT,
    timestamp DATETIME DEFAULT CURRENT_TIMESTAMP
)
''')

cursor.execute('''
INSERT INTO Temperature (reading) VALUES (22.5)
''')

connection.commit()
```

```
connection.close()
```

- **5. Data Analysis and Visualization:** After data storage, the data pipeline might include steps for data analysis and visualization, which can be pivotal for decision-making processes. Analysis techniques such as statistical analyses, real-time analytics, or machine learning models can be implemented at the edge to provide immediate insights. Visualization tools can also be incorporated for monitoring and reporting.

```python
import matplotlib.pyplot as plt

def plot_temperature_data(data):
    timestamps = [x['timestamp'] for x in data]
    readings = [x['reading'] for x in data]

    plt.plot(timestamps, readings)
    plt.xlabel('Timestamp')
    plt.ylabel('Temperature (C)')
    plt.title('Temperature Readings over Time')
    plt.show()

sensor_data = [
    {'timestamp': '2023-01-01 00:00:00', 'reading': 22.5},
    {'timestamp': '2023-01-01 01:00:00', 'reading': 22.7},
    {'timestamp': '2023-01-01 02:00:00', 'reading': 23.1}
]
plot_temperature_data(sensor_data)
```

- **6. Data Pipeline Orchestration:** Managing the end-to-end workflow of data pipelines involves orchestrating various tasks and ensuring their timely execution. Tools such as Apache NiFi, Azure IoT Edge, and Kubernetes can aid in this orchestration by providing robust mechanisms for task scheduling, resource allocation, and error handling.

```
az iot edge deployment create --resource-group MyResourceGroup --name
    MyDeployment --template-file deployment.json --target-condition "tags.
    environment='prod'" --priority 10
```

Data pipelines in edge computing benefit from modularity, scalability, and fault tolerance to achieve efficient data processing and reduced latency. Best practices include leveraging edge-specific hardware acceleration, deploying lightweight containers, and using asynchronous processing to optimize performance.

4.10 Optimizing Data Storage for Performance and Scalability

Edge computing environments necessitate efficient data storage strategies to handle large volumes of data generated by numerous edge devices, ensuring both high performance and scalability. These optimizations are critical to minimize latency, maximize throughput, and maintain reliable service quality. This section delves into various techniques and best practices for optimizing data storage to meet the stringent demands of edge computing.

- **1. Data Compression Techniques**

  Applying data compression can significantly reduce the storage footprint and improve data transfer rates. Common compression algorithms include gzip, LZ4, and Bzip2. The choice of compression algorithm depends on the required compression ratio and computational overhead.

  ```python
  import gzip
  import shutil

  def compress_file(input_file, output_file):
      with open(input_file, 'rb') as f_in:
          with gzip.open(output_file, 'wb') as f_out:
              shutil.copyfileobj(f_in, f_out)

  compress_file('data.txt', 'data.txt.gz')
  ```

- **2. Data Partitioning**

  Data partitioning involves dividing a dataset into smaller, manageable segments. This technique enhances query performance and enables parallel processing. In time-series databases like InfluxDB, partitioning data by time intervals can be particularly effective.

  ```sql
  CREATE TABLE measurements (
      sensor_id INT,
      reading_time TIMESTAMP,
      reading_value FLOAT
  ) PARTITION BY RANGE (extract(year FROM reading_time));

  CREATE TABLE measurements_2021 PARTITION OF measurements
      FOR VALUES FROM ('2021-01-01') TO ('2022-01-01');
  ```

- ## 3. Using In-Memory Datastores

  In-memory datastores like Redis and Memcached provide rapid read and write access to data by storing it in RAM. These are particularly useful for caching frequently accessed data.

```
import redis

r = redis.Redis(host='localhost', port=6379, db=0)

# Set data
r.set('key', 'value')

# Get data
value = r.get('key')
```

- ## 4. Leveraging Edge-Specific Database Solutions

  Edge-specific databases, such as SQLite for lightweight local storage and InfluxDB for time-series data, offer features optimized for edge environments. They are designed to run on limited-resource devices and handle intermittent connectivity.

```
import sqlite3

conn = sqlite3.connect('example.db')

c = conn.cursor()
c.execute('''CREATE TABLE readings (sensor_id int, value real, timestamp
    text)''')

c.execute("INSERT INTO readings VALUES (1, 23.7, '2023-10-10 10:00:00')")

conn.commit()
conn.close()
```

- ## 5. Implementing Efficient Indexing

  Indexes accelerate data retrieval operations. However, improper indexing can degrade write performance and consume excessive storage. It's crucial to balance indexing needs based on query patterns. B-trees and hash indexes are commonly used structures.

```
CREATE INDEX idx_reading_time ON measurements (reading_time);
```

- ## 6. Data Redundancy and Deduplication

  Storing multiple copies of data enhances fault tolerance but increases storage requirements. Deduplication processes can identify and eliminate redundant data, thus optimizing storage utilization while maintaining data redundancy.

```
def deduplicate_data(data):
    seen = set()
    deduplicated_data = []
    for item in data:
        if item not in seen:
            seen.add(item)
            deduplicated_data.append(item)
    return deduplicated_data

data = [1, 2, 2, 3, 4, 4, 5]
deduplicated_data = deduplicate_data(data)
print(deduplicated_data) # Output: [1, 2, 3, 4, 5]
```

- **7. Asynchronous Data Writing**

Asynchronous data writing allows the main application to continue processing without waiting for data to be written to storage. Implementing write-back or write-through caching strategies can further optimize performance.

```
import asyncio

async def write_data(file, data):
    with open(file, 'a') as f:
        f.write(data)

loop = asyncio.get_event_loop()
data = 'sample data'
loop.run_until_complete(write_data('data.txt', data))
loop.close()
```

- **8. Utilizing Content Delivery Networks (CDNs)**

CDNs distribute data across geographically dispersed servers, reducing latency and enhancing data access speed for distributed edge devices. Leveraging a CDN for static content can offload traffic from the primary edge storage.

To effectively optimize data storage for performance and scalability in edge computing, it is crucial to balance between the techniques described, tailoring them to the specific requirements and constraints of the edge environment.

131

4.11 Data Backup and Disaster Recovery in Edge Computing

In the scope of edge computing, data backup and disaster recovery are critical to ensure data integrity and service continuity. Implementing robust backup and recovery mechanisms is essential to mitigate the risks of data loss or system failures that could disrupt operations. This section delves into the concepts and methodologies tailored for edge computing environments, ensuring an adept handling of the unique challenges posed by decentralized architectures.

Backup strategies can be broadly categorized into full backups, incremental backups, and differential backups. Each strategy offers distinct advantages and trade-offs, particularly when applied to edge computing, where network constraints and storage limitations must be considered.

Full Backups involve copying all data from the source to the backup location. While this method provides comprehensive data redundancy, it requires significant storage space and bandwidth, which may not be feasible for edge devices with limited resources. Thus, full backups are typically scheduled less frequently, complemented by more efficient incremental or differential backups.

Incremental Backups copy only the data that has changed since the last backup. This approach significantly reduces the amount of data transferred and stored, making it an ideal choice for edge devices. However, restoration from incremental backups can be time-consuming, as it involves applying a series of changes starting from the last full backup.

Differential Backups represent a middle ground, storing all changes made since the last full backup. This method strikes a balance between the frequency and volume of data saved. Restoring from a differential backup is faster than an incremental backup as it requires only the last full backup and the last differential backup.

For edge computing environments, backup strategies need to be designed to handle intermittent network connectivity and limited bandwidth. One effective method is leveraging local storage for primary backup operations and asynchronously synchronizing with a central cloud repository. This ensures that data protection is maintained even during network outages.

```
# Example cron job for periodic local backups:
0 2 * * * /usr/bin/rsync -a /data/ /backup/
```

In edge-computing environments, redundancy and data distribution are fundamental for resilience. Multi-tier backup architectures, encompassing both local and cloud components, are often employed. Local storage provides quick access to recent backups while the cloud ensures protection from physical damage to edge devices.

Disaster Recovery (DR) mechanisms must consider the step-by-step process to restore normal operations within the specified Recovery Time Objective (RTO) and Recovery Point Objective (RPO). RTO denotes the maximum acceptable delay before the restoration of service, while RPO indicates the maximum permissible data loss in terms of time.

```
# Restoring data from local backup
/usr/bin/rsync -a /backup/ /data/

# Synchronizing with cloud backup
/usr/bin/aws s3 sync s3://mycloudbackup/ /data/
```

Edge devices may have varying RTO and RPO based on the criticality of services they support. It is imperative to design DR plans accordingly, ensuring high-priority services have minimal downtime and data loss.

Automated failover systems enhance disaster recovery capabilities by allowing services to switch to backup resources without manual intervention. Similarly, seamless integration with cloud services for backup and DR facilitates centralized management and monitoring, crucial for scalability.

```
import boto3
client = boto3.client('cloudwatch')

def monitor_and_failover(instance_id, backup_instance_id):
    response = client.describe_instance_status(InstanceIds=[instance_id])
    if response['InstanceStatuses'][0]['InstanceState']['Name'] != 'running':
        client.start_instances(InstanceIds=[backup_instance_id])
```

Considerations for security and compliance, such as encryption and data sovereignty, must be incorporated in the backup and DR planning. Encryption ensures that data remains secure both in transit and at rest, while respecting data sovereignty laws ensures compliance with regulations like GDPR.

```
from cryptography.fernet import Fernet

# Encryption key
key = Fernet.generate_key()
cipher_suite = Fernet(key)

# Encrypt data before backup
plaintext = b"Sensitive data"
ciphertext = cipher_suite.encrypt(plaintext)
```

Testing the backup and recovery procedures regularly ensures that the processes are reliable and that the employees are trained to carry out necessary steps during an actual disaster. It is advisable to document all backup and disaster recovery procedures comprehensively for consistency and accuracy in execution.

```
Backup completed successfully.
Restoration verified: all data restored accurately.
```

Continuous improvements and periodic reviews of the backup and DR plan help adapt to evolving requirements and potential new threats, ensuring robust data protection and resilience in an edge computing environment.

Chapter 5

Security and Compliance in Edge Computing

This chapter provides an in-depth analysis of security and compliance in edge computing. It examines the various security threats specific to edge environments and outlines strategies for device security, data encryption, and network protection. The importance of access control, identity management, and adherence to compliance standards such as GDPR is emphasized. Additionally, it covers best practices for incident response and recovery to maintain robust security postures and ensure regulatory compliance in edge deployments.

5.1 Introduction to Edge Security

The proliferation of edge computing devices, comprising sensors, gateways, and edge servers, necessitates the rigorous safeguarding of these systems against evolving security threats. Edge computing diverges significantly from traditional centralized cloud architectures by decentralizing computation and storage, thus introducing unique security challenges. This section outlines the fundamental principles and considerations pertinent to securing edge computing environments, laying the foundation for subsequent discussions on detailed security strategies and compliance measures.

A central facet of edge computing security is the inherent complexity and heterogeneity of edge devices. Unlike homogeneous, well-managed cloud data centers, edge environments can include a diverse array of devices, each with varying capabilities and security vulnerabilities. This diversity mandates a robust, adaptable security framework capable of accommodating the distinct characteristics of different device types. Furthermore, edge devices are often deployed in less controlled environments, such as remote locations or public spaces, increasing their susceptibility to physical tampering and unauthorized access.

Primary among the security concerns for edge computing is ensuring the integrity and confidentiality of data in transit and at rest. As data flows between edge devices and centralized cloud services, it is vital to implement strong encryption mechanisms to prevent interception and unauthorized modifications. Establishing end-to-end encryption ensures that even if data is intercepted during transmission, the contents remain secure and inaccessible without proper decryption keys.

Authentication and authorization mechanisms are critical components of a secure edge computing environment. Each device must be authenticated to verify its identity before being allowed to communicate with other devices or the central cloud. This prevents malicious actors from masquerading as legitimate devices. Authorization, on the other hand, ensures that authenticated devices have appropriate permissions to access specific resources and perform designated actions. Utilizing multi-factor authentication (MFA) and public key infrastructure (PKI) significantly enhances the security of these processes.

Another salient aspect is the need for continual monitoring and updating of edge devices. Due to their distributed nature, edge devices frequently operate outside the traditional IT security perimeter. This requires the implementation of remote management capabilities, enabling administrators to deploy security patches and updates efficiently. Automated update mechanisms can ensure that devices remain protected against newly discovered vulnerabilities without requiring direct physical access.

Device security also encompasses protecting the physical hardware from tampering. Tamper-resistant designs, secure boot processes, and hardware-based security modules (such as Trusted Platform Modules, or TPMs) provide robust defenses against physical attacks. These measures ensure that even if a device is physically compromised, the attacker is unable to extract sensitive information or alter the device's behavior without detection.

In terms of data confidentiality, employing data encryption is paramount. Encrypted data storage ensures that sensitive information stored on edge devices remains secure even if the device is compromised. This is particularly important for use cases involving personal or sensitive data, such as healthcare or financial applications. Encryption algorithms and key management protocols must be carefully selected to balance security requirements with the computational limitations of edge devices.

Network security is another critical pillar of edge computing security. Utilizing virtual private networks (VPNs), secure communication protocols (such as TLS/SSL), and intrusion detection and prevention systems (IDS/IPS) helps fortify the network against attacks. Network segmentation can also mitigate risks by isolating different segments of the network, thereby containing potential breaches.

Proactive threat detection and response capabilities are essential to maintaining the security posture of edge computing environments. Integrating real-time threat intelligence and anomaly detection systems can help identify and mitigate threats before they cause significant damage. Additionally, developing and enforcing comprehensive incident response plans ensures that organizations can swiftly and effectively respond to security breaches, minimizing their impact.

Compliance with regulatory standards and best practices is critical for organizations leveraging edge computing. Adhering to regulations such as the General Data Protection Regulation (GDPR) ensures that personal data is handled responsibly, and appropriate measures are in place to protect individual privacy. Establishing a culture of compliance and security awareness within the organization further strengthens the overall security framework.

Edge computing security is a multifaceted and dynamic field requiring continuous adaptation and vigilance. As the landscape evolves, so too must the strategies employed to secure it. By thoroughly understanding and addressing the unique challenges of edge environments, organizations can better protect their assets and data, ensuring the benefits of edge computing are realized without compromising security.

5.2 Security Threats in Edge Computing

Edge computing introduces specific security challenges due to its decentralized nature, the diversity of edge devices, and the potential for physical attacks. These threats necessitate a comprehensive understanding to develop robust security measures. This section systematically explores the primary security threats in edge computing, encompassing physical attacks, network threats, software vulnerabilities, and data-related risks.

Physical attacks are a prevalent threat due to the often remote and unattended deployment of edge devices. These devices can be tampered with, leading to hardware manipulation or theft. Examples include:

- **Device Tampering:** Physical access to devices can allow attackers to modify hardware components or install malicious software directly.

- **Environmental Damage:** Deliberate exposure to harmful environmental conditions such as extreme temperatures or moisture to disrupt operations.

- **Hardware Theft:** Stealing edge devices to extract sensitive data or intellectual property stored locally.

Network-related threats are significant in edge computing due to the reliance on network interconnectivity. Such threats include:

- **Man-in-the-Middle Attacks (MitM):** Attackers intercept communication between edge devices and the central cloud or other devices to eavesdrop or manipulate data exchanges.

138

- **Denial of Service (DoS) Attacks:** Overloading network components or devices with a flood of traffic to disrupt service availability.

- **Eavesdropping:** Unencrypted network communications may be monitored by attackers, exposing sensitive information.

Software vulnerabilities represent another considerable category of threats in edge computing. Such vulnerabilities can be exploited to gain unauthorized access or disrupt services. Key examples include:

- **Unpatched Software:** Edge devices often run software that may not receive timely updates and patches, leaving known vulnerabilities unaddressed.

- **Malware:** Malicious software can be introduced through various vectors, compromising device integrity, data, and network communications.

- **Unsecured APIs:** Application Programming Interfaces (APIs) that lack proper security measures can be exploited to gain unauthorized access.

Data-related threats in edge computing stem from the sensitive nature of data processed locally. Threats in this domain include:

- **Data Breaches:** Unauthorized access to sensitive data stored on edge devices due to inadequate security controls.

- **Data Leakage:** Accidentally or maliciously exposing private data through poorly secured communication channels or storage mechanisms.

- **Data Tampering:** Alteration of data on edge devices, leading to erroneous computations or reports.

The diversity and scale of edge environments further compound these threats. Edge devices vary widely in terms of capabilities, operating systems, and use cases, which increases the attack surface. Additionally, the sheer number of devices in a typical edge deployment poses scalability challenges for managing security updates and monitoring.

To mitigate these threats, a multi-layered security approach is often essential. This includes employing hardware-based security features like Trusted Platform Modules (TPMs), implementing robust encryption protocols for data in transit and at rest, and ensuring regular software updates. Furthermore, continuous network monitoring and anomaly detection can help in identifying and responding to unusual activities promptly.

Below is an example of how a DoS attack could be launched against an edge network, demonstrating the ease with which network security can be compromised if not properly secured. The Python code snippet simulates a basic DoS attack by sending numerous requests to an edge device's IP address, overwhelming its resources:

```
import socket
import threading

target_ip = '192.168.1.1'
target_port = 80
fake_ip = '182.21.20.32'

def attack():
    while True:
        s = socket.socket(socket.AF_INET, socket.SOCK_STREAM)
        s.connect((target_ip, target_port))
        s.sendto(("GET /" + target_ip + " HTTP/1.1\r\n").encode('ascii'), (target_ip
            , target_port))
        s.sendto(("Host: " + fake_ip + "\r\n\r\n").encode('ascii'), (target_ip,
            target_port))
        s.close()

for i in range(500):
    thread = threading.Thread(target=attack)
    thread.start()
```

The output of this code will not be visible here, but in a real scenario, launching this script would lead to the target device being inundated with requests, potentially causing service disruption:

(launching multiple threads targeting 192.168.1.1)

Attention to these threats is crucial for maintaining the integrity, confidentiality, and availability of edge computing environments.

5.3 Device Security and Authentication

In the context of edge computing, device security and authentication are paramount due to the geographically distributed nature of edge devices, which often operate in less controlled environments compared to centralized data centers. Ensuring that edge devices are secure from unauthorized access and tampering is critical to maintaining the overall integrity and confidentiality of data processed at the edge.

Device security entails securing the hardware, firmware, and software components of the device. Hardware security can be achieved through several mechanisms, such as the use of Trusted Platform Modules (TPMs), secure boot processes, and hardware-based encryption. TPMs are specialized chips that provide secure cryptographic operations and can securely store keys and certificates. The secure boot process ensures that the device boots only using trusted software, thereby preventing the execution of compromised or malicious code.

Firmware security involves ensuring that the firmware running on the device is authentic and has not been tampered with. This can be enforced through code signing, where the firmware is digitally signed by a trusted authority. During the boot process, the device verifies this signature before executing the firmware code. Additionally, regular firmware updates and patches are essential to fix vulnerabilities and improve security features.

Software security is another critical aspect, encompassing the operating system and any applications running on the device. It is vital to follow secure coding practices, employ regular vulnerability assessments, and apply necessary updates and patches promptly. Using virtualization and containerization techniques can also help isolate different software components, reducing the risk of a compromise spreading across the system.

Authentication mechanisms ensure that only authorized devices and users can access the system. Device authentication verifies the identity of the device trying to connect to the network or service. This can be achieved using certificates, keys, and other cryptographic methods. Similarly, user authentication ensures that only authorized personnel can access and manage the edge devices. This involves implementing strong, multi-factor authentication (MFA) processes.

141

```
import hmac
import hashlib

def create_hmac(key, message):
    return hmac.new(key, message.encode('utf-8'), hashlib.sha256).hexdigest()

key = b'secret_key'
message = 'Device_Authentication_Message'
hmac_code = create_hmac(key, message)
print(f"HMAC: {hmac_code}")
```

In the example above, the Python code generates an HMAC (Hash-based Message Authentication Code) using a secret key and a message. HMAC is commonly used in various authentication protocols to ensure data integrity and authenticity. The key and message are provided to the create_hmac function, which uses the hashlib library to generate the HMAC using the SHA-256 hash function.

HMAC: 816c6bfaa6766d19e2cb1d5e32c60aa5d504bbc5f47d9f5eab2051a1ba14e7b6

Encryption of communication between devices and control centers is also vital to prevent eavesdropping and tampering. Transport Layer Security (TLS) can be used to secure communications, ensuring data is encrypted during transmission. Proper management of certificates and keys is fundamental to maintaining secure connections. Certificate authorities (CAs) can issue digital certificates that validate the authenticity of devices and services.

Access control mechanisms must be enforced to restrict who or what can access the edge devices and their resources. Role-based access control (RBAC) and attribute-based access control (ABAC) are effective methods. RBAC assigns permissions based on roles within the organization, while ABAC uses attributes of users or devices to determine access rights. Implementing the principle of least privilege ensures that entities have only the necessary permissions required to perform their tasks.

To enhance device security further, regular security audits and penetration testing should be conducted. These assessments help identify and mitigate potential vulnerabilities before they can be exploited. Additionally, maintaining a robust incident response plan ensures that any security breaches are addressed swiftly, minimizing the impact on the overall system.

Integrating secure development lifecycle (SDL) practices into the development process ensures that security considerations are addressed at every stage of device development. This includes threat modeling, secure coding practices, code reviews, and regular security testing.

Logging and monitoring are crucial for detecting and responding to security incidents. Implementing comprehensive logging on edge devices allows for the collection of important security events, which can be analyzed to detect suspicious activities. Automated monitoring tools help in real-time detection and response to potential threats, ensuring the security posture is maintained.

Strict adherence to industry standards and best practices, such as those outlined by the National Institute of Standards and Technology (NIST) and the International Organization for Standardization (ISO), provides a structured approach to device security and authentication. By following these guidelines, organizations can ensure that their edge devices are secure and resilient against evolving threats.

5.4 Data Encryption at the Edge

Data encryption at the edge is a critical component of maintaining the confidentiality and integrity of sensitive information. Edge computing environments often process and store data closer to the data source, which necessitates robust encryption mechanisms to protect data from unauthorized access or tampering as it travels across networks and when it is stored on edge devices.

Encryption transforms readable data (plaintext) into an unreadable format (ciphertext) using an algorithm and a key. Only those who possess the appropriate decryption key can revert the ciphertext back into its original plaintext form. There are mainly two types of encryption used in edge computing: symmetric encryption and asymmetric encryption.

Symmetric Encryption involves a single key for both encryption and decryption. The security of symmetric encryption relies on keeping this key secret. Common symmetric encryption algorithms include the Advanced Encryption Standard (AES) and the Data Encryption Standard (DES).

```
from Crypto.Cipher import AES
from Crypto.Random import get_random_bytes

# Generate a random 256-bit key
key = get_random_bytes(32)
cipher = AES.new(key, AES.MODE_GCM)

plaintext = b'Edge computing is powerful but needs encryption!'
ciphertext, tag = cipher.encrypt_and_digest(plaintext)
```

In this example, the AES algorithm is used to encrypt a string of plain-text. The get_random_bytes function generates a 256-bit key, ensuring a high level of security. AES.MODE_GCM is one of the modes of AES that provides authenticated encryption, combining both encryption and integrity verification.

Asymmetric Encryption, also known as public-key encryption, uses a pair of keys: a public key for encryption and a private key for decryption. One of the most commonly used asymmetric encryption algorithms is the RSA (Rivest–Shamir–Adleman) algorithm. Asymmetric encryption is particularly useful in edge computing for secure key exchange and identity verification.

```
from Crypto.PublicKey import RSA
from Crypto.Cipher import PKCS1_OAEP

# Generate RSA key pair
key = RSA.generate(2048)
public_key = key.publickey()

# Encrypt data with the public key
cipher = PKCS1_OAEP.new(public_key)
ciphertext = cipher.encrypt(b'Confidential data at the edge')

# Decrypt data with the private key
cipher = PKCS1_OAEP.new(key)
plaintext = cipher.decrypt(ciphertext)
```

As shown, RSA can securely encrypt data at the edge using a public key, ensuring that only the corresponding private key can decrypt it. This is essential for scenarios where secure communication channels are required between devices and central systems.

Data-at-Rest Encryption protects data stored on disks and databases in edge devices. Technologies like Transparent Data Encryption (TDE) and full disk encryption are commonly employed. For instance, Microsoft Azure offers Azure Disk Encryption which utilizes BitLocker to encrypt Windows Virtual Machine disks and dm-crypt for Linux Virtual Machine disks.

```
# Example command to enable Azure Disk Encryption on a VM
az vm encryption enable --resource-group MyResourceGroup --name MyVM --disk-
    encryption-keyvault MyKeyVault
```

Data-in-Transit Encryption ensures that data being transmitted over the network is secure. Secure transport protocols such as HTTPS, SSL/TLS, and IPsec are utilized to protect data in transit. Implementing strong encryption standards such as TLS 1.2 or 1.3 is recommended to avoid vulnerabilities associated with older versions of these protocols.

```
# Example command to set up HTTPS with Let's Encrypt
sudo certbot --nginx -d myedgeapplication.com
```

Encrypted communication channels not only protect data from interception but also ensure data integrity and authenticity through certificates and mutual authentication.

Key Management is another pivotal aspect of data encryption at the edge. Secure key management practices involve generating, distributing, storing, rotating, and retiring encryption keys in a secure manner. Solutions like Azure Key Vault provide centralized key management and minimize the risks associated with local key storage.

```
# Create a key vault
az keyvault create --name MyKeyVault --resource-group MyResourceGroup --location
    eastus

# Create a key
az keyvault key create --vault-name MyKeyVault --name MyKey --protection software
```

Azure Key Vault alleviates the complexity of managing keys, secrets, and certificates by providing a secure space for their storage and access through authenticated API calls.

Implementing robust data encryption mechanisms at the edge is non-negotiable. It ensures that even if data is intercepted or accessed by unauthorized entities, it remains unintelligible and protected. As the edge computing landscape evolves, so must the encryption strategies, ensuring compliance with regulatory frameworks and maintaining the highest standards of data security.

5.5 Network Security for Edge Devices

In edge computing environments, network security is paramount as data is processed closer to the data source rather than in centralized data centers. This paradigm entails unique security challenges stemming from the heterogeneous and distributed nature of edge devices. This section explores the various aspects of ensuring robust network security for edge devices, highlighting practical strategies and technological tools available.

Network Segmentation: Network segmentation is a critical strategy for reducing the attack surface in edge environments. By dividing the network into smaller, isolated segments, each segment can be individually secured and monitored. This division confines potential security breaches to a limited part of the network, preventing lateral movement by threat actors.

A typical configuration might involve segregating the network into subnets for different types of devices or functions—for example, one subnet for sensors, another for actuators, and another for edge servers. Employing VLANs (Virtual Local Area Networks) and ACLs (Access Control Lists) further enhances the granularity of segmentation and control.

Firewalls and Intrusion Detection Systems: The implementation of firewalls is fundamental in controlling the ingress and egress network traffic based on predetermined security rules. At the edge, firewalls should be configured to allow only necessary traffic and block all others, thereby minimizing exposure to malicious entities.

Integrating Intrusion Detection Systems (IDS) and Intrusion Prevention Systems (IPS) helps in monitoring network traffic for suspicious activities. These systems can be signature-based or anomaly-based. Signature-based IDS/IPS identifies threats by comparing patterns against a database of known attack signatures, while anomaly-based systems learn the normal behavior of the network and alert deviations.

```
sudo ufw default deny incoming
sudo ufw default allow outgoing
sudo ufw allow from 192.168.1.0/24 to any port 22
sudo ufw enable
```

The above commands configure a basic Uncomplicated Firewall (UFW) on an edge server, allowing only SSH traffic from a specific subnet while denying all other incoming traffic.

Secure Communication Protocols: Encryption of data in transit is essential to protect against interception and man-in-the-middle attacks. Utilizing secure communication protocols such as HTTPS, TLS, and DTLS (Datagram Transport Layer Security) ensures that data transferred between edge devices, gateways, and the cloud is encrypted.

A common practice involves generating and managing digital certificates to establish secure channels. Certificate Authorities (CAs) or self-signed certificates can be utilized depending on the scale and security requirements.

```
openssl req -new -newkey rsa:2048 -nodes -keyout myserver.key -out myserver.csr
openssl x509 -req -days 365 -in myserver.csr -signkey myserver.key -out myserver.crt
```

These commands generate a private key, a Certificate Signing Request (CSR), and a self-signed certificate for secure communications.

Zero Trust Architecture: Adopting a Zero Trust Architecture (ZTA) principle fundamentally shifts the security model from "trust but verify" to "never trust, always verify". In edge computing, this involves continuously authenticating and authorizing devices and users rather than providing blanket access after a single verification event. It mandates stringent identity verification, device integrity checks, and compliance with security policies before granting access.

Major components of ZTA include multi-factor authentication (MFA), micro-segmentation, and dynamic, context-aware access controls. The enforcement of least-privilege access ensures that entities only have permissions necessary for their roles, reducing potential attack vectors.

Virtual Private Networks (VPNs) and Software-Defined Perimeters (SDP): Utilizing VPNs for encrypting data transmission between edge devices and cloud resources offers an added layer of security. However, traditional VPNs have scalability issues, particularly with a large number of devices.

SDP, as a modern alternative, provides more granular and dynamic control over network security. It decouples the control plane from the data plane, enabling the establishment of a secure perimeter around each device. The SDP model can dynamically create an end-to-end encrypted connection, effectively mitigating attack vectors such as network scanning and unauthorized access.

```
# Example of configuring OpenVPN
sudo apt-get install openvpn
sudo openvpn --config /etc/openvpn/server.conf
```

Network Monitoring and Threat Intelligence: Continuous monitoring of network traffic using advanced analytics helps in the early detection and mitigation of security incidents. Deploying Security Information and Event Management (SIEM) systems equipped with machine learning algorithms enhances the ability to identify anomalous activities and potential threats in real-time.

Integrating threat intelligence feeds with network monitoring tools allows for proactive defense by providing up-to-date information on emerging threats. These feeds can automatically update security policies to defend against known malicious activities, thereby strengthening the overall security posture of the network.

Edge-to-Cloud Security Integration: Securing the communication between edge devices and cloud infrastructure is critical. Implementing secure APIs and leveraging edge-to-cloud frameworks with built-in security features ensures seamless, secure data flow. Utilizing cloud-based security services such as AWS IoT Device Defender or Azure Security Center for IoT can provide extended protection, including threat detection, posture management, and compliance monitoring.

```
{
  "rules": [
    {
      "ruleName": "LimitAllocatedCPUCores",
      "ruleCondition": {
        "conditionType": "DeviceAttribute",
        "deviceAttribute": "allocatedCpuCores",
        "operator": "GREATER_THAN",
        "comparisonValue": "4"
      }
    }
  ]
}
```

The provided JSON snippet is a sample rule for AWS IoT Device Defender to ensure resource usage limits on edge devices, contributing to resource availability and security.

Integrating the above-discussed measures into a comprehensive network security strategy significantly enhances the security of edge devices. These practices help to protect sensitive data, ensure the reliable operation of edge systems, and maintain compliance with regulatory requirements.

5.6 Securing Edge Applications and Modules

Edge computing deployments necessitate the integration of secure applications and modules to protect sensitive data and maintain the integrity and availability of the services provided. This section focuses on the myriad techniques and considerations critical to ensuring the security of edge applications and modules.

One of the foremost considerations in securing edge applications is the implementation of robust secure coding practices. Secure coding involves writing software in a manner that prevents the introduction or exploitation of vulnerabilities. Common strategies include input validation, output encoding, and error handling to mitigate risks such as injection attacks, cross-site scripting (XSS), and buffer overflows. In numerous programming languages, libraries and frameworks exist to facilitate these security measures, although due diligence is required to ensure their correct application.

```
def validate_input(user_input):
    if not isinstance(user_input, str):
        raise ValueError("Input must be a string")
    if len(user_input) > 100:
        raise ValueError("Input exceeds maximum length")
    return user_input.strip()
```

Another essential aspect of securing edge applications is the use of containerization and microservices. By deploying applications within containers (e.g., Docker), it is possible to achieve significant improvements in isolation and the management of dependencies. Containers encapsulate an application along with its runtime environment, which includes libraries and environment variables, thus ensuring consistency across different deployments. This isolation reduces the blast radius in the event of a security breach, confining the impact to the container instead of affecting the entire system.

```
docker run -d --name secure_app -p 80:80 my_secure_application:latest
```

Applying the principle of least privilege is another critical practice, whereby edge applications and modules run with the minimum permissions necessary to perform their functions. This approach minimizes the potential damage resulting from successful exploitation. Configuring Role-Based Access Control (RBAC) ensures that privileges are assigned judiciously and that access to functions and data is restricted based on the user's role.

```
apiVersion: rbac.authorization.k8s.io/v1
kind: Role
metadata:
  namespace: default
  name: read-only-role
rules:
- apiGroups: [""]
  resources: ["pods"]
  verbs: ["get", "list"]
```

Regular updates and patch management are vital in maintaining the security of edge applications. Timely application of patches ensures that known vulnerabilities are mitigated before they can be exploited. It is advisable to automate the update process using tools such as Ansible, Puppet, or Chef to achieve consistency and reduce human error.

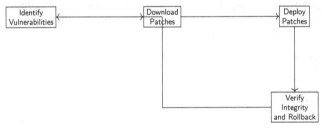

Secure application development for edge computing also demands thorough testing, including static code analysis, dynamic analysis, and penetration testing. These tests help in identifying and mitigating security weaknesses in code before deployment. Static code analysis tools like SonarQube and Fortify inspect the source code for potential vul-

150

nerabilities without executing the application, while dynamic analysis tools such as OWASP ZAP assess the running application for security flaws.

Test Type	Status
SQL Injection	Not Detected
XSS Vulnerabilities	Not Detected
CSRF Vulnerabilities	Detected and Mitigated

Implementing secure communication protocols is crucial to ensure data integrity and confidentiality during transit. Protocols such as Transport Layer Security (TLS) encrypt data between edge devices and central servers or other edge nodes, thus protecting data from eavesdropping and tampering. The use of mutual TLS (mTLS) further enhances security by providing bidirectional authentication, confirming the identity of both communicating parties.

```
openssl req -new -newkey rsa:2048 -nodes -keyout domain.key -out domain.csr
openssl x509 -req -days 365 -in domain.csr -signkey domain.key -out domain.crt
```

Furthermore, monitoring and logging are indispensable to the security of edge applications and modules. Continuous monitoring allows for the early detection of anomalies and potential security incidents, while comprehensive logging ensures that system activities can be audited and analyzed post-incident. Solutions such as the Elastic Stack (Elasticsearch, Logstash, Kibana) or Splunk facilitate real-time monitoring and log management, providing insights into system health and security posture.

```
{
  "timestamp": "2023-10-04T15:21:01.241Z",
  "level": "ERROR",
  "message": "Failed login attempt for user admin",
  "ip_address": "192.168.1.105"
}
```

Finally, employing secure deployment practices is paramount. Edge applications should be deployed using Continuous Integration/Continuous Deployment (CI/CD) pipelines that integrate automated security checks and scans. These pipelines enforce security policies and ensure that only code meeting predefined security standards progresses through the stages of development and deployment.

All these measures, from secure coding and containerization to regular updates and secure communication protocols, collectively contribute to the robust security of edge applications and modules, safeguarding the integrity, confidentiality, and availability of data and services across edge computing environments.

5.7 Access Control and Identity Management

Access control and identity management are critical components in securing edge computing environments. The distributed nature of edge computing requires robust mechanisms to ensure that only authorized entities can access and manipulate resources. Identity management involves creating, maintaining, and managing user and device identities, while access control governs the permissions and restrictions associated with these identities.

Identity Management:

Identity management in edge computing involves the establishment and administration of user identities and the associated credentials. This process includes user registration, authentication, authorization, and identity repositories. Implementing strong identity management practices ensures that only authenticated users and devices can access the system.

The following steps are typically involved in identity management:

- *Identity Provisioning*: This process involves creating and configuring user accounts and profiles for both human users and devices. For devices, identity provisioning might include the assignment of device certificates and credentials.

- *Authentication*: This is the process of validating an identity claim typically through passwords, biometrics, or cryptographic keys. Multi-factor authentication (MFA) is highly recommended to enhance security.

- *Authorization*: After authentication, this step determines the rights and permissions of the authenticated entity. Role-based access control (RBAC) and attribute-based access control (ABAC) are common models used.

- *Identity Repository*: This is a system or database where identities and credentials are stored securely. Examples include Microsoft Azure Active Directory (Azure AD) and other LDAP (Lightweight Directory Access Protocol) directories.

Access Control:

Access control mechanisms in edge computing ensure that users and devices can only access resources they are permitted to. It is essential to define and enforce comprehensive policies to mitigate unauthorized access risks. There are several models of access control utilized in edge environments:

1. *Role-Based Access Control (RBAC)*: In RBAC, access permissions are assigned based on roles within the organization. A role represents a set of permissions, and users are assigned roles, thus inheriting the role's permissions. An example in Azure is the use of Azure RBAC, which allows fine-grained access management for Azure resources.

```
from azure.identity import DefaultAzureCredential
from azure.mgmt.authorization import AuthorizationManagementClient

credential = DefaultAzureCredential()
subscription_id = 'your_subscription_id'
client = AuthorizationManagementClient(credential, subscription_id)

role_definition = {
    "roleName": "EdgeDeviceOperator",
    "description": "Can manage edge devices within a resource group",
    "permissions": [
        {
            "actions": [
                "Microsoft.Resources/subscriptions/resourceGroups/read",
                "Microsoft.Devices/IotHubs/devices/read",
                "Microsoft.Devices/IotHubs/devices/write"
            ],
            "notActions": []
        }
    ],
    "assignableScopes": ["/subscriptions/{subscriptionId}/resourceGroups/{
        resourceGroupName}"]
}

role_created = client.role_definition.create_or_update(
    scope="/subscriptions/{subscriptionId}",
    role_definition_id="roleDefinitionID",
    role_definition_params=role_definition
)

print("Role created:", role_created)
```

2. *Attribute-Based Access Control (ABAC)*: ABAC uses policies that evaluate attributes (such as user, resource, and environment attributes) to determine access decisions. Attributes might include time of day, IP address, or user department. ABAC allows more dynamic and context-aware access management compared to RBAC.

3. *Discretionary Access Control (DAC)*: In DAC, the control of access is at the discretion of the owner or administrator of the resource. This model provides flexibility but can become complex to manage in large environments.

4. *Mandatory Access Control (MAC)*: MAC enforces policies that define access rules based on information sensitivity and user clearance levels. This model is commonly used in environments that require higher security and tight control, such as governmental and military applications.

Access control lists (ACLs) are often used to manage permissions in various models. An ACL specifies which users or system processes can access the objects and what operations they can perform.

Principal	Permissions
Alice	["read", "write"]
Bob	["read"]

Implementing strong access control and identity management practices involves regular monitoring and auditing of access logs to ensure compliance with security policies. The use of centralized identity management systems and integration with edge devices enhances the security posture by enabling consistent and scalable management of user and device identities.

Technologies like federated identity management can further extend these capabilities by allowing users to use the same credentials across multiple systems or domains, facilitating seamless and secure interactions in complex, distributed edge environments. Services like Azure Active Directory support federation and can be integrated with various edge devices and services for unified identity and access management.

5.8 Compliance Standards and Regulations

In the context of edge computing, adherence to compliance standards and regulations is paramount for ensuring the protection of data and adherence to legal requirements. Compliance standards provide frameworks and guidelines that organizations must follow to safeguard information and maintain trust with their customers and stakeholders. This section delves into the various compliance standards relevant to edge computing, discussing key aspects and requirements for each.

Among the most prominent standards are the General Data Protection Regulation (GDPR), the Health Insurance Portability and Accountability Act (HIPAA), the Payment Card Industry Data Security Standard (PCI-DSS), and the Federal Information Security Management Act (FISMA). Each of these standards addresses different aspects of data security and privacy, necessitating careful consideration and implementation in edge computing environments.

General Data Protection Regulation (GDPR):

GDPR is a regulation in EU law designed to protect the data privacy of individuals within the European Union and the European Economic Area. Implementing GDPR in edge computing involves several key components:

- Data Processing: Organizations must ensure that personal data is collected, processed, and stored legally and transparently. This encompasses having explicit consent from data subjects and ensuring data usage aligns with the consent provided.

- Data Protection: Adequate technical and organizational measures must be in place to protect personal data against unauthorized access, processing, and disclosure.

- Right to Access and Erasure: Individuals have the right to request access to their data and to request its deletion. Edge computing solutions must provide mechanisms for data retrieval and deletion upon request.

155

Health Insurance Portability and Accountability Act (HIPAA):

For organizations handling health information in the United States, HIPAA sets standards for the protection of health information. Key requirements under HIPAA for edge computing:

- Data Encryption: Protected Health Information (PHI) should be encrypted both at rest and in transit to prevent unauthorized access.

- Access Controls: Edge devices and applications must implement strict access controls to ensure that only authorized personnel can access sensitive health information.

- Audit Controls: Organizations need to maintain detailed audit logs of access and modifications to PHI, enabling the detection and investigation of potential breaches.

Payment Card Industry Data Security Standard (PCI-DSS):

PCI-DSS applies to organizations that handle credit card transactions and aims to protect cardholder data. Edge computing solutions dealing with payment processing must comply with the following PCI-DSS requirements:

- Secure Network: Implement and maintain a secure network environment, including firewall configuration to protect cardholder data.

- Encryption: Ensure cardholder data is encrypted during transmission across open, public networks.

- Monitoring and Testing: Regularly test security systems and processes, including using automated monitoring tools to detect and alert on suspicious activities.

Federal Information Security Management Act (FISMA):

FISMA is a United States federal law that stipulates a framework for protecting government information, operations, and assets against natural or man-made threats. FISMA compliance in edge computing involves:

- Risk Management: Establishing a comprehensive risk management framework that identifies potential security threats and im-
  plements appropriate safeguards.

- Incident Response: Developing and maintaining an incident response plan to swiftly address and mitigate security breaches.

- Continuous Monitoring: Implementing continuous monitoring
  controls to regularly assess the security posture of edge devices
  and networks.

Given the diversity and specificity of these standards, edge computing
solutions must integrate compliance from the design phase through
to deployment and maintenance. A combination of robust access controls, data encryption, continuous monitoring, and incident response
strategies ensures adherence to relevant standards while safeguarding sensitive information. Organizations must remain vigilant in their
compliance efforts, staying informed of updates to regulations and continually refining their security practices to align with evolving standards.

5.9   GDPR and Data Privacy at the Edge

The General Data Protection Regulation (GDPR) is a comprehensive
data protection law that mandates stringent requirements for data
privacy and security for organizations operating within the European
Union (EU) or handling data of EU citizens. In the context of edge
computing, adherence to GDPR necessitates additional considerations
due to the decentralized nature of data processing across various edge
devices and locations.

GDPR compliance revolves around several key principles, including
data minimization, purpose limitation, consent, data accuracy, storage limitation, integrity and confidentiality, and accountability. These
principles must be seamlessly integrated into edge computing architectures to maintain compliance and protect individual privacy.

Data minimization is the practice of collecting only the necessary data
required for a specific purpose. In edge computing, this principle can

be implemented by ensuring that only relevant data is processed and stored on edge devices. This reduces the risk of data breaches and ensures that unnecessary personal data is not exposed. Techniques like data aggregation and anonymization can be utilized to meet this requirement.

Purpose limitation refers to the clear definition of the purpose for which personal data is collected and processed. Edge devices should be configured to process data strictly for the defined purpose, with safeguards to prevent unauthorized use. Explicit consent must be obtained from individuals for data processing, and they should be informed about the specific purposes for which their data will be used.

Consent management is a critical component of GDPR compliance. In edge environments, obtaining and managing consent can be challenging due to the distributed nature of the devices. Implementing robust consent management systems that handle consent collection, storage, and withdrawal across all edge devices is essential. Consent should be as easy to withdraw as it is to give, and edge applications must incorporate mechanisms to respect and act upon withdrawn consent immediately.

Data accuracy under GDPR mandates that personal data must be accurate and up-to-date. Edge computing applications should incorporate validation and verification mechanisms to maintain data accuracy. This can include automated processes that check for data consistency and correctness at the point of capture and throughout the data lifecycle.

Storage limitation requires that personal data be kept only for as long as necessary for the purposes for which it was collected. In an edge computing context, this means implementing appropriate data retention and deletion policies across all edge devices and ensuring that outdated or redundant data is securely erased.

Integrity and confidentiality are essential to protect personal data against unauthorized or unlawful processing and accidental loss, destruction, or damage. Implementing data encryption both at rest and in transit is a fundamental requirement. Strong encryption protocols should be used to secure data storage on edge devices, and secure communication channels should be established for data transmission between edge devices and central cloud servers.

Accountability is a principle that mandates organizations to demonstrate compliance with GDPR. This involves maintaining detailed records of data processing activities and conducting regular audits to ensure compliance. In edge computing, this translates to logging data processing events across all edge nodes and ensuring that these logs are centrally aggregated and analyzed to detect any anomalies or breaches.

One specific challenge of GDPR compliance in edge computing is ensuring that data subjects can exercise their rights effectively. These rights include the right to access, rectification, erasure, restriction of processing, data portability, and objection. Edge applications must be designed to facilitate these rights, allowing data subjects to easily manage their personal data no matter where it is processed.

Implementing GDPR compliance in edge computing necessitates a multi-faceted approach:

- **Data Encryption and Protection:** As edge devices process and store sensitive personal data, implementing AES (Advanced Encryption Standard) and TLS (Transport Layer Security) for protecting data in transit and at rest is paramount.

- **Anonymization and Pseudonymization:** Utilizing techniques such as anonymization and pseudonymization can reduce the risk if data is compromised. These techniques should be incorporated into the data-processing pipeline at the edge.

- **Intrusion Detection Systems (IDS):** Deploying IDS on edge devices to monitor and alert for suspicious activities can enhance data protection. These systems must be capable of operating efficiently in decentralized environments.

- **Edge Compliance Frameworks:** Integrating frameworks that provide templates and guidelines for GDPR compliance specific to edge computing can streamline the compliance process.

Edge computing adds a layer of complexity to GDPR compliance, but with meticulous planning and implementation of robust privacy and security controls, organizations can effectively protect personal data and maintain compliance with GDPR regulations.

5.10 Security Best Practices and Strategies

Effective security in edge computing requires a comprehensive approach that integrates various best practices and strategic methodologies to protect systems from a myriad of threats. This section delves into the essential practices that should be employed to fortify edge environments, ensuring robustness and compliance.

Adopt a Zero Trust Architecture (ZTA) Zero Trust Architecture (ZTA) is based on the principle of "never trust, always verify." In edge computing, where devices are distributed across a vast landscape, adopting ZTA mitigates risks associated with implicit trust in network boundaries. Every access request in a ZTA must be authenticated, authorized, and encrypted, regardless of its origin within or outside the network. This approach involves continuous monitoring and validation, leveraging tools such as Multi-Factor Authentication (MFA) and micro-segmentation to minimize attack surfaces.

Implement Strong Encryption Protocols Data at rest, in transit, and in use requires robust encryption to prevent unauthorized access. AES (Advanced Encryption Standard) with 256-bit keys is recommended for encrypting sensitive data at the edge.

```
from Crypto.Cipher import AES
from Crypto.Random import get_random_bytes

data = b'Edge computing data to encrypt'
key = get_random_bytes(32) # AES-256 key
cipher = AES.new(key, AES.MODE_GCM)
nonce = cipher.nonce
ciphertext, tag = cipher.encrypt_and_digest(data)
```

Utilizing TLS (Transport Layer Security) v1.3 for secure data transmission ensures that data remains confidential and immune to interception during transit.

Regular Vulnerability Assessments and Penetration Testing (VAPT) Conducting regular Vulnerability Assessments and Penetration Testing (VAPT) is essential for identifying and addressing security weaknesses in edge devices and networks. Automated tools such as Nessus or OpenVAS can be used to scan for vulnerabilities,

160

whereas manual penetration testing can help to discover complex security flaws.

```
openvas-start
omp --username admin --password admin --xml='<create_task>'
```

Deploy Endpoint Detection and Response (EDR) Solutions

Endpoint Detection and Response (EDR) solutions provide continuous monitoring and analysis of endpoint activities to detect and respond to security incidents swiftly. EDR tools can capture detailed activity logs, trace the origins of a breach, and automate responses to contain and mitigate threats.

Secure Device Boot and Firmware Integrity Ensuring the security of the boot process and the integrity of the device firmware is crucial. Secure Boot technology verifies the digital signatures of the bootloader and firmware, ensuring only trusted software can initialize. Trusted Platform Module (TPM) can be employed to provide hardware-based security functions, including secure boot and disk encryption.

Continuous Monitoring and Anomaly Detection Employing continuous monitoring tools enables the detection of anomalous behaviors that may indicate a security breach. Machine learning algorithms can be implemented to analyze patterns and detect deviations from normal operations. Integration with Security Information and Event Management (SIEM) systems enhances the ability to correlate incidents and respond appropriately.

Patch Management and Software Updates Timely application of security patches and software updates is fundamental to protecting edge devices from exploits that take advantage of known vulnerabilities. Implement an automated patch management system to ensure all devices in the network are up-to-date.

Least Privilege and Role-Based Access Control (RBAC) Enforcing the principle of least privilege ensures that users and devices are granted only the permissions necessary to perform their functions. Role-Based Access Control (RBAC) facilitates organized and manageable assignment of permissions based on user roles, reducing the risk of privilege escalation attacks.

Implementing Secure APIs APIs are often employed in edge computing for communication between devices and cloud services. Ensuring secure API design includes using OAuth for authentication, regular security assessments of API endpoints, and encryption of API traffic using TLS.

Regular Training and Awareness Programs Human factors often contribute significantly to security vulnerabilities. Regular training and awareness programs equip personnel with the knowledge to recognize phishing attempts, understand secure coding practices, and adhere to security protocols.

Utilizing these best practices and strategies forms a robust defense framework capable of addressing the dynamic and distributed nature of edge computing environments, ensuring continuous protection against evolving threats.

5.11 Incident Response and Recovery

Effective incident response and recovery are crucial aspects of maintaining a secure edge computing environment. As edge computing operates with decentralized data processing and various devices, it presents unique challenges in identifying, managing, and mitigating security incidents. This section explores the structured approach to incident response and details the best practices necessary for a robust recovery strategy.

An incident response plan must be well-defined and comprise of structured phases: Preparation, Identification, Containment, Eradication, Recovery, and Lessons Learned. Each phase must be meticulously planned to ensure a prompt and efficient response to security incidents.

Preparation: Preparation involves establishing and documenting policies, procedures, and agreements for incident response. This includes creating an incident response team equipped with the necessary tools and clearly defined roles and responsibilities.

```
# Basic Incident Response Preparation Checklist
- Establish and train an incident response team
- Develop an incident response plan and communication strategy
- Deploy monitoring tools and technologies for threat detection
- Regularly update and patch systems to mitigate vulnerabilities
```

Identification: The identification phase is critical in recognizing incidents promptly. By leveraging advanced monitoring tools and anomaly detection algorithms, potential threats can be identified early. These tools should be configured to generate alerts for any unusual activity that might indicate a security breach.

```python
# Example of a Python Script for Anomaly Detection using scikit-learn
from sklearn.ensemble import IsolationForest

# Sample data for anomaly detection
data = [[0.1], [0.2], [1.0], [0.15], [0.22], [10.0], [0.23]]

# Create Isolation Forest model
model = IsolationForest(contamination=0.1)
model.fit(data)

# Predict anomalies (-1 indicates anomaly)
predictions = model.predict(data)
print(predictions)
```

```
[ 1  1  1  1  1 -1  1]
```

Containment: The containment phase aims to limit the damage inflicted by the incident. This involves strategies to isolate affected components while ensuring business continuity. Short-term containment strategies focus on immediate isolation, whereas long-term strategies address the root causes and prevent recurrence.

Eradication: Eradication entails the removal of the source of the incident from the network. This requires a thorough investigation to identify all affected areas and the implementation of measures to eliminate threats. For example, eradicating malware may involve comprehensive system scans and the application of advanced antivirus solutions.

Recovery: Recovery is the process of restoring and validating system functionality after an incident. The recovery plan should include steps to restore systems to normal operations while verifying that they are free from any remaining threats. For edge computing environments, this involves validating remote devices, configurations, and data integrity.

```
# Sample Recovery Steps for Edge Devices
- Assess and document the impact of the incident
- Restore affected systems from clean backups
- Reconfigure and revalidate network settings
- Perform comprehensive vulnerability assessments
```

Lessons Learned: The lessons learned phase is vital for identifying the strengths and weaknesses of the incident response plan. Post-incident analysis helps in improving response strategies and implementing modifications to prevent future incidents. Documentation and sharing of insights with relevant stakeholders form an essential part of this phase.

Key practices for incident response and recovery in edge computing include leveraging automation for faster incident detection and response, using machine learning for predictive analytics, and ensuring consistent communication across all teams involved. Regular training and simulations help in maintaining readiness and improving the effectiveness of the incident response plan.

Incident response teams must remain agile and adaptive, consistently updating their methodologies to keep pace with evolving threats. They must establish clear lines of communication and collaboration with all stakeholders, including developers, IT operations, and management, to ensure a unified approach to incident handling.

Ensuring effective incident response and recovery in edge computing environments demands a comprehensive and proactive approach, supported by continuous improvement and adaptability to emerging threats and technologies.

Chapter 6

Scalability and Performance Optimization

This chapter focuses on designing scalable edge architectures and optimizing performance. It discusses techniques for load balancing, resource management, and efficient data processing. Strategies for maximizing network bandwidth utilization and implementing edge caching are presented. The chapter also covers tools for performance monitoring, profiling, and tuning, along with methods for handling device failures and scaling edge deployments effectively. Best practices for achieving optimal performance in varied operational scenarios are highlighted.

6.1 Introduction to Scalability and Performance in Edge Computing

Edge computing represents a paradigm shift in data processing and storage, moving closer to the source of data generation to reduce latency and bandwidth use. As the edge computing landscape continues to evolve, attention to scalability and performance becomes paramount. Scalability refers to the system's capacity to handle growing amounts of work or its potential to be enlarged to accommodate that growth. Performance pertains to how efficiently a system processes data and tasks, often measured in terms of latency, throughput, and resource utilization.

Edge computing applications must address specific challenges that differentiate them from traditional cloud computing. The distribution of resources across various locations necessitates robust and scalable architectures that can dynamically adjust to changing workloads, ensure high availability, and deliver low-latency processing.

The primary factors influencing scalability and performance in edge environments include:

- **Computational Resources:** Edge devices vary widely in computational power, from low-power microcontrollers to powerful servers. Optimizing the use of these heterogeneous resources is crucial for scalable edge solutions.

- **Network Constraints:** While cloud environments benefit from high-speed, high-bandwidth internal networks, edge environments often rely on less reliable and slower public networks. Efficient use of available network resources must be a focal point.

- **Data Volume and Velocity:** The volume of data generated at the edge can be substantial, and the velocity at which data needs to be processed can vary, requiring flexible and responsive system designs.

- **Fault Tolerance and Recovery:** Given the distributed nature of edge networks, fault tolerance and rapid recovery from node failures are essential to maintain system stability and performance.

In the context of these factors, several core techniques and strategies are utilized to enhance scalability and performance in edge computing:

- **1. Load Balancing:** Essential for distributing workloads evenly across available resources, load balancing ensures no single node becomes a bottleneck, enhancing both performance and scalability. Load balancing can be implemented using various algorithms and mechanisms, such as round-robin, least connections, and resource-based distribution.

- **2. Resource Management:** Effective resource management involves dynamically allocating and deallocating resources based on current demand. Techniques such as containerization, orchestration, and adaptive resource provisioning are commonly used in edge environments to manage computational workloads efficiently.

- **3. Data Processing Optimization:** Optimizing data processing involves leveraging local computation at the edge to preprocess data before transmitting it to the cloud. This reduces bandwidth usage and processing time. Techniques such as data filtering, aggregation, and compression are commonly applied.

- **4. Network Bandwidth Utilization:** Maximizing network bandwidth utilization is critical in constrained environments. Techniques like edge caching, efficient data routing, and protocol optimization help in reducing the bandwidth required for data transmissions.

- **5. Edge Caching:** Storing frequently accessed data closer to end-users can significantly reduce latency and bandwidth usage. Content Delivery Networks (CDNs) and peer-to-peer caching strategies are useful in implementing efficient edge caching mechanisms.

- **6. Performance Monitoring and Profiling:** Continuous monitoring and profiling of edge devices and applications help identify performance bottlenecks and optimize resource utilization. Tools and frameworks for performance monitoring, such as Prometheus, Grafana, and Azure Monitor, provide essential insights into the operational status of edge deployments.

The rest of this chapter delves deeper into each of these strategies, exploring techniques and best practices for designing scalable and high-

167

performance edge computing solutions. We will examine methods for load balancing, resource management, data processing optimization, network bandwidth utilization, and edge caching. Additionally, we will address how performance monitoring and profiling tools can be leveraged to maintain and enhance system performance. By understanding and implementing these strategies, developers and architects can create edge computing solutions that are not only scalable and performant but also reliable and adaptable to varying operational scenarios.

6.2 Scalable Edge Architecture Design

Designing a scalable edge architecture involves careful consideration of multiple factors to ensure efficient and reliable processing of data. This section examines the principles and components necessary for developing a flexible and robust edge architecture that can scale with increasing data loads and evolving computational requirements.

The primary objective in designing scalable edge architectures is to distribute workloads effectively across edge devices while maintaining low latency and high availability. Several architectural patterns and best practices can be utilized, including microservices architecture, containerization, and serverless computing.

Microservices Architecture: A microservices architecture divides an application into small, independently deployable services. Each service runs its own process and communicates with other services typically via HTTP or messaging queues. This architectural pattern enhances scalability by isolating the performance and scaling concerns of individual services. If a particular service experiences increased load, such as a data processing component, it can be scaled independently without affecting other parts of the system.

The benefits of microservices architecture include:

- *Isolation of failures:* Failures in one service do not propagate to others, enhancing the system's robustness.

- *Independent scaling:* Each service can be scaled independently based on its load and performance requirements.

- *Polyglot persistence:* Different services can use different data storage technologies optimized for their specific needs.

Containerization: Containers provide a lightweight, portable, and consistent environment for deploying microservices. Tools such as Docker enable the packaging of applications and their dependencies into containers, ensuring that they run consistently across various environments. Kubernetes can be employed to orchestrate containers, providing automated deployment, scaling, and management of containerized applications.

```
# Use an official Python runtime as a parent image
FROM python:3.8-slim

# Set the working directory to /app
WORKDIR /app

# Copy the current directory contents into the container at /app
COPY . /app

# Install any needed packages specified in requirements.txt
RUN pip install -r requirements.txt

# Make port 80 available to the world outside this container
EXPOSE 80

# Define environment variable
ENV NAME World

# Run app.py when the container launches
CMD ["python", "app.py"]
```

Serverless Computing: Serverless computing abstracts server management by automatically scaling compute resources in response to incoming requests. Examples include AWS Lambda, Azure Functions, and Google Cloud Functions. Serverless architectures are inherently scalable and cost-effective, as resources are only consumed when the function is executed. For edge computing, serverless functions can be deployed closer to the data source, reducing latency and improving performance.

Edge Device Management: Managing a fleet of edge devices at scale requires robust device management capabilities. Azure IoT Hub can be used to connect, monitor, and control edge devices securely. It supports features such as device twins, which maintain the state of devices, and direct methods for executing commands on devices remotely.

```
from azure.iot.hub import IoTHubRegistryManager

# Connection string to Azure IoT Hub
CONNECTION_STRING = "HostName=example.azure-devices.net;
    SharedAccessKeyName=iothubowner;SharedAccessKey=examplekey"

# Device ID to manage
DEVICE_ID = "myEdgeDevice"

# Initialize IoTHubRegistryManager
registry_manager = IoTHubRegistryManager(CONNECTION_STRING)

# Get the device twin
device_twin = registry_manager.get_twin(DEVICE_ID)

# Print the device twin
print("Device Twin: {}".format(device_twin))
```

Data Flow Management: Efficient data flow management is crucial in edge architectures. Apache Kafka is a distributed streaming platform that can handle high throughput and fault-tolerant data pipelines. Kafka can be deployed at the edge to collect, store, and process data streams in real-time. Edge nodes can act as Kafka producers, sending data to Kafka topics, while downstream applications or cloud services can consume and process this data.

Resilience and Fault Tolerance: Ensuring resilience and fault tolerance in edge architectures involves implementing strategies such as redundancy, failover mechanisms, and data replication. Edge devices should be capable of operating independently if they lose connectivity to the central cloud infrastructure. Techniques such as edge-to-edge replication allow data to be mirrored across multiple edge nodes, enhancing the system's overall fault tolerance.

In summary, scalable edge architecture design leverages modern architectural patterns and technologies such as microservices, containerization, and serverless computing. Effective edge device management and resilient data flow mechanisms are key to supporting scalability and ensuring robust performance in edge environments. These considerations are critical for the successful deployment and operation of scalable edge solutions in a variety of application scenarios.

6.3 Load Balancing and Resource Management

Load balancing and resource management are critical facets of scalable edge computing solutions. These techniques ensure optimal distribution of computational tasks and efficient utilization of available resources, thereby enhancing performance and reliability. This section delves into the principles and practices of load balancing and resource management within the context of edge computing, specifically leveraging Azure services.

Load balancing involves distributing incoming network traffic across multiple servers or nodes to ensure no single server is overwhelmed, thereby maintaining service availability and performance. In the context of edge computing, load balancing is essential due to the distributed nature of edge devices and the need to process data close to the data source.

$$\sum_{i=1}^{n} L_i = S(t) \quad \text{where} \quad L_i \text{ is the load on node } i \text{ and } S(t) \text{ is the total system load at time } t$$

The total system load $S(t)$ must be balanced across all nodes i to prevent hotspots and underutilization.

Azure offers several services that aid in load balancing for edge computing environments:

- **Azure Load Balancer:** This service provides high availability by distributing incoming traffic among healthy VMs configured in backend pools.

- **Azure Traffic Manager:** A DNS-based traffic load balancer that enables global distribution of network traffic.

- **Azure Application Gateway:** Offers application-level load balancing for HTTP and HTTPS traffic, including Web Application Firewall (WAF) features.

Resource management in edge computing consists of several vital tasks, including resource allocation, scaling, and monitoring to ensure

171

efficient utilization and performance. Resource allocation aims to assign available resources in a manner that maximizes performance and minimizes costs. The decision process can be formulated as an optimization problem:

$$\min_{x} C(x) \quad \text{subject to} \quad x \in R, U(x) \geq D$$

Here, $C(x)$ represents the cost function, x are the resource allocation decisions, R is the set of available resources, and $U(x)$ denotes the utility derived from the resources meeting the demands D.

Azure provides robust tools and services for resource management:

- **Azure Resource Manager (ARM):** Enables deployment, management, and monitoring of Azure resources through a unified interface.

- **Azure Virtual Machine Scale Sets (VMSS):** Facilitates the creation and management of a group of load-balanced VMs. VMSS enables auto-scaling in response to demand alterations based on pre-defined metrics.

- **Azure Kubernetes Service (AKS):** Manages containerized applications with Kubernetes, automating deployment, scaling, and operations of application containers across clusters of hosts.

To illustrate the implementation of load balancing and resource management in Azure, consider the following example using Azure Application Gateway for HTTP traffic load balancing and Azure Virtual Machine Scale Sets for resource scaling.

```
az network application-gateway create --resource-group MyResourceGroup --name
    MyAppGateway --capacity 2 --sku Standard_v2 --vnet-name MyVNet --subnet
    MySubnet
```

This command deploys an Azure Application Gateway in the specified resource group with a Standard_v2 SKU and initial capacity of 2 instances.

```
az vmss create --resource-group MyResourceGroup --name MyScaleSet --image
    UbuntuLTS --vm-sku Standard_B1ms --instance-count 2 --upgrade-policy-mode
    automatic
```

This command creates a Virtual Machine Scale Set with an initial instance count of 2 and automatic upgrade policy mode.

Resource monitoring is essential to maintain and optimize performance. Azure Monitor and Azure Log Analytics provide comprehensive monitoring solutions, enabling real-time visibility into resource utilization, performance bottlenecks, and potential failures. These insights facilitate proactive adjustments to resource allocation and load balancing strategies.

```python
from azure.mgmt.monitor import MonitorManagementClient
from azure.identity import DefaultAzureCredential

credential = DefaultAzureCredential()
monitor_client = MonitorManagementClient(credential, subscription_id)

metrics_data = monitor_client.metrics.list(
    resource_uri=vmss_resource_id,
    timespan='2022-12-01T00:00:00Z/2022-12-01T01:00:00Z',
    interval='PT1M',
    metricnames='Percentage CPU',
    aggregation='Average'
)

for item in metrics_data.value:
    for timeseries in item.timeseries:
        for data in timeseries.data:
            print(data.time_stamp, data.average)
```

This Python script utilizes the Azure SDK to retrieve and print average CPU utilization metrics for a Virtual Machine Scale Set, aiding in performance assessment and management.

Efficient load balancing and resource management in edge computing systems are foundational to achieving high availability, reliability, and performance. Leveraging Azure's powerful tools and services, developers can implement scalable, responsive, and optimized edge solutions that meet varying workload demands effectively.

6.4 Optimizing Data Processing at the Edge

Edge computing necessitates the efficient handling of data closer to the source of its generation. Effective data processing at the edge can significantly reduce latency and bandwidth usage, enhance real-time processing capabilities, and ensure higher reliability and autonomy. This section explores various methodologies and technologies designed to optimize data processing in edge computing environments.

Data Preprocessing Techniques: Data preprocessing at the edge involves filtering, aggregating, and transforming raw data before being sent to central cloud services, thereby reducing the amount of data that needs to be transmitted. Common data preprocessing techniques include:

- **Filtering:** Only the relevant data is forwarded, while extraneous or redundant information is discarded. For instance, IoT sensors may generate high-frequency data where only anomalies or specific events are of interest.

- **Aggregation:** Combining multiple data points into a summary form can significantly reduce data volume. Aggregation techniques include averaging, min-max calculations, and statistical summaries.

- **Transformation:** Data may need to be transformed into a more suitable format or structure for further processing or analysis. This includes normalization, encoding, or feature extraction techniques that enhance the efficiency of machine learning models running at the edge.

Utilizing Edge AI and Machine Learning: By leveraging machine learning models at the edge, devices can make intelligent decisions locally, reducing reliance on central servers. This approach also improves real-time processing and response times. Key considerations for deploying machine learning models at the edge include:

- **Model Selection:** Lightweight models such as MobileNet, TinyML, or pruned versions of larger networks are more suitable for resource-constrained edge devices.

- **Model Quantization:** Converting models into lower bit-width representations (e.g., 8-bit integers) can significantly reduce their size and computational requirements without sacrificing much accuracy.

174

- **Incremental Learning:** Implementing models that can adapt based on new data received can improve predictive performance over time without needing full retraining.

Efficient Data Serialization Formats: Choosing the correct data serialization format is crucial for optimizing both the speed of data processing and the utilization of network bandwidth. Common formats used in edge computing include:

- **Protocol Buffers:** Google's Protocol Buffers (Protobuf) offer a compact and efficient binary serialization format suitable for serialized data exchange between devices.

- **Apache Avro:** Predominantly used in data-intensive applications, Avro is a compact, fast, and schema-based serialization system.

- **FlatBuffers:** Developed by Google, FlatBuffers is an efficient cross-platform serialization library that enables data access without parsing/unpacking.

```
syntax = "proto3";

message SensorData {
    string sensor_id = 1;
    double temperature = 2;
    double humidity = 3;
    int64 timestamp = 4;
}
```

```
$ protoc --python_out=. sensor_data.proto
```

Edge-Oriented Data Processing Frameworks: Several frameworks have been developed to facilitate efficient data processing at the edge. These include:

- **Apache NiFi:** Apache NiFi supports real-time data ingestion, routing, and transformation. With a focus on providing a user-friendly interface, NiFi is suitable for complex data flows and prioritizes back-pressure handling.

- **EdgeX Foundry:** An open-source project under the Linux Foundation, EdgeX provides an extensible framework for plugging in various microservices for data ingestion, transformation, and analytics.

- **Azure IoT Edge:** Azure's IoT Edge extends cloud intelligence and analytics to the edge by deploying containerized workloads to edge devices and enabling seamless integration with Azure services.

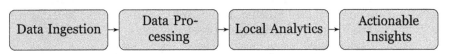

Figure 6.1: Data Processing Flow at the Edge

Real-Time Stream Processing: Applications that handle data streams in real-time can benefit from edge frameworks specifically designed for low-latency processing. Technologies such as Apache Flink, Apache Kafka Streams, and Azure Stream Analytics can be effectively utilized to process incoming data streams near the edge. These frameworks support complex event processing, windowed operations, and consistency guarantees, crucial for applications demanding high reliability and low latency.

Consider the example of processing a high-throughput data stream from multiple IoT sensors in an edge environment:

```
import org.apache.kafka.streams.KafkaStreams;
import org.apache.kafka.streams.StreamsBuilder;
import org.apache.kafka.streams.kstream.KStream;

public class SensorDataProcessor {
    public static void main(String[] args) {
        StreamsBuilder builder = new StreamsBuilder();
        KStream<String, String> source = builder.stream("sensor-data");

        KStream<String, String> processed = source
            .filter((key, value) -> isValidData(value))
            .mapValues(value -> processData(value));

        processed.to("processed-sensor-data");

        KafkaStreams streams = new KafkaStreams(builder.build(), getStreamsConfig()
            );
        streams.start();
```

```
    }

    private static boolean isValidData(String value) {
        // Validation logic here
        return true;
    }

    private static String processData(String value) {
        // Data processing logic here
        return value;
    }

    private static Properties getStreamsConfig() {
        // Configuration properties here
        Properties props = new Properties();
        props.put(StreamsConfig.APPLICATION_ID_CONFIG, "sensor-data-processor
            ");
        props.put(StreamsConfig.BOOTSTRAP_SERVERS_CONFIG, "localhost:9092"
            );
        return props;
    }
}
```

Containerization and Orchestration: To achieve optimal resource utilization and flexibility, deploying data processing workloads in containers at the edge, orchestrated by Kubernetes or other container orchestration platforms, is highly effective. Containerization allows isolated execution environments, efficient scaling, and reliable deployment processes.

Overall, optimizing data processing at the edge is a multifaceted endeavor that incorporates data preprocessing techniques, edge AI, efficient serialization formats, powerful data processing frameworks, and containerization. Employing these techniques collectively ensures that edge devices perform efficiently, making timely and intelligent decisions while minimizing dependency on central cloud resources.

6.5 Efficient Network Bandwidth Utilization

Efficient network bandwidth utilization is crucial in edge computing to ensure that data transmission between edge devices and central cloud services is optimized, minimizing latency and maximizing throughput. Effective bandwidth utilization reduces operational costs and enhances user experience by quick data accessibility and faster response times.

- **1. Data Compression Techniques:** Employing data compression is one of the foremost methods to utilize network bandwidth efficiently. Compression reduces the size of data being transmitted, thereby decreasing the amount of bandwidth needed.

```
import gzip
import shutil

# Original data size
input_file = 'data.txt'

# Gzipped data size
output_file = 'data.txt.gz'

with open(input_file, 'rb') as f_in:
    with gzip.open(output_file, 'wb') as f_out:
        shutil.copyfileobj(f_in, f_out)
```

- **2. Adaptive Bitrate Streaming:** Adaptive Bitrate Streaming (ABR) is a technique predominantly used in the delivery of multimedia content. ABR dynamically adjusts the quality of the media stream being delivered to match the end user's network conditions.

Algorithm 2 Adaptive Bitrate Streaming

---

1. Divide the video into multiple segments.
2. Encode each segment at multiple bitrates.
3. Monitor the network conditions.
4. Adjust the bitrate of the next segment based on the network's current status.

- **3. Utilizing HTTP/2 and QUIC Protocols:** HTTP/2 and QUIC (Quick UDP Internet Connections) are modern protocols that enhance bandwidth utilization. HTTP/2 reduces latency by allowing multiplexing of streams over a single TCP connection. QUIC, built on UDP, further reduces latency through quicker handshake and improved congestion control.

178

Example setup for a server supporting HTTP/2 can be done using Apache:

```
sudo a2enmod http2
sudo systemctl restart apache2
<VirtualHost *:443>
    Protocols h2 http/1.1
</VirtualHost>
```

Using these protocols ensures that bandwidth is used more effectively and typical issues such as Head-Of-Line (HOL) blocking are mitigated.

- **4. Efficient Data Routing:** Edge computing environments can benefit significantly from optimized data routing strategies. Implementing intelligent routing policies based on real-time network conditions helps in balancing the load and reducing congestion.

Diagrammatic representation:

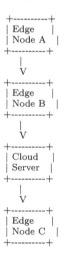

```
+----------+
| Edge     |
| Node A   |
+----------+
    |
    V
+----------+
| Edge     |
| Node B   |
+----------+
    |
    V
+----------+
| Cloud    |
| Server   |
+----------+
    |
    V
+----------+
| Edge     |
| Node C   |
+----------+
```

- **5. Caching Strategies:** Implementing caching reduces the amount of data transmitted over the network. Edge caching involves storing frequently accessed data closer to the user, which minimizes the network load.

An example of configuring caching in an NGINX server:

179

```
http {
    proxy_cache_path /data/nginx/cache levels=1:2
                     keys_zone=my_cache:10m
                     max_size=10g
                     inactive=60m
                     use_temp_path=off;
    server {
        location / {
            proxy_pass http://backend;
            proxy_cache my_cache;
            proxy_cache_bypass $http_cache_control;
        }
    }
}
```

- **6. Traffic Shaping and QoS:** Implementing traffic shaping and Quality of Service (QoS) policies helps to manage bandwidth effectively. Traffic shaping involves controlling the volume of traffic being sent over the network to avoid congestion, while QoS ensures that critical applications receive the necessary bandwidth.

QoS policy application using tc in Linux:

```
sudo tc qdisc add dev eth0 root handle 1: htb default 30
sudo tc class add dev eth0 parent 1: classid 1:1 htb rate 1gbit
sudo tc class add dev eth0 parent 1:1 classid 1:10 htb rate 100mbit
sudo tc class add dev eth0 parent 1:1 classid 1:20 htb rate 200mbit
```

Effectively utilizing network bandwidth involves leveraging a mixture of these techniques, adapted to specific use cases and operational requirements. By implementing these methods, edge computing environments can achieve optimal network performance and resource allocation.

6.6 Edge Caching and Content Delivery Networks

Edge caching and Content Delivery Networks (CDNs) play a pivotal role in enhancing the performance and scalability of edge computing applications. By placing frequently accessed data closer to the end-users, these technologies significantly reduce latency and improve user experience. The following section details the mechanisms and strategies involved in implementing edge caching and leveraging CDNs in an edge computing environment.

Edge caching involves storing data at various edge nodes, allowing quick access from geographically dispersed locations. This approach reduces the round-trip time by eliminating the need to fetch data from a central server for every user request. As such, it is essential to understand the types of caching mechanisms available and how to configure them effectively.

CDNs, on the other hand, are a network of distributed servers strategically placed to deliver content efficiently. These networks are designed to serve content with high availability and performance. CDNs handle vast amounts of web traffic, distributing the load across multiple servers, thus preventing bottlenecks and ensuring seamless delivery of content.

Implementing edge caching requires an understanding of various caching strategies, such as:

- **Cache Invalidation Policies:** These policies determine when cached data should be refreshed or removed. Common strategies include time-to-live (TTL), where data is considered stale after a certain period, and event-based invalidation, which updates the cache when specific events occur.

- **Cache Replacement Policies:** When the cache reaches its storage limit, older data must be replaced with new data. Popular replacement policies include Least Recently Used (LRU), where the least recently accessed data is replaced first, and First-In-First-Out (FIFO), where the oldest data enqueued is replaced first.

- **Data Consistency:** Maintaining consistency between cached data and the original data source is crucial. Techniques such as write-through and write-back caches ensure that updates to the data are appropriately propagated to the cache and the original source.

An example of configuring an edge caching solution in Azure is provided below. This example demonstrates setting up Azure CDN to optimize the delivery of content.

```
from azure.mgmt.cdn import CdnManagementClient
from azure.identity import DefaultAzureCredential

cd_client = CdnManagementClient(credential=DefaultAzureCredential(),
    subscription_id='your_subscription_id')

# Create a CDN profile
cd_profile = cd_client.profiles.create(
    resource_group_name='your_resource_group',
    profile_name='your_cdn_profile',
    profile={
        'location': 'your_location',
        'sku': {'name': 'Standard_Verizon'}
    }
)

# Create a CDN endpoint
cd_endpoint = cd_client.endpoints.create(
    resource_group_name='your_resource_group',
    profile_name='your_cdn_profile',
    endpoint_name='your_cdn_endpoint',
    endpoint={
        'origin_host_header': 'your_origin_host_header',
        'origins': [{
            'name': 'your_origin_name',
            'host_name': 'your_origin_hostname'
        }]
    }
)
```

The output of this script will show the successful creation of a CDN profile and endpoint.

```
Creating CDN profile...
CDN profile created: your_cdn_profile
Creating CDN endpoint...
CDN endpoint created: your_cdn_endpoint
```

Using the CDN, content can be distributed across multiple edge locations, significantly reducing latency. Cache configuration for the CDN can be managed through Azure's portal or programmatically.

Beyond CDNs, edge caching can also involve storing data on edge devices, allowing for even faster access. This type of caching is beneficial in scenarios where internet connectivity is intermittent or where ultra-low latency is required.

In the context of edge caching, several challenges arise, such as determining optimal cache placement, managing cache size, and ensuring data consistency across distributed caches. Advanced algorithms and machine learning models can be employed to predict data access patterns and optimize cache utilization.

Furthermore, the integration of edge caching with CDNs can be enhanced by using other Azure services, such as Azure Blob Storage for origin storage, and Azure Front Door for load balancing and global routing. These integrations help create a robust edge architecture capable of handling high traffic volumes and delivering content with minimal latency.

Understanding and implementing edge caching and CDNs effectively is crucial for any edge computing application aiming to achieve high performance and scalability. By leveraging these technologies, applications can deliver a better user experience, reduce latency, and efficiently manage network bandwidth.

6.7 Performance Monitoring and Profiling

Performance monitoring and profiling constitutes a critical aspect of maintaining and optimizing edge computing systems. Ensuring that edge devices and applications perform efficiently requires continuous observation and fine-tuning based on gathered performance data. This section delves into the specific methodologies and tools utilized for monitoring and profiling within Azure-based edge deployments.

Performance monitoring encompasses the ongoing collection of data related to system and application behavior under varying operational conditions. This data is foundational for understanding resource utilization, identifying bottlenecks, and forecasting future performance trends. Profiling, on the other hand, is a more targeted approach used to obtain detailed information about specific aspects of an application's performance, such as execution time, memory usage, and I/O operations.

Azure provides a comprehensive suite of tools and services tailored for performance monitoring and profiling in edge computing environments. Core among these are Azure Monitor, Azure Log Analytics, Application Insights, and Azure Diagnostics. These tools enable developers and administrators to gather, analyze, and react to performance metrics efficiently.

Azure Monitor is the centralized service for monitoring resources in the Azure ecosystem, including edge devices. It can aggregate data from multiple sources, creating a unified view of the system's health and performance. Azure Monitor allows the configuration of alerts, dashboards, and automated responses to specific conditions, ensuring timely intervention when performance issues are detected.

Azure Monitor's capabilities can be extended using **Azure Log Analytics**, which helps in querying and analyzing log data. By writing custom queries, users can gain deep insights into performance metrics and identify trends that may not be immediately apparent from raw data.

The use of *Kusto Query Language (KQL)* in Azure Log Analytics is pivotal for constructing complex queries. Below is an example of a KQL query that retrieves CPU utilization data from edge devices over the past 24 hours:

```
AzureMetrics
| where TimeGenerated > ago(24h)
| where ResourceId contains "edgeDevice"
| where MetricName == "Percentage CPU"
| summarize avg(CounterValue) by bin(TimeGenerated, 1h), ResourceId
```

The query identifies and averages the CPU usage, offering a clear timeline of how resources have been consumed.

For application-specific monitoring, **Azure Application Insights** is instrumental. It collects telemetry data from applications, providing insights into request rates, response times, failure rates, and more. Integrating Application Insights with edge applications involves adding a small instrumentation package to the application's code.

Consider the following snippet for integrating Application Insights with a Python-based edge application:

```
from opencensus.ext.azure.log_exporter import AzureLogHandler
import logging

logger = logging.getLogger(__name__)
logger.addHandler(AzureLogHandler(connection_string='InstrumentationKey=<KEY
    >'))
```

```python
def process_data():
    try:
        # Data processing logic
        pass
    except Exception as e:
        logger.exception("Data processing error: {}".format(e))

process_data()
```

This integration ensures that any performance anomalies, exceptions, or custom metrics within the process_data function are logged and sent to Azure Application Insights for further analysis.

Azure Diagnostics complements the monitoring tools by collecting diagnostic data, such as event logs, performance counters, and crash dumps. Configuring Azure Diagnostics can be achieved via the Azure portal or by using configuration files in an application. A JSON configuration setup for diagnostic data collection on an Azure virtual machine is as follows:

```json
{
  "diagnosticsMonitorConfiguration": {
    "overallQuotaInMB": 4096,
    "scheduledTransferPeriod": "PT1H",
    "performanceCounters": {
      "performanceCounterConfiguration": [
        {
          "counterSpecifier": "\\Processor(_Total)\\% Processor Time",
          "sampleRate": "PT1M"
        },
        {
          "counterSpecifier": "\\Memory\\Available MBytes",
          "sampleRate": "PT1M"
        }
      ]
    },
    "windowsEventLog": {
      "dataSource": [
        {
          "name": "Application!*",
          "scheduledTransferPeriod": "PT1H"
        }
      ]
    }
  }
}
```

With this JSON configuration, CPU utilization and memory availability are monitored at 1-minute intervals, and event logs from the Application log are transferred hourly.

185

Proactive utilization of these monitoring and profiling tools enables system administrators to preempt performance degradation by observing key metrics and identifying trends. Correlating events, setting alerts, and automating responses are essential steps in maintaining seamless edge operations.

Moreover, edge computing systems often operate under varying network conditions and loads. Profiling allows developers to micro-optimize application performance. Tools like **Visual Studio Profiler**, **dotTrace**, and **Py-Spy** can be integrated into the development process to obtain granular performance data. For instance, using Visual Studio Profiler with a .NET edge application, developers can analyze CPU and memory usage or track synchronous and asynchronous call patterns.

Continuous integration and deployment (CI/CD) pipelines should integrate performance testing and monitoring to ensure code changes contribute positively to performance metrics. By embedding profiling into development iterations, teams can identify and address performance issues early in the development lifecycle.

In sum, performance monitoring and profiling enable the maintenance of high-performing edge computing systems by providing actionable insights derived from comprehensive metric collection and detailed application analysis. Proper implementation of these practices ensures that edge deployments remain responsive, scalable, and resilient under various operational scenarios.

6.8   Scaling Edge Deployments in Azure

Scaling edge deployments within the Azure ecosystem requires a thorough understanding of both the architectural principles and the specific tools provided by the Azure platform. The need to effectively manage, monitor, and expand edge operations necessitates a strategic approach to resources, orchestration, and deployment pipelines.

Azure provides a suite of services and frameworks that allow for the horizontal and vertical scaling of edge applications, ensuring that they can handle varying loads and operational demands.

- **Azure IoT Edge:** One of the primary services for edge deployment within Azure is Azure IoT Edge. Azure IoT Edge extends cloud intelligence and analytics to edge devices. To enable scaling, IoT Edge supports module management and deployment across multiple devices.

```
# Example to deploy a module to multiple IoT Edge devices
az iot edge deployment create --content deployment.json --target-condition tags.
    environment='production' --priority 10
```

- **Automated Deployment Pipelines:** Azure DevOps and GitHub Actions can be utilized to automate the deployment processes. This integration ensures that updates, scaling operations, and configuration changes can be propagated efficiently across numerous edge devices.

```
# Example GitHub Actions workflow for deployment
name: Edge Module CI/CD

on:
  push:
    branches:
      - main

jobs:
  deploy:
    runs-on: ubuntu-latest
    steps:
    - name: Checkout code
      uses: actions/checkout@v2

    - name: Build and Push Docker Image
      run: |
        docker build -t edge-module .
        docker tag edge-module <container-registry>/edge-module:latest
        docker push <container-registry>/edge-module:latest

    - name: Deploy to IoT Edge
      run: |
        az iot edge set-modules --device-id <device-id> --hub-name <hub-name
            > --content deployment.json
```

- **Azure Kubernetes Service (AKS) at the Edge:** For scenarios requiring scaling beyond the capacity of traditional IoT devices, Azure Kubernetes Service (AKS) can be deployed at the edge. AKS allows for the orchestration of containerized applications, providing mechanisms for scaling pods and nodes as necessary.

```
# Example AKS deployment file
apiVersion: apps/v1
kind: Deployment
metadata:
  name: edge-app
spec:
  replicas: 3
  selector:
    matchLabels:
      app: edge-app
  template:
    metadata:
      labels:
        app: edge-app
    spec:
      containers:
      - name: edge-app-container
        image: <container-registry>/edge-app:latest
        resources:
          requests:
            cpu: "250m"
            memory: "64Mi"
          limits:
            cpu: "500m"
            memory: "128Mi"
```

- **Resource Management:** Effective resource management is crucial in scaling edge deployments. Azure's vertical scaling capabilities allow for the adjustment of resource allocations in response to changing computational and storage requirements of edge applications.

```
# Example to resize an Azure VM scale set for vertical scaling
az vmss scale --resource-group <resource-group-name> --name <vmss-name> --
    new-capacity 5
```

- **Monitoring and Analytics:** Continuous monitoring is indispensable for maintaining optimal performance during scaling operations. Azure Monitor, combined with Azure IoT Hub metrics, provides a comprehensive suite of tools for real-time monitoring, logging, and analytics.

```
# Example to set up Azure Monitor alert for CPU usage
az monitor metrics alert create --name "HighCPUUsage" --resource-group <
    resource-group-name> --scopes <vmss-id> --condition "avg Percentage
    CPU > 80" --window-size 5m --evaluation-frequency 1m
```

- **Automated Remediation:** Responding to anomalies and failures in a scalable manner ensures the continuity and reliability

188

of edge deployments. Utilizing Azure Logic Apps or Azure Functions, automated remediation processes can be established to handle issues dynamically.

```
# Example to create an Azure Logic App for automatic remediation
az logicapp create --resource-group <resource-group-name> --location <location
    > --name <logicapp-name>
```

Azure's comprehensive set of tools and services support scaling edge deployments efficiently and effectively, allowing for robust and resilient application performance across diverse and distributed environments. Properly leveraging these capabilities enhances the adaptability and scalability of edge solutions, enabling them to meet the evolving demands of modern applications.

6.9 Optimizing Edge Storage Solutions

In edge computing, storage optimization is critical due to constraints on physical resources such as disk space, I/O bandwidth, and access latency. Efficient storage at the edge ensures rapid access to critical data, minimizes latency, and supports high-availability requirements essential for edge applications.

To achieve optimal storage solutions, several strategies need to be considered: data locality, compression, deduplication, hierarchical storage management, and intelligent data placement.

1. Data Locality

One of the key principles in edge storage is data locality, which refers to keeping frequently accessed data close to the edge devices where computations are performed. This minimizes the data transfer time and reduces network load. Techniques to improve data locality include:

- **Caching frequently accessed data**: Leveraging local caches to store recently or frequently accessed data can significantly boost access speed. Implementing a Least Recently Used (LRU) policy for cache management can help maintain an up-to-date and efficient cache.

189

- **Pre-fetching strategies**: Based on prediction algorithms, pre-fetching data that is likely to be accessed soon can reduce access latency. For instance, machine learning models can be employed to predict and preload data based on usage patterns.

- **Data replication**: Replicating critical data across multiple edge nodes ensures high availability and fault tolerance. However, this must be balanced against the overhead of maintaining consistency across replicas.

2. Data Compression

Compressing data before storing it on edge devices can save significant storage space and reduce the amount of data that needs to be transferred over the network. Common methods include:

- **Lossless compression**: Algorithms such as Gzip, Brotli, and LZ4 compress data without losing any information, making them ideal for scenarios where it is crucial to retain the integrity of the original data.

- **Lossy compression**: Techniques like JPEG and MP3 can be used where some loss of data is acceptable. These methods typically offer higher compression ratios compared to lossless methods.

3. Data Deduplication

Data deduplication reduces storage consumption by eliminating redundant copies of data, storing only the unique instances, and referring back to them as needed. This can be implemented at various levels:

- **File-level deduplication**: Identifies and removes duplicate files across the storage system.

- **Block-level deduplication**: Works by dividing files into smaller blocks and identifying duplicates among these blocks, allowing for finer granularity and more substantial savings in storage space.

190

- **Inline deduplication**: Executes deduplication in real-time as data is written to storage, ensuring continuous optimization without requiring additional post-process steps.

4. Hierarchical Storage Management

Hierarchical storage management (HSM) automates the movement of data between high-cost and low-cost storage media based on usage patterns. This system uses a tiered approach, placing frequently accessed data on faster storage systems (e.g., SSDs) while migrating less critical or older data to slower, more cost-effective solutions (e.g., HDDs or cloud storage).

- Implementation of policies that determine the criteria for migration can help ensure seamless data accessibility and resource utilization.

- Leveraging solid-state drives (SSDs) for high-velocity, frequently accessed data and hard disk drives (HDDs) for archival purposes maximizes cost efficiency and performance.

5. Intelligent Data Placement

Intelligent data placement involves using knowledge about the data and the workload to determine the most suitable location for storing data. This can be achieved through:

- **Workload characterization**: Understanding the characteristics of the workload such as read/write ratios, access patterns, and data temperature can guide how data is placed and tiered.

- **Context-aware placement algorithms**: Employing algorithms that consider the context, such as geographical location, network bandwidth, and latency requirements, can optimize placement decisions to ensure minimal access times and optimal resource usage.

```
class LRUCache:
    def __init__(self, capacity: int):
        self.cache = {}
        self.capacity = capacity
```

```
    self.order = []

def get(self, key: int) -> int:
    if key in self.cache:
        self.order.remove(key)
        self.order.append(key)
        return self.cache[key]
    return -1

def put(self, key: int, value: int) -> None:
    if key in self.cache:
        self.order.remove(key)
    elif len(self.cache) == self.capacity:
        oldest = self.order.pop(0)
        del self.cache[oldest]
    self.cache[key] = value
    self.order.append(key)

# Usage example
capacity = 2
lru_cache = LRUCache(capacity)
lru_cache.put(1, 1)
lru_cache.put(2, 2)
print(lru_cache.get(1)) # returns 1
lru_cache.put(3, 3) # evicts key 2
print(lru_cache.get(2)) # returns -1
```

Efficiently handling edge storage solutions requires a multi-faceted approach that incorporates advanced techniques to optimize data storage and retrieval. By applying strategies such as improving data locality, utilizing compression and deduplication, leveraging hierarchical storage management, and employing intelligent data placement, one can significantly enhance the performance and reliability of edge computing deployments. Consequently, this enables edge devices to handle more substantial workloads, ensuring that applications remain responsive and robust even under varying operational conditions.

6.10 Strategies for Handling Device Failures

In edge computing environments, device failures can significantly impact the overall performance and reliability of distributed systems. To mitigate these issues, it is essential to develop robust strategies for handling device failures. This section delves into various techniques and best practices that enhance system resilience, ensuring continuity of service despite potential hardware or software malfunctions.

The first step in addressing device failures involves understanding the common causes and types of failures that can occur. Device failures may include hardware defects, software bugs, network issues, or power outages. Each type of failure requires specific handling strategies to minimize disruption and data loss.

Redundancy and fault tolerance are crucial components in designing resilient edge architectures. By incorporating redundant systems, such as duplicate hardware components or parallel processing units, the system can continue to operate even if one component fails. For example, using a cluster of edge devices to distribute workloads ensures that if one device becomes unresponsive, others can seamlessly take over.

```yaml
apiVersion: apps/v1
kind: Deployment
metadata:
  name: edge-app
spec:
  replicas: 3
  selector:
    matchLabels:
      app: edge-app
  template:
    metadata:
      labels:
        app: edge-app
    spec:
      containers:
      - name: app-container
        image: edge-app:latest
        ports:
        - containerPort: 8080
```

Monitoring and alerting systems are essential for the timely detection of device failures. Implementing tools such as Azure Monitor or Prometheus can help track the health and performance of edge devices in real-time. These systems can generate alerts for anomalies or failures, enabling prompt response and remediation.

```python
from prometheus_client import start_http_server, Gauge
import random
import time

# Define metrics
device_temperature = Gauge('device_temperature', 'Temperature of the edge device')
device_status = Gauge('device_status', 'Operational status of the edge device', ['
    status'])
```

```
# Start the Prometheus server
start_http_server(8000)

# Simulation of device metric updates
while True:
    temperature = random.uniform(20.0, 80.0)
    status = 'up' if temperature < 75 else 'down'

    # Update Prometheus metrics
    device_temperature.set(temperature)
    device_status.labels(status=status).set(1 if status == 'up' else 0)

    time.sleep(5)
```

Implementing automated recovery mechanisms is another vital strategy for handling device failures. Automated recovery can include actions such as restarting failed services, reallocating resources, or migrating workloads to healthy devices. Utilizing container orchestration platforms such as Kubernetes facilitates automated recovery through features like self-healing, where the orchestrator detects failed containers and restarts them automatically.

Data integrity and consistency are critical during device failures. Employing distributed databases and ensuring data redundancy across multiple devices can safeguard against data loss. Techniques such as data replication and distributed consensus protocols (e.g., Raft or Paxos) can help maintain data integrity. Consistency models, like eventual consistency and strong consistency, should be chosen based on application requirements and failure scenarios.

```
-- Create a replica of the primary database
CREATE DATABASE edge_replica AS COPY OF edge_primary;

-- Set up replication settings
ALTER DATABASE edge_replica SET ENABLED_LAG_ALERTS = ON;

-- Monitor replication status
SELECT * FROM sys.dm_database_copies
WHERE database_id = DB_ID('edge_replica');
```

The use of predictive maintenance can further reduce the risk of device failures. By analyzing historical performance data and leveraging machine learning algorithms, it is possible to predict and pre-emptively address potential device failures before they occur. Azure Machine Learning can be utilized to build predictive maintenance models that forecast failures and suggest maintenance activities.

Load balancing is yet another strategy that contributes to resilience. Distributing workloads evenly across multiple devices reduces the risk of overload and subsequent failure. Load balancers can dynamically route traffic based on device health and performance metrics, ensuring that no single device becomes a point of failure.

To implement these strategies effectively, a clear incident response plan should be established. This plan outlines the procedures to follow during device failures, including roles and responsibilities, communication protocols, and recovery steps. Regular testing and updating of the incident response plan ensure preparedness for real-world scenarios.

These strategies collectively enhance the robustness and reliability of edge computing deployments, ensuring that device failures do not compromise system performance or data integrity.

6.11 Best Practices for Performance Tuning

Performance tuning in edge computing environments necessitates a meticulous approach to ensure that applications run optimally under varying loads and conditions. This section delineates essential best practices that facilitate efficient performance tuning.

Profiling and Benchmarking

Profiling is the foundational step in performance tuning. Using application profilers and benchmarking tools, engineers can identify performance bottlenecks. Profiling tools such as Azure Monitoring and Application Insights provide detailed insights into CPU utilization, memory consumption, and I/O operations.

```
# Install the Azure Monitor CLI extension
az extension add --name application-insights

# Create an Application Insights resource
az monitor app-insights component create --app <app_name> --location <location> --
    resource-group <resource_group>

# Retrieve performance metrics
az monitor metrics list --resource <resource_id> --metric-names "CPU Usage,"
    Memory Usage" --interval PT1M
```

Code Optimization

Optimizing the application code itself is crucial. Review and refactor code to remove inefficiencies. Use concurrency and parallelism where applicable to leverage multi-core processors effectively. For example, employing asynchronous programming models can significantly enhance performance by preventing blocking calls. In Python, using asyncio can improve the throughput of I/O-bound tasks.

```
import asyncio

async def fetch_data():
    await asyncio.sleep(1) # Simulates an I/O-bound operation

async def main():
    await asyncio.gather(fetch_data(), fetch_data())

# Run the asynchronous event loop
asyncio.run(main())
```

Efficient Resource Management

Efficient resource allocation and utilization are paramount. Employ auto-scaling features provided by Azure, ensuring resources are dynamically allocated based on current demand. This prevents both under-provisioning and over-provisioning of resources.

```
# Create a scaling rule based on CPU usage
az monitor autoscale rule create --resource-group <resource_group> --resource <
    resource_id> --condition "Percentage CPU > 75 avg 5m" --scale out 1

# Set auto-scaling settings
az monitor autoscale create --resource-group <resource_group> --name <
    autoscale_setting_name> --resource <resource_id> --min-count 1 --max-count
    10 --count 1
```

Data Locality and Caching

Reducing latency through data locality and caching mechanisms can significantly improve performance. Implement edge caching strategies, where frequently accessed data is cached locally on edge devices. Utilizing Azure's Content Delivery Network (CDN) also minimizes latency by delivering content from geographically dispersed edge nodes.

```
# Create a CDN profile
az cdn profile create --name <cdn_profile_name> --resource-group <resource_group>
    --location <location> --sku Standard_Akamai

# Create a CDN endpoint
az cdn endpoint create --resource-group <resource_group> --profile-name <
```

```
cdn_profile_name> --name <endpoint_name> --origin <origin_hostname>
```

Minimizing Latency

Network latency can profoundly impact performance. Optimize network configurations and choose proximity to end-users for edge deployments. Utilize Azure Traffic Manager to route requests efficiently based on the lowest latency by setting up geographic routing.

```
# Create a Traffic Manager profile
az network traffic-manager profile create --name <tm_profile_name> --resource-group
    <resource_group> --routing-method Geographic --unique-dns-name <
    unique_dns_name> --ttl 30

# Add an endpoint to the Traffic Manager
az network traffic-manager endpoint create --resource-group <resource_group> --
    profile-name <tm_profile_name> --type externalEndpoints --name <
    endpoint_name> --target <fqdn_target>
```

Monitoring and Alerting

Continuous monitoring combined with alerting mechanisms enables proactive identification of performance degradation. Utilizing Azure Monitor and setting up alert rules ensures timely interventions are made to mitigate performance issues.

```
# Create an alert rule for CPU usage
az monitor metrics alert create --name <alert_name> --resource-group <
    resource_group> --scopes <resource_id> --condition "avg Percentage CPU > 80
    " --window-size 5m --evaluation-frequency 1m
```

Capacity Planning

Proper capacity planning ensures that the infrastructure can handle peak loads without performance degradation. Utilize historical data and predictive analytics to forecast demand and scale resources accordingly, leveraging tools such as Azure Advisor.

Application Configuration Tuning

Fine-tuning application configurations can also yield performance gains. Adjusting thread pools, connection limits, and garbage collection settings are examples of tweaks that can optimize application throughput and responsiveness.

Performance tuning is an iterative and ongoing process that benefits significantly from continuous monitoring, efficient resource management, effective caching strategies, and proactive capacity planning. Integrating these best practices ensures robust and scalable edge computing solutions that deliver optimal performance across diverse operational scenarios.

Chapter 7

Edge AI and Machine Learning

This chapter explores the integration of AI and machine learning at the edge. It discusses the benefits of localized AI processing, the necessary hardware and accelerators, and the steps for building and deploying machine learning models on edge devices. Key applications such as real-time inference, computer vision, and natural language processing are presented. The chapter also covers model optimization, compression techniques, and the use of Azure Machine Learning to manage and deploy AI models effectively at the edge.

7.1   Introduction to Edge AI and Machine Learning

Edge AI and Machine Learning represent a significant advancement in the realm of artificial intelligence, leveraging localized processing capabilities to ameliorate the demand for extensive cloud-based data transmissions. The edge computing paradigm aims to bring computation and data storage closer to the location where it is needed, improving response times and saving bandwidth.

Edge AI incorporates these principles by executing AI algorithms directly on devices situated at the network edge (e.g., IoT devices, smartphones, gateways). In contrast to traditional frameworks, which rely on centralized cloud computing, edge AI processes data locally. This reduces latency, enhances privacy, and can provide more reliable service in areas with intermittent or low-bandwidth connectivity.

A foundational aspect of edge AI is understanding the hardware that enables such computations. Devices at the edge commonly include embedded systems with specialized AI accelerators such as GPUs (Graphics Processing Units), TPUs (Tensor Processing Units), or more domain-specific accelerators. These components are designed to handle the computationally intensive workloads required by machine learning and deep learning algorithms.

```
import tensorflow as tf
from tensorflow import lite

# Load the pretrained model
model = tf.keras.models.load_model('model_path.h5')

# Convert the model
converter = lite.TFLiteConverter.from_keras_model(model)
tflite_model = converter.convert()

# Save the model
with open('model.tflite', 'wb') as f:
    f.write(tflite_model)
```

One of the dominant approaches employed in Edge AI involves the use of TensorFlow Lite, a lightweight library that enables the deployment of TensorFlow models on mobile and edge devices. This deployment is feasible due to quantization and model optimization techniques that make the models less resource-intensive without significantly compromising accuracy.

From a machine learning perspective, Edge AI follows the paradigm where models are first trained on powerful cloud-based systems using extensive datasets. Subsequently, these trained models undergo a transformation—optimizations such as pruning, quantization, and conversion to formats compatible with edge devices. Once the model is made efficient, it can be deployed to edge devices where inference can be performed.

```
Successful Edge AI deployment results:
Inference time: 50ms
Model size: Reduced from 20MB to 5MB
```

An integral part of this process is the ability to handle real-time data streams. Edge devices, embedded with AI models, facilitate instantaneous data processing and decision-making, which is critical in applications demanding low-latency responses, such as autonomous driving, medical diagnostics, and industrial automation.

The local nature of processing also inherently provides a layer of data security and privacy. Since data is processed locally rather than transmitted to a central server, the risk of data interception or unauthorized access is minimized. This is particularly beneficial in sectors where data sensitivity and confidentiality are paramount.

Azure offers robust support for deploying AI at the edge through its suite of tools collectively known as Azure IoT and Azure Machine Learning. With Azure IoT Edge, developers can run Azure services and custom code on cross-platform IoT devices. Additionally, Azure Machine Learning facilitates the training and subsequent deployment of models to edge devices, ensuring management and updates remain seamless and centralized.

Underpinning these capabilities are several essential services such as Azure IoT Hub, which acts as a central message hub for bi-directional communication between IoT applications and the devices it manages, and Azure Machine Learning service, which provides end-to-end management of the machine learning lifecycle.

An example of deploying a model with Azure IoT Edge involves creating a containerized version of the model and deploying it to the target edge device via the Azure IoT Edge runtime. This integration demonstrates the high degree of flexibility and functionality provided by cloud services in managing edge deployments.

Through combining the principles of edge computing with advanced AI models, edge AI is set to revolutionize various industries, offering more responsive, reliable, and secure AI-powered applications.

This chapter will delve further into these concepts, exploring in detail the benefits and challenges associated with running AI models at the edge, examining the hardware involved, and providing compre-

201

hensive guidelines on deploying and optimizing these models. Practical applications within computer vision and natural language processing domains will be addressed, alongside real-world examples utilizing Azure's rich ecosystem's tools and services.

7.2   Benefits of Running AI Models at the Edge

Implementing AI models at the edge offers significant advantages in terms of performance, security, and operational efficiency. Understanding the specific benefits is crucial for designing optimal edge computing solutions.

Low Latency and Real-Time Processing:

One of the foremost benefits of edge AI is the reduction in latency due to decentralized processing. When AI models operate directly on edge devices such as IoT sensors or gateways, data processing occurs closer to the data source. This proximity diminishes the need to transfer substantial data volumes to centralized cloud servers for analysis. Consequently, decisions based on AI models, especially those requiring real-time processing such as autonomous vehicles or industrial automation systems, are executed with minimal delay.

Example:
Autonomous vehicles need immediate response mechanisms to dodge obstacles.
Edge AI facilitates sub-millisecond reaction times, crucial for vehicle navigation.

Reduced Bandwidth Usage:

As AI tasks move to the edge, the demand for data bandwidth is significantly lowered. Typically, transmitting raw data to the cloud for analysis necessitates considerable bandwidth, particularly with high-resolution video streams in computer vision or extensive datasets in industrial IoT implementations. By conducting initial data processing and inference at the edge, only pertinent information, such as summarized insights or alerts, is sent to cloud servers, hence optimizing bandwidth usage.

Bandwidth Usage Scenario:

> Edge Devices: Process raw video streams locally.
> Cloud: Receives occasional event alerts instead of continuous video streams.

Improved Data Privacy and Security:

Edge AI enhances data privacy and security by limiting the data travers-
ing over the network. Sensitive information remains within local systems, reducing exposure to potential cyber threats encountered during
data transmission. This model is particularly beneficial in healthcare
applications where patient information needs to be secured, and in financial services where transaction data should be protected from interception.

- **Healthcare Example:** Medical devices equipped with edge
  AI analyze patient vitals locally, ensuring sensitive data such as
  heart rate or ECG metrics remains on-device.

- **Financial Services Example:** Edge AI can analyze ATM transaction patterns locally to detect fraud without broadcasting sensitive user information over unsecured networks.

Increased Reliability:

Edge AI solutions are more reliable in environments with intermittent or limited network connectivity. By performing computations locally, edge devices continue operations uninterrupted despite network
issues. This self-sufficiency is vital in remote locations or critical applications, such as remote monitoring systems in agriculture or disaster
response tools.

- **Remote Monitoring:** Agricultural drones with embedded AI
  can analyze crop health on-site, without reliance on network connectivity.

- **Disaster Response:** In natural disasters, edge AI solutions empower rescue robots to make immediate decisions even when disconnected from central networks.

Scalability:

Edge AI facilitates scalable and distributed system architectures. By decentralizing the computational load, network and central computing resources face reduced strain, thereby efficiently handling growing numbers of edge devices. This decentralized approach also allows incremental scaling, where edge devices or capabilities can be added without significant overhauls to the entire system architecture.

Cost Efficiency:

Operating AI models on edge devices reduces operational costs associated with extensive data transmission and cloud processing. On-device processing minimizes the need for expansive cloud infrastructure, reducing continuous operational expenses. This financial efficiency is complemented by the advanced computational power and energy efficiency of modern edge hardware accelerators, such as GPUs, TPUs, and FPGAs.

Cost Saving Illustration:
Cloud-Only Model: High recurring charges for continuous video stream analysis.
Edge-AI Model: Once-off investment in edge hardware with lower operational expenditures.

Customization and Adaptability:

Edge AI empowers businesses with the ability to tailor and adapt AI models to specific local requirements and contexts. Since models operate within the local environment, they can be customized to better address local conditions and requirements, leading to more accurate and relevant insights.

With these comprehensive benefits, deploying AI models at the edge serves as a transformative strategy, markedly enhancing performance, reliability, and operational efficiency in numerous real-world applications.

7.3 Edge AI Hardware and Accelerators

Edge AI involves executing artificial intelligence (AI) and machine learning (ML) algorithms directly on edge devices, such as smartphones, IoT devices, and industrial machinery, rather than relying on centralized data centers. This can drastically reduce latency, enhance privacy, and reduce dependence on network connectivity. To achieve this, devices must be equipped with specialized hardware and accelerators capable of handling the computational demands of AI workloads in a resource-constrained environment.

Edge AI hardware typically includes microcontrollers, system-on-chips (SoCs), and dedicated AI accelerators. These hardware components are designed to optimize energy efficiency and computational power, providing essential support for running AI models locally. Key features of edge hardware include low power consumption, high processing capabilities, and the ability to perform on-device inference.

- Microcontrollers and SoCs form the backbone of edge devices. A microcontroller is a compact integrated circuit designed to govern a specific operation in an embedded system. Microcontrollers can include a processor core, memory, and programmable input/output peripherals. Examples include the ARM Cortex-M series, ESP32, and ATmega328.

- SoCs, on the other hand, integrate all components of a computer or other electronic systems into a single chip. This includes processors, memory, input/output ports, and secondary storage. Popular SoCs used in edge AI applications include the NVIDIA Jetson family, Google Coral, and Raspberry Pi. These SoCs leverage multicore CPUs and GPUs to provide substantial computational resources necessary for AI workloads.

- GPUs, traditional components of gaming and graphics applications, have become crucial in AI and machine learning tasks due to their parallel processing capabilities. They are designed to handle multiple tasks simultaneously, making them suitable for training and inference of deep learning models.

- On edge devices, GPUs must be optimized for low power consumption. The NVIDIA Jetson Nano and the Jetson Xavier NX are exemplary devices in this category, providing performance capabilities suitable for AI applications while maintaining a low power envelope.

205

```
import tensorflow as tf
from tensorflow.keras.models import load_model
from tensorflow.keras.preprocessing import image

model = load_model('model.h5')
img = image.load_img('image.jpg', target_size=(224, 224))
x = image.img_to_array(img)
x = tf.expand_dims(x, axis=0)
x = tf.keras.applications.mobilenet_v2.preprocess_input(x)

predictions = model.predict(x)
print(predictions)
```

- Tensor Processing Units (TPUs) are specialized hardware accelerators designed specifically for AI workloads. They are engineered to optimize the performance of tensor operations, which are fundamental to deep learning. Google's Coral Edge TPU, a compact device tailored for edge applications, exemplifies the impactful integration of TPUs in edge computing. Designed to perform high-speed inference of neural networks, the Coral Edge TPU focuses on power efficiency.

The following code snippet demonstrates how to leverage a Coral Edge TPU to perform inference:

```
import tensorflow as tf
import tflite_runtime.interpreter as tflite

interpreter = tflite.Interpreter(model_path="model.tflite",
                        experimental_delegates=[tflite.load_delegate('libedgetpu.
                                so.1')])
interpreter.allocate_tensors()

input_details = interpreter.get_input_details()
output_details = interpreter.get_output_details()

# Input preprocessing
input_data = np.array(img, dtype=np.float32)
interpreter.set_tensor(input_details[0]['index'], input_data)
interpreter.invoke()

# Output postprocessing
output_data = interpreter.get_tensor(output_details[0]['index'])
print(output_data)
```

- NPUs are specialized chips that accelerate artificial neural network computations. These units are explicitly designed to im-

206

prove the efficiency of deep learning applications on edge devices. NPUs like the Huawei Ascend and the Amlogic A311D are equipped with capabilities to handle complex deep learning models.

- FPGAs are configurable integrated circuits that can be programmed to perform specific computations. FPGAs offer flexibility and can be fine-tuned for AI applications to provide both high performance and low power usage. An example is the Xilinx Zynq UltraScale+ MPSoCs, which can be customized for a wide range of AI workloads.

Deploying AI models on an FPGA generally follows these steps:

- Convert the trained neural network model into a form suitable for FPGA implementation.

- Program the FPGA to perform the inference tasks.

- Integrate the programmed FPGA with the edge device for on-device inference.

```
from vitis_ai_vart import Runner

dpu = Runner('/path/to/dpu/model.xmodel')
input_data = preprocess_input('image.jpg')
output = dpu.run(input_data)
```

- Comparing Edge TPUs and GPUs for edge AI applications involves evaluating criteria such as power consumption, computational power, latency, and ease of integration. While GPUs offer versatility and high performance, TPUs are designed for specialized tensor operations, providing higher efficiency and reduced power usage for specific deep learning tasks.

Overall, the choice of hardware accelerators for edge AI depends on the specific requirements of the application, including the desired balance of computational power, power efficiency, and the complexity of the AI models to be deployed.

207

7.4 Building and Training Machine Learning Models

To implement machine learning capabilities at the edge, it is crucial to comprehend the process of building and training models effectively. This encompasses selecting appropriate datasets, preprocessing data, choosing suitable algorithms, and training the models prior to deployment. This section elaborates on these steps in detail.

Dataset Selection and Preparation

The foundation of any machine learning model is the dataset used to train it. The right dataset must accurately represent the patterns and context that the model will encounter in a real-world scenario. For edge AI applications, datasets should ideally be relevant to the specific environment and conditions where the model will be deployed.

Dataset Characteristics: A high-quality dataset should:

- Be comprehensive and sufficiently large.

- Include diverse and representative samples.

- Be labeled accurately if supervised learning is used.

Data Preprocessing

Data preprocessing is a critical step that ensures the success of machine learning models by transforming raw data into a suitable format. It involves several key steps:

- *Normalization*: Ensures that features are on a similar scale, improving convergence speed in training.

```
from sklearn.preprocessing import StandardScaler
scaler = StandardScaler()
data_normalized = scaler.fit_transform(data)
```

- *Data Augmentation*: Especially important in computer vision, it generates new training samples by augmenting the original data.

```
from tensorflow.keras.preprocessing.image import ImageDataGenerator
```

208

```
datagen = ImageDataGenerator(rotation_range=10,
                             width_shift_range=0.1,
                             height_shift_range=0.1,
                             horizontal_flip=True)
datagen.fit(training_images)
```

- *Feature Extraction*: Identifies and retains useful features from data, enhancing model performance.

Algorithm Selection

Choosing the right machine learning algorithm is pivotal. The selection depends on the problem type, dataset size, and computational constraints of edge devices. Edge AI often demands lightweight, efficient models:

- *Convolutional Neural Networks (CNNs)*: Effective for image and video processing tasks.

- *Recurrent Neural Networks (RNNs)*: Suitable for sequence prediction tasks such as natural language processing.

- *Decision Trees and Random Forests*: Useful for classification and regression tasks with lower computational overhead.

Model Training

Training the model involves feeding the preprocessed data through the selected algorithm to learn the underlying patterns. This process is computationally intensive and typically performed on powerful cloud resources or local high-performance computing setups before deploying to edge devices.

Training Process:

1. Initialize model parameters.

2. Select a loss function appropriate to the task.

3. Use optimization algorithms such as Stochastic Gradient Descent (SGD) to minimize the loss function.

4. Run the training data through multiple iterations (epochs) to refine the model parameters.

Example of training a CNN using TensorFlow:

```
import tensorflow as tf

model = tf.keras.models.Sequential([
    tf.keras.layers.Conv2D(32, (3,3), activation='relu', input_shape=(128, 128, 3)),
    tf.keras.layers.MaxPooling2D((2, 2)),
    tf.keras.layers.Conv2D(64, (3, 3), activation='relu'),
    tf.keras.layers.MaxPooling2D((2, 2)),
    tf.keras.layers.Flatten(),
    tf.keras.layers.Dense(128, activation='relu'),
    tf.keras.layers.Dense(10, activation='softmax')
])

model.compile(optimizer='adam',
              loss='sparse_categorical_crossentropy',
              metrics=['accuracy'])

model.fit(training_images, training_labels, epochs=10)
```

Model Evaluation

Post-training, the model must be evaluated to ensure it generalizes well to new, unseen data. This is done using validation and test datasets:

- *Validation Set*: Used during training to monitor model performance and prevent overfitting.

- *Test Set*: Evaluates the model after training, providing an unbiased performance estimate.

Evaluation metrics can vary depending on the task:

- *Accuracy, Precision, Recall, and F1-score*: Commonly used for classification problems.

- *Mean Squared Error (MSE) and R-squared*: Used for regression problems.

Evaluating model performance using confusion matrix for classification:

```
from sklearn.metrics import confusion_matrix, classification_report

predictions = model.predict(test_images)
print(confusion_matrix(test_labels, predictions))
print(classification_report(test_labels, predictions))
```

Hyperparameter Tuning

Fine-tuning hyperparameters improves model performance. Techniques such as grid search or randomized search are frequently employed:

```
from sklearn.model_selection import GridSearchCV

param_grid = {
    'batch_size': [16, 32, 64],
    'epochs': [10, 20, 30],
    'optimizer': ['adam', 'sgd']
}

grid_search = GridSearchCV(estimator=model, param_grid=param_grid, cv=3)
grid_search.fit(training_images, training_labels)
```

Upon completing these steps, the model is prepared for deployment to edge devices, ensuring efficient and effective performance in real-time, resource-constrained environments.

7.5   Deploying AI Models to Edge Devices

The deployment of AI models to edge devices necessitates a comprehensive understanding of several integral components and processes. This section explicates the pivotal steps involved, the tools and frameworks available, and the considerations for effective deployment.

To begin with, the key steps in deploying AI models to edge devices encompass model conversion, selection of runtime environments, packaging, and orchestrating the deployment.

Model Conversion: Typically, AI models are developed and trained using high-level frameworks such as TensorFlow, PyTorch, or Keras. However, these models often need conversion into formats compatible with edge devices, such as TensorFlow Lite, ONNX, or Core ML. This conversion is vital to ensure that the models can be executed within the hardware constraints of edge devices and to leverage any hardware accelerators available.

The TensorFlow model conversion to TensorFlow Lite format can be achieved using the TFLite Converter:

```
import tensorflow as tf
```

```
# Load the pre-trained model
model = tf.keras.models.load_model('model.h5')

# Convert the model to TensorFlow Lite format
converter = tf.lite.TFLiteConverter.from_keras_model(model)
tflite_model = converter.convert()

# Save the converted model
with open('model.tflite', 'wb') as f:
    f.write(tflite_model)
```

Runtime Environments: The next step is to select an appropriate runtime environment for executing the AI model on the edge device. Several runtime environments are specialized for different hardware configurations, such as TensorFlow Lite Interpreter, ONNX Runtime, and Core ML Runtime.

The runtime environment must support the target device's operating system and hardware capabilities. These environments are optimized for minimal latency and resource utilization, ensuring efficient execution of inference tasks on edge devices.

Packaging: Once the model is converted and the runtime environment is selected, the model and its dependencies need to be packaged. This involves bundling the model file(s), runtime libraries, and any additional resources required for model execution into a deployable package. Containerization technologies like Docker can be used to encapsulate the model and its runtime environment, ensuring consistent deployment across different edge devices.

An example of a Dockerfile for packaging a TensorFlow Lite model:

```
FROM tensorflow/tensorflow:2.4.0

# Copy the TensorFlow Lite model file to the container
COPY model.tflite /models/

# Set the working directory
WORKDIR /app

# Install necessary Python dependencies
RUN pip install tensorflow tensorflow-lite

# Copy the application code to the container
COPY app.py /app/

# Define the entry point for the container
CMD ["python", "app.py"]
```

Deployment Orchestration: The final step is orchestrating the deployment of the packaged model to the edge devices. This can be managed using various deployment platforms and services, such as Azure IoT Hub, AWS IoT Greengrass, or Google Cloud IoT Core. These platforms facilitate seamless distribution, version control, and monitoring of deployed AI models across numerous edge devices.

Azure IoT Hub, for instance, enables deployment through device twins and direct methods, allowing precise control over model distribution and device configurations. The following steps outline the deployment process using Azure IoT Hub:

- Register Edge Device: Register the edge device on Azure IoT Hub and install Azure IoT Edge runtime on the device.

- Create Deployment Manifest: Define the deployment manifest specifying the model, its version, container settings, and runtime requirements.

- Deploy via Azure IoT Hub: Deploy the manifest to the registered device from the Azure IoT Hub portal or using Azure CLI commands.

Example CLI commands for creating a deployment manifest:

```
# Create an IoT Edge deployment manifest
az iot edge deployment create --config-id myEdgeDeployment --hub-name myIoTHub --
    content deployment.json

# Assign the deployment to the IoT Edge device
az iot edge set-modules --device-id myEdgeDevice --hub-name myIoTHub --content
    deployment.json
```

Effective deployment also involves continuous monitoring and updating of AI models. With edge devices often operating in isolated environments, it is crucial to establish robust monitoring mechanisms to track model performance and resource usage. Automated update pipelines can be set up to push incremental updates and patches, thereby ensuring the edge devices run the most up-to-date and efficient versions of the AI models.

The deployment of AI models to edge devices is a multifaceted process requiring meticulous attention to model conversion, runtime environment selection, packaging, and deployment orchestration. By leveraging advanced tools and services, such as those offered by Azure, these steps can be streamlined, ensuring efficient and scalable deployment of AI models at the edge.

7.6 Inference and Real-Time Processing at the Edge

Inference represents the phase where a pre-trained machine learning model processes new data to generate predictions or classifications, typically termed as real-time inference when applied directly in production environments. Real-time processing at the edge refers to executing these inferences on edge devices, rather than in centralized cloud infrastructures. This section delves into the intricacies of running inference at the edge, emphasizing practical implementations, latency considerations, resource management, and integration with Azure services.

1. Architectural Considerations

Edge devices often feature a heterogeneous architecture that includes a combination of CPUs, GPUs, and specialized AI accelerators like TPUs or FPGAs. Selecting the right combination of hardware elements is paramount for achieving efficient inference at the edge. Central processing units (CPUs), though versatile, may not always meet the processing demands of heavy AI workloads due to their relatively limited parallel processing capabilities. Graphics processing units (GPUs) can handle parallel tasks more efficiently, making them suitable for high-throughput inference operations. Tensor processing units (TPUs) and field-programmable gate arrays (FPGAs) offer specialized processing capabilities, optimized for specific types of neural network computations.

2. Latency and Throughput

Latency, the time taken for an input to be processed and an inference to be generated, is a critical metric in real-time edge applications. Low latency is essential for applications such as autonomous driving, where decisions must be made within milliseconds. Throughput, measured in inferences per second (IPS), determines how many inference operations can be performed in a given time span. Balancing latency and throughput often involves trade-offs; optimizing one may compromise the other.

The equation for computing latency L can be given by:

$$L = \frac{D}{R}$$

where D is the data payload size and R is the data transfer rate. The aim is to minimize L to ensure prompt inference results.

3. Resource Management

Efficient resource management is essential for sustainable real-time processing. Edge devices usually have constrained computational resources, memory, and power. Effective resource management techniques include:

- *Model Pruning*: Reducing model size by eliminating redundant parameters without significantly affecting model accuracy.

- *Quantization*: Converting model weights from floating-point precision to lower precision (e.g., INT8), thus reducing computational load and memory footprint.

- *Edge Caching*: Storing frequently accessed data and model parameters in fast, easily accessible storage to reduce processing times.

```
import tensorflow as tf

converter = tf.lite.TFLiteConverter.from_saved_model(saved_model_dir)
converter.optimizations = [tf.lite.Optimize.DEFAULT]
tflite_model = converter.convert()

with open('quantized_model.tflite', 'wb') as f:
    f.write(tflite_model)
```

4. Real-Time Processing Frameworks

Frameworks like TensorFlow Lite, ONNX Runtime, and OpenVINO are pivotal for deploying AI models on edge devices. These frameworks

215

provide optimized inference engines that leverage hardware acceleration and ensure models run efficiently on limited resource devices.

Implementing real-time processing using TensorFlow Lite involves the
following steps:

- Convert the trained model to a TensorFlow Lite format.

- Deploy the TFLite model onto the edge device.

- Execute the inference using TensorFlow Lite interpreter.

```
import numpy as np
import tensorflow as tf

# Load TFLite model and allocate tensors
interpreter = tf.lite.Interpreter(model_path="model.tflite")
interpreter.allocate_tensors()

# Get input and output tensors
input_details = interpreter.get_input_details()
output_details = interpreter.get_output_details()

# Prepare the input data
input_data = np.array(data, dtype=np.float32)

# Perform the inference
interpreter.set_tensor(input_details[0]['index'], input_data)
interpreter.invoke()
output_data = interpreter.get_tensor(output_details[0]['index'])
```

5. Integration with Azure Services

Azure IoT Edge provides a robust platform for deploying and managing
edge computing applications. Integration with Azure Machine Learning allows seamless deployment of AI models to edge devices. Azure
IoT Edge can be configured to push updates, collect telemetry data, and
orchestrate workflows.

To deploy a model to an edge device using Azure IoT Edge, follow these
steps:

- Containerize the pre-trained model.

- Define an IoT Edge deployment manifest that specifies the model
  and associated services.

- Push the deployment to the edge device using Azure IoT Hub.

```
# Build and push Docker image
docker build -t mymodel:latest .
docker tag mymodel:latest <azure-container-registry>/mymodel:latest
docker push <azure-container-registry>/mymodel:latest

# Create IoT Edge deployment manifest
az iot edge deployment create --content configuration.json --target-condition "tags.
    environment='edge'" --priority 10 --output table
```

Executing the aforementioned steps ensures that the AI model is efficiently deployed and managed for real-time inference at the edge. The model deployment workflow leverages containerization for portability and Azure IoT services for orchestration, thus enabling scalable and responsive AI applications.

Overall, running real-time inference at the edge requires a holistic approach encompassing hardware selection, latency optimization, resource management, framework utilization, and seamless integration with cloud services. Each component plays a critical role in ensuring the precision, efficiency, and reliability of AI-driven edge applications.

7.7 Using Azure Machine Learning for Edge AI

Azure Machine Learning (Azure ML) provides a comprehensive platform for managing the end-to-end lifecycle of machine learning models, including those deployed to edge devices. Leveraging Azure ML for edge AI allows developers to seamlessly build, train, optimize, and deploy models, ensuring efficient management and orchestration. This section elaborates on how to use Azure ML to facilitate edge AI workflows, emphasizing key features and practical implementations.

Creating and Registering Models

At the core of deploying machine learning models to the edge is the process of creating and registering models. Azure ML offers robust tools for these tasks. The following demonstrates the essential steps for creating and registering a machine learning model using the Azure ML SDK.

```
from azureml.core import Workspace
```

```
from azureml.core.model import Model

# Connect to Azure ML workspace
ws = Workspace.from_config()

# Register the model
model = Model.register(workspace=ws,
                       model_name='my_edge_model',
                       model_path='./model_dir/model.onnx',
                       description='Edge AI ONNX Model')
```

Model Packaging and Deployment

Once a model is registered, the next step is preparing it for deployment to edge devices. Azure ML supports the packaging of models into a Docker image that can be deployed efficiently.

```
from azureml.core.image import ContainerImage, Image

# Define Docker image configuration
image_config = ContainerImage.image_configuration(
    runtime="python",
    execution_script="score.py",
    dependencies=["my_edge_model.onnx"]
)

# Build the image
image = Image.create(
    name="edge-ai-container",
    models=[model],
    image_config=image_config,
    workspace=ws
)

image.wait_for_creation(show_output=True)
```

The score.py script referenced in the execution_script parameter should include the necessary inference logic, ensuring the edge device can execute the model properly.

Deployment to Azure IoT Hub

After creating a Docker image, it can be deployed to an edge device via Azure IoT Hub. This step involves creating an IoT Edge deployment manifest and deploying the model as a module.

```
{
  "modulesContent": {
    "$edgeAgent": {
      "properties.desired": {
        "modules": {
          "edge-ai-container": {
```

```
    "type": "docker",
    "settings": {
      "image": "<registry-url>/edge-ai-container:latest",
      "createOptions": "{}"
    }
   }
  }
 }
},
"$edgeHub": { ... },
"edge-ai-container": {
 "properties.desired": {
  "input": "camera-feed",
  "output": "processed-output"
 }
}
}
}
```

Deploying the model to Azure IoT Hub involves configuring both edge-Hub and edgeAgent modules to handle communication and execution commands. Review Azure IoT Hub documentation for details on configuring these modules.

Remote Monitoring and Management

Azure ML enables continuous monitoring and management of deployed edge models. By integrating with Azure IoT Hub and Azure Monitor, developers can retrieve logs, monitor performance metrics, and update models remotely.

```
from azureml.core.webservice import Webservice

# List deployed services
services = Webservice.list(workspace=ws)

# Access specific web service
service = Webservice(name='edge-ai-service', workspace=ws)

# Get logs
logs = service.get_logs()

print(logs)
```

Remote management capabilities simplify the process of updating existing models with newly trained versions or modifying configurations to enhance performance. Models are updated by re-registering and redeploying, following similar steps shown earlier.

Automated ML Pipelines

Azure ML also supports automated machine learning pipelines, facilitating streamlined training and deployment processes. Developers can design pipelines to automate data ingestion, model training, validation, and deployment stages, integrating seamlessly with CI/CD practices.

```python
from azureml.pipeline.core import Pipeline, PipelineData
from azureml.pipeline.steps import PythonScriptStep

# Define a data input
datastore = ws.get_default_datastore()
data_input = PipelineData(name='data_input', datastore=datastore)

# Define a training step
train_step = PythonScriptStep(
    name="train_step",
    source_directory="./scripts",
    script_name="train.py",
    arguments=['--input', data_input],
    outputs=[PipelineData(name='trained_model')],
    compute_target='cpu-cluster'
)

# Build pipeline
pipeline = Pipeline(workspace=ws, steps=[train_step])

# Submit pipeline run
pipeline_run = pipeline.submit('training-pipeline')
pipeline_run.wait_for_completion(show_output=True)
```

Utilizing automated ML pipelines increases productivity by reducing manual intervention, ensuring consistency, and fostering reproducibility in the model training and deployment processes.

Azure Machine Learning's capabilities significantly facilitate the deployment and management of machine learning models at the edge, ensuring robust performance, scalability, and easy integration with enterprise systems. These features enable developers to focus on enhancing model accuracy and efficiency while Azure ML manages the complexities of deployment and orchestration.

7.8 Computer Vision Applications at the Edge

Computer vision, a pivotal subset of artificial intelligence, involves enabling machines to interpret and make decisions based on visual input from the world. Edge computing enhances the efficacy of computer vision by allowing the processing to occur closer to the source of data generation, thereby reducing latency, bandwidth usage, and potentially providing better security and privacy by minimizing data transfer. This section will explore various applications, technologies, and methodologies for implementing computer vision at the edge.

- **Object Detection and Recognition** In edge computing, object detection and recognition serve as fundamental tasks. Object detection involves identifying instances of semantic objects of a certain class in digital images or videos. The need for responsive and real-time systems makes edge computing particularly suitable for these tasks. Consider the example of an autonomous vehicle that must process images from its cameras to detect pedestrians, other vehicles, or obstacles. By using edge devices, the vehicle can process this information rapidly, thereby enhancing safety.

  The prevalent models for object detection, such as YOLO (You Only Look Once), SSD (Single Shot MultiBox Detector), and Faster R-CNN, can be optimized to run on edge hardware. These models can be quantized to reduce their size and increase inference speed while maintaining a high level of accuracy. Below is a sample Python code snippet using TensorFlow Lite for running an object detection model on an edge device:

```python
import tensorflow as tf
import numpy as np
from PIL import Image

# Load the TFLite model and allocate tensors.
interpreter = tf.lite.Interpreter(model_path="model.tflite")
interpreter.allocate_tensors()

# Get input and output tensors.
input_details = interpreter.get_input_details()
output_details = interpreter.get_output_details()

# Load and preprocess the image.
def load_image(image_path):
    img = Image.open(image_path).resize((300, 300))
    img = np.array(img, dtype=np.float32)
    img = np.expand_dims(img, axis=0)
    return img

# Perform inference
image = load_image("image.jpg")
```

221

```
interpreter.set_tensor(input_details[0]['index'], image)
interpreter.invoke()

# Output results
output_data = interpreter.get_tensor(output_details[0]['index'])
print(output_data)
```

The output from the above code will be processed to detect and recognize objects within the given image, an operation pivotal in real-time applications like surveillance systems and smart cities.

- **Facial Recognition** Facial recognition technologies are extensively used for authentication and security purposes. These systems benefit significantly from local processing at the edge due to the sensitive nature of biometric data. Edge AI facilitates instantaneous face recognition while ensuring the data remains on the device, enhancing both speed and security.

For instance, consider a smart lock system in a high-security area that ensures instant access based on facial features. OpenCV and pre-trained models, such as MobileNetV2, are often used for this purpose. Below is a simplified Python implementation utilizing OpenCV and a pre-trained face detector:

```
import cv2

# Load the pre-trained face detector model
face_cascade = cv2.CascadeClassifier(cv2.data.haarcascades + '
    haarcascade_frontalface_default.xml')

# Open a video capture
cap = cv2.VideoCapture(0)

while True:
    # Capture frame-by-frame
    ret, frame = cap.read()
    gray = cv2.cvtColor(frame, cv2.COLOR_BGR2GRAY)

    # Detect faces
    faces = face_cascade.detectMultiScale(gray, scaleFactor=1.1, minNeighbors
        =5, minSize=(30, 30))

    # Draw rectangle around the faces
    for (x, y, w, h) in faces:
        cv2.rectangle(frame, (x, y), (x + w, y + h), (255, 0, 0), 2)

    # Display the resulting frame
    cv2.imshow('Face Detection', frame)

    # Break the loop on 'q' key press
    if cv2.waitKey(1) & 0xFF == ord('q'):
        break
```

```
# Release the capture and close windows
cap.release()
cv2.destroyAllWindows()
```

In this example, the edge device captures video frames, processes each frame to detect faces, and displays the detection results in near real-time. This process underscores the importance of reduced latency and the ability to perform complex processing locally.

- **Industrial Applications** Computer vision at the edge is instrumental in industrial inspection and automation. In manufacturing, edge devices equipped with computer vision can inspect products on the production line to identify defects. This enables rapid quality control, reducing the need for manual inspections and enhancing overall efficiency.

  High-speed cameras and edge-ready AI models detect product inconsistencies such as cracks, deformation, or misalignment. Integrating these systems within the production environment minimizes delays caused by data transmission to centralized servers and ensures rapid decision-making. For instance, a conveyor belt can halt the production process immediately upon detecting a defect, preventing further resource wastage.

- **Healthcare Monitoring** Healthcare applications benefit substantially from the deployment of computer vision at the edge, including patient monitoring, diagnostic assistance, and surgery aid. Edge-based computer vision systems can continuously monitor patients for critical signs and alert medical staff promptly in case of emergencies.

  Consider an edge device continuously analyzing video feeds from a patient's room to ensure their safety or alert caregivers if the patient shows signs of distress. Technologies such as infrared cameras and depth sensors capturing 3D data can be leveraged for more nuanced patient monitoring. The computational responsibility lies in the edge device, maintaining patient privacy and immediate response capabilities.

```
import numpy as np
import cv2
```

223

```
# Sample function to process video for patient monitoring
def monitor_patient(video_capture):
    while True:
        ret, frame = video_capture.read()
        if not ret:
            break

        # Example processing - Convert frame to grayscale
        gray_frame = cv2.cvtColor(frame, cv2.COLOR_BGR2GRAY)

        # Display the processed frame
        cv2.imshow('Patient Monitoring', gray_frame)

        if cv2.waitKey(1) & 0xFF == ord('q'):
            break

# Start patient monitoring
cap = cv2.VideoCapture("patient_room_video.mp4")
monitor_patient(cap)
cap.release()
cv2.destroyAllWindows()
```

The integration of computer vision applications at the edge harnesses the full potential of localized AI processing. By leveraging edge computing, industries, healthcare, surveillance, and autonomous systems can experience enhanced performance, reduced latency, and improved security, making these applications invaluable in the modern world.

7.9 Natural Language Processing at the Edge

Natural Language Processing (NLP) at the edge enables the execution of language-based computational models directly on edge devices, providing various benefits including reduced latency, enhanced privacy, and decreased dependency on cloud connectivity. This section will delve into the methodologies for deploying NLP models on edge devices, the challenges encountered, and the strategies to mitigate them, emphasizing practical implementations using Azure Machine Learning.

Executing NLP models at the edge involves numerous tasks such as text classification, sentiment analysis, entity recognition, and machine translation. The deployment procedure necessitates a confluence of optimized hardware and software, model optimization, and a clear understanding of the constraints imposed by edge devices, such as limited computational power and memory.

```
import nltk
from nltk.tokenize import word_tokenize

nltk.download('punkt')
text = "Processing natural language at the edge requires robust techniques."
tokens = word_tokenize(text)
print(tokens)
```

['Processing', 'natural', 'language', 'at', 'the', 'edge', 'requires', 'robust', 'techniques', '.']

Key steps in deploying NLP models at the edge include model selection, optimization, deployment, and inference. Below are the detailed steps involved in each process.

- **Model Selection**: Choosing an appropriate model is crucial. Smaller models like DistilBERT or MobileBERT are preferable for edge deployment due to their reduced size and faster inference times compared to BERT or GPT-3. The chosen model should be pre-trained on relevant datasets to achieve satisfactory accuracy without extensive computational overhead.

- **Model Optimization**: The optimization phase focuses on reducing the model size and improving inference speed. Techniques such as quantization, pruning, and knowledge distillation are employed. Quantization involves reducing the precision of the model's weights and activations from 32-bit floats to lower-precision formats such as 8-bit integers, which accelerates inference and reduces model size.

```
import torch
from torchvision import models

model = models.resnet18(pretrained=True)
model.eval()
quantized_model = torch.quantization.quantize_dynamic(
    model, {torch.nn.Linear}, dtype=torch.qint8
)
```

- **Deployment**: Deploying NLP models using Azure Machine Learning involves creating an Azure IoT Edge deployment manifest and configuring the device with the required runtime environment. An Azure IoT Hub is used to manage the deployed models and devices. Below is an example of a deployment script.

```json
{
  "modulesContent": {
    "$edgeAgent": {
      "properties.desired": {
        "modules": {
          "nlpModule": {
            "type": "docker",
            "settings": {
              "image": "myregistry.azurecr.io/nlp-module:latest",
              "createOptions": {}
            }
          }
        }
      }
    },
    "$edgeHub": {
      "properties.desired": {
        "routes": {
          "route1": "FROM /messages/* INTO $upstream"
        },
        "schemaVersion": "1.0"
      }
    },
    "nlpModule": {
      "properties.desired": {
        "config": {
          "batchSize": 16,
          "device": "CPU"
        }
      }
    }
  }
}
```

- **Inference**: The inference phase involves processing text inputs through the deployed model to obtain predictions. Efficient inference at the edge necessitates mindful resource management to ensure timely and accurate outputs. For instance, running a sentiment analysis model on a constrained device could be optimized by batching inputs and leveraging hardware accelerators where available.

```python
from transformers import pipeline
```

```
# Assuming the model is already downloaded and optimized
nlp_pipeline = pipeline("sentiment-analysis", model="distilbert-base-uncased")

text = "Azure Edge AI enables robust NLP at the edge."
result = nlp_pipeline(text)
print(result)
```

[{'label': 'POSITIVE', 'score': 0.999437}]

Challenges in NLP at the edge are non-trivial and multifaceted, encompassing hardware limitations, energy consumption, and security concerns. Hardware limitations include reduced computational power and restricted memory footprint on edge devices, which impede the deployment of large-scale models. Energy consumption is also critical as edge devices, often battery-powered, need to operate efficiently. Security concerns pertain to safeguarding the data handled by these models, ensuring encryption and compliance with data privacy regulations.

Mitigating these challenges involves leveraging model compression techniques, choosing efficient runtime environments, and implementing robust security protocols. Additionally, updating the models frequently and monitoring their performance ensures continuous improvement and relevance of the NLP tasks being executed at the edge.

NLP at the edge, facilitated by Azure Machine Learning, enhances real-time processing capabilities, providing scalability and flexibility for diverse applications ranging from customer service automation to smart home devices. Developing a robust strategy for model optimization and deployment is essential for harnessing the full potential of NLP at the edge.

7.10 Model Optimization and Compression Techniques

Model optimization and compression are crucial for the efficient deployment of machine learning models on edge devices, which are often resource-constrained. The goal is to reduce the model size and computational load while maintaining acceptable levels of accuracy and performance.

The optimization and compression processes encompass a variety of techniques, including quantization, pruning, knowledge distillation, and low-rank factorization.

Quantization reduces the precision of the numbers used to represent the model's weights and activations. Typically, weights and activations are stored as 32-bit floating-point numbers, but quantization can reduce this to 16-bit or even 8-bit integers, thus significantly lowering the model's memory footprint and accelerating execution.

```
import tensorflow as tf

# Load the model
model = tf.keras.models.load_model('path/to/your_model.h5')

# Convert the model to TensorFlow Lite format with quantization
converter = tf.lite.TFLiteConverter.from_keras_model(model)
converter.optimizations = [tf.lite.Optimize.DEFAULT]
tflite_model = converter.convert()

# Save the quantized model
with open('model_quantized.tflite', 'wb') as f:
    f.write(tflite_model)
```

The above script demonstrates the conversion of a Keras model to a TensorFlow Lite model with quantization. The quantized model is smaller and more efficient for edge deployment.

Pruning involves removing weights from the neural network that are not critical during the inference phase. By setting less important weights to zero, the model's sparsity increases, which can lead to significant reductions in model size and computational load.

```
import tensorflow as tf
import tensorflow_model_optimization as tfmot

# Annotate the model with pruning
pruning_params = {
    'pruning_schedule': tfmot.sparsity.keras.PolynomialDecay(
        initial_sparsity=0.30, final_sparsity=0.75, begin_step=2000, end_step=10000)
}
model_for_pruning = tfmot.sparsity.keras.prune_low_magnitude(model, **
    pruning_params)

# Compile the model
model_for_pruning.compile(optimizer='adam', loss='sparse_categorical_crossentropy'
    , metrics=['accuracy'])

# Train the model
model_for_pruning.fit(x_train, y_train, epochs=2, validation_data=(x_test, y_test))
```

```
# Update model sparsity
model_for_pruning = tfmot.sparsity.keras.strip_pruning(model_for_pruning)
```

In this example, the TensorFlow Model Optimization Toolkit is used to prune a Keras model, inducing sparsity which can lead to reduced model size and improved performance on edge devices.

Knowledge Distillation is an optimization technique where a smaller model (student) is trained to mimic the predictions of a larger, pre-trained model (teacher). This process allows the smaller model to achieve similar accuracy to the larger model while being more computationally efficient.

```
import tensorflow as tf
import numpy as np

# Define the teacher model (assuming it is pre-trained)
teacher_model = tf.keras.models.load_model('path/to/teacher_model.h5')

# Define a smaller student model
student_model = tf.keras.Sequential([
    tf.keras.layers.Flatten(input_shape=(28, 28)),
    tf.keras.layers.Dense(128, activation='relu'),
    tf.keras.layers.Dense(10, activation='softmax')
])

# Custom training loop for distillation
def distillation_loss(y_true, y_pred, teacher_logits, alpha=0.1, temperature=10.0):
    teacher_probs = tf.nn.softmax(teacher_logits / temperature)
    student_probs = tf.nn.softmax(y_pred / temperature)
    distillation_loss = tf.reduce_mean(tf.keras.losses.KLD(teacher_probs,
        student_probs))
    student_loss = tf.reduce_mean(tf.keras.losses.sparse_categorical_crossentropy(
        y_true, y_pred))
    return alpha * distillation_loss + (1 - alpha) * student_loss

# Training process
for epoch in range(epochs):
    for step, (x_batch, y_batch) in enumerate(train_dataset):
        teacher_logits = teacher_model(x_batch)
        with tf.GradientTape() as tape:
            student_logits = student_model(x_batch)
            loss = distillation_loss(y_batch, student_logits, teacher_logits)
        gradients = tape.gradient(loss, student_model.trainable_variables)
        optimizer.apply_gradients(zip(gradients, student_model.trainable_variables))
```

This script outlines the knowledge distillation process where the student model learns from the teacher model using a custom distillation loss function.

Low-Rank Factorization leverages the idea that the weight matrices in neural networks are often high-dimensional but can be decomposed into products of lower-dimensional matrices with minimal loss of accuracy. This technique reduces the model size and speeds up computation.

The common approach involves singular value decomposition (SVD) of the weight matrices.

```
import numpy as np
from scipy.linalg import svd

# Original dense weight matrix (W)
W = np.random.randn(256, 256)

# Singular Value Decomposition
U, S, Vt = svd(W, full_matrices=False)
rank = 64 # Desired rank for approximation

# Low-rank approximations
W_low_rank = np.dot(U[:, :rank], np.dot(np.diag(S[:rank]), Vt[:rank, :]))

# New factorized layers can replace the original dense layer in the model
```

Using SVD, the dense weight matrix W is decomposed into lower-rank approximations, reducing model complexity while preserving most of the information.

These techniques, when applied judiciously, can lead to substantial improvements in model efficiency and make the deployment of AI models on edge devices more feasible.

7.11 Challenges and Best Practices for Edge AI

Edge AI, while offering significant advantages in terms of latency reduction and enhanced privacy, also presents a complex set of challenges that must be meticulously addressed to ensure deployment and operational success. Understanding these challenges and adopting best practices can dramatically improve the robustness and efficiency of edge AI implementations.

A primary challenge in edge AI deployment is the constraint on computational resources. Contrary to centralized cloud environments, edge devices often have limited processing capabilities, memory, and stor-

230

age. This necessitates the use of optimized and lightweight models that can run efficiently on such constrained hardware. Model optimization techniques, such as quantization and pruning, are crucial. Quantization reduces the numerical precision of model weights, which can significantly decrease the model size and computational load. Pruning removes less-important connections in a network, thus decreasing the number of operations required.

```python
import tensorflow as tf

# Load the pre-trained model
model = tf.keras.models.load_model('model.h5')

# Convert to TensorFlow Lite model with quantization
converter = tf.lite.TFLiteConverter.from_keras_model(model)
converter.optimizations = [tf.lite.Optimize.DEFAULT]
tflite_model = converter.convert()

# Save the quantized model
with open('model_quantized.tflite', 'wb') as f:
    f.write(tflite_model)
```

Another significant challenge is energy consumption. Edge devices are often battery-powered or have strict power budgets, necessitating energy-efficient solutions. Optimizing for energy efficiency involves selecting appropriate hardware platforms and ensuring that the software workloads are optimized for low-power execution. Utilizing dedicated AI accelerators, such as Google's Coral Edge TPU or NVIDIA's Jetson modules, can provide substantial performance improvements while keeping energy usage within acceptable limits.

Data privacy and security are also critical considerations. Processing data locally on edge devices reduces the exposure of sensitive information to potential breaches that can occur during data transmission to centralized servers. However, this introduces new security challenges, such as ensuring the integrity of the models and the data they process. Techniques such as secure boot, hardware encryption, and regular software updates are imperative for maintaining security.

Network connectivity remains an intermittent challenge in edge environments. Edge devices might operate in areas with unreliable or intermittent network access, impacting data synchronization and model updates. Implementing robust data caching and synchronization mechanisms can mitigate issues arising from network unreliability. Utilizing asynchronous communication patterns and local data storage ensures

231

that edge devices can continue to operate effectively even in the absence of network connectivity.

Deploying and managing AI models across a diverse fleet of edge devices introduces the challenge of scalability. The diversity in hardware, operating systems, and network conditions necessitates a flexible deployment pipeline. Containerization technologies such as Docker can facilitate this process by encapsulating models and their dependencies. Azure IoT Edge provides a framework for deploying containers to edge devices, allowing for consistent and scalable management.

```
# Create an IoT Edge deployment manifest
az iot edge deployment create --config-file deployment.json --name myEdgeDeployment

# Check deployment status
az iot edge deployment show --deployment-id myEdgeDeployment --device-id
    myEdgeDevice
```

Updating models in the field is another challenge, necessitating a balance between the frequency of updates and the operational stability of the edge devices. Continuous integration and continuous deployment (CI/CD) pipelines tailored for edge environments are essential. These pipelines should include extensive testing suites to verify model performance and stability before any update is rolled out. Over-the-air (OTA) updates should be securely transmitted and should include rollback mechanisms to return to a previous stable state in case of failure.

To address these challenges effectively, several best practices have emerged. Comprehensive monitoring and logging systems are essential for tracking model performance, device health, and environmental conditions. Azure Monitor and Application Insights can be integrated with edge deployments to provide real-time analytics and diagnostics.

Edge AI systems must also embrace modular and scalable software architectures. Using containerized microservices facilitates independent deployment and scalability of multiple AI models and components. Adopting a modular architecture supports component reuse and simplifies maintenance.

Equally important is the adoption of rigorous testing methodologies in edge AI deployments. This includes unit testing, integration testing, and performance testing under various network conditions and hardware configurations. Automated testing pipelines should simulate the edge environment as closely as possible to identify potential issues early in the development cycle.

Lastly, collaboration between hardware, software, and data science teams is critical to the success of edge AI projects. Cross-functional teams should work closely through the entire lifecycle of edge AI deployment, from model development to field deployment and monitoring. Effective communication and collaboration ensure that all potential challenges are addressed holistically, leading to more robust and efficient edge AI solutions.

Implementing these best practices ensures that the deployment of AI models to edge devices can scale effectively while maintaining performance, security, and reliability.

Chapter 8

Networking and Communication Protocols

This chapter examines the networking requirements and communication protocols essential for edge computing. It covers various network topologies and protocols such as MQTT, CoAP, and HTTP/HTTPS, along with industrial protocols like OPC UA. The role of 5G in enhancing edge capabilities, network security protocols, and Quality of Service (QoS) considerations are also discussed. The chapter provides insights into network configuration and management practices required to support robust and efficient edge deployments.

8.1 Introduction to Networking in Edge Computing

Edge computing represents a paradigm shift from centralized data processing to localized, distributed data handling near the data source.

The essential principle is to process data closer to where it is generated, which can significantly reduce latency, save bandwidth, and improve the overall efficiency of the computing infrastructure. Networking plays a critical role in this paradigm by linking edge devices, edge nodes, and the broader cloud infrastructure.

At the core of edge computing is the network—a robust, scalable, and resilient network is required to support the myriad of devices and applications connected in an edge architecture. This section delves into the fundamental concepts of networking within the context of edge computing, exploring the necessary requirements and considerations for deploying an effective edge network.

The first consideration in networking for edge computing is the reduction of latency. Traditional cloud computing models often involve significant data transmission times between the end devices and cloud data centers, leading to network latency that can be detrimental to real-time applications. Edge networks address this by placing processing capabilities closer to the devices, thus minimizing the distance data must travel.

Bandwidth efficiency is another crucial factor, as the explosion of IoT devices leads to an enormous amount of data generation. Transmitting all raw data to a centralized cloud for processing can be impractical and costly. By performing preliminary processing at the edge, only essential data or summarized information needs to be sent across the network, thereby conserving bandwidth and reducing congestion.

A well-designed edge network also ensures enhanced reliability and resilience. Distributed architectures are inherently more fault-tolerant because multiple nodes can take over the responsibilities of a failed node, ensuring uninterrupted service. This resilience is particularly important in mission-critical applications such as autonomous vehicles, healthcare, and industrial automation.

Security is a paramount concern in edge networking. Decentralization introduces new attack vectors, as each edge device or node could potentially be a point of entry for malicious activities. Effective network designs for edge computing incorporate robust security protocols, including encryption, authentication, and secure data transmission practices to protect against vulnerabilities and breaches.

Interoperability is essential in the heterogeneous environment of edge computing, where devices from different vendors using various communication protocols must work seamlessly together. Open standards and protocols enable this interoperability, ensuring that devices can communicate efficiently regardless of their underlying technology.

Quality of Service (QoS) mechanisms are vital for maintaining the performance and reliability of the network. QoS involves prioritizing traffic, ensuring that critical data packets are transmitted with the necessary speed and reliability. Techniques such as traffic shaping and bandwidth allocation are employed to manage network resources efficiently, providing consistent service levels even under high load conditions.

The topology of an edge network dictates how devices and nodes are interconnected. Different topologies, such as star, mesh, and hybrid configurations, offer various advantages and trade-offs in terms of performance, scalability, ease of management, and fault tolerance. Selecting an appropriate topology is crucial for optimizing the network infrastructure to meet specific application requirements.

Edge networks rely heavily on various communication protocols to facilitate data exchange between devices and cloud services. Protocols like MQTT (Message Queuing Telemetry Transport), CoAP (Constrained Application Protocol), and HTTP/HTTPS are employed based on the requirements of the edge applications. Each protocol has its unique strengths, such as low overhead, high security, or simplicity, which are matched to the needs of the use case.

Advancements in networking technologies, particularly the advent of 5G, further enhance the capabilities of edge computing. 5G provides unprecedented data transfer speeds, lower latency, greater bandwidth, and the ability to support a massive number of connected devices. These characteristics make it well-suited to meet the demands of edge computing, enabling applications that require real-time processing and high data throughput.

To summarize, networking is the backbone of edge computing, enabling efficient, reliable, and secure data communication across distributed devices and nodes. Understanding the networking requirements and selecting the appropriate technologies and protocols are imperative for leveraging the full benefits of edge computing. By addressing latency, bandwidth usage, reliability, security, interoperability, and QoS, a well-architected edge network can markedly enhance the performance and capabilities of edge applications.

8.2 Types of Network Topologies in Edge Architecture

In edge computing, the choice of network topology plays a critical role in determining the efficiency, scalability, and reliability of the overall system. Network topology refers to the arrangement of various elements (links, nodes, etc.) in a computer network. Several types of network topologies are applicable to edge architectures, each with its own advantages and trade-offs. This section provides an in-depth analysis of different network topologies, including star, mesh, and hybrid topologies, and their implications for edge computing environments.

Star Topology

In a star topology, each edge node (device) is connected to a central node (hub or switch). This central node acts as a mediator for data transmission between edge nodes.

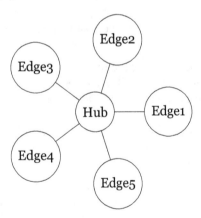

Figure 8.1: Star Topology in Edge Architecture

The primary advantages of a star topology include:

- *Simplicity of implementation*: Simple to set up and manage, making it a popular choice for small to medium-sized edge deployments.

- *Fault isolation*: A malfunction in one edge node does not affect the entire network, as data flows through the central hub.

However, the star topology has notable disadvantages:

- *Single point of failure*: The central hub is a critical node; its failure can disrupt the entire network.

- *Scalability limitations*: Adding more nodes can lead to congestion and potential performance degradation at the hub.

Mesh Topology

A mesh topology involves direct connections between edge nodes. This can be achieved in either a full mesh or a partial mesh configuration. In a full mesh, every node is directly connected to every other node, while in a partial mesh only some nodes have direct connections.

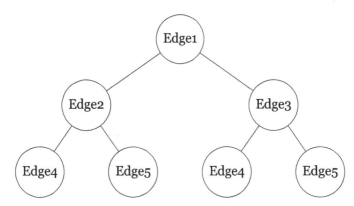

Figure 8.2: Mesh Topology in Edge Architecture

Mesh topologies provide several benefits:

- *High reliability and redundancy*: Multiple paths exist for data transmission, ensuring network reliability and fault tolerance.

239

- *Enhanced scalability*: The addition of new nodes does not significantly impact existing nodes, as data can be rerouted through multiple paths.

The disadvantages of mesh topology include:

- *Complexity*: Managing connections in a full mesh network is complex and requires significant resources.

- *High cost*: The infrastructure costs are higher due to the need for multiple connections between nodes.

Hybrid Topology

A hybrid topology combines elements of various topologies to leverage their respective strengths and mitigate their weaknesses. A common example is the combination of star and mesh topologies to form a more balanced approach to network design.

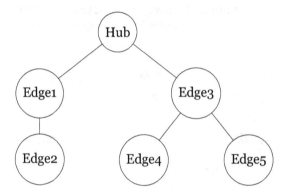

Figure 8.3: Hybrid Topology in Edge Architecture

Advantages of hybrid topology:

- *Flexibility*: Can be adapted based on specific requirements of the edge computing environment, providing a tailored approach.

- *Scalability and fault tolerance*: Balances the simplicity of star topology with the robustness of mesh topology.

The potential drawbacks of hybrid topology are:

- *Design complexity*: Designing and maintaining a hybrid topology can be intricate due to the combination of different topologies.

- *Resource requirements*: Can be more resource-intensive both in terms of hardware and management overhead.

Tree Topology

Tree topology, also known as hierarchical topology, is another structure where nodes are arranged in a hierarchy. This consists of multiple star topologies connected together, forming a tree-like structure.

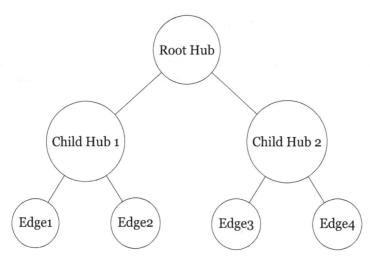

Figure 8.4: Tree Topology in Edge Architecture

Tree topologies have distinct advantages:

- *Scalability*: Easily scaled by adding more nodes or branches to the tree structure.

- *Structured hierarchy*: Facilitates efficient data management and routing through defined hierarchical layers.

However, tree topologies also have some limitations:

- *Dependence on root node*: The root hub is a critical node. Its failure can significantly impact the network.

- *Increased latency*: Data must often traverse multiple layers, potentially increasing latency.

Each network topology provides unique benefits and challenges in the context of edge computing. The selection of an appropriate topology should be guided by factors such as the scale of deployment, fault tolerance requirements, latency considerations, and the specific use cases of the edge environment.

8.3   Communication Protocols Overview

A comprehensive understanding of communication protocols is crucial for developing robust and efficient edge computing applications. In this section, we will delve into the essential communication protocols that enable data exchange between edge devices, gateways, and cloud systems. These protocols vary in their design, purpose, and suitability for different use cases, particularly in terms of latency, reliability, and resource constraints.

At the core of edge communication lie several key protocols: Message Queuing Telemetry Transport (MQTT), Constrained Application Protocol (CoAP), Hypertext Transfer Protocol (HTTP/HTTPS), and Open Platform Communications Unified Architecture (OPC UA). Each of these protocols brings distinct advantages and is optimized for specific scenarios in edge computing.

Message Queuing Telemetry Transport (MQTT) is a lightweight, publish-subscribe network protocol that is highly effective for machine-to-machine (M2M) and Internet of Things (IoT) communications. MQTT operates on top of TCP/IP and is designed to minimize bandwidth and device resource usage while ensuring reliability and some level of delivery assurance.

The following code snippet illustrates a basic MQTT client setup in Python using the paho-mqtt library:

```
import paho.mqtt.client as mqtt

# Callback function when the client receives a CONNACK response from the server
def on_connect(client, userdata, flags, rc):
    print("Connected with result code "+str(rc))
    client.subscribe("topic/test")

# Callback function for when a PUBLISH message is received from the server
def on_message(client, userdata, msg):
    print(msg.topic+" "+str(msg.payload))

client = mqtt.Client()
client.on_connect = on_connect
client.on_message = on_message

client.connect("mqtt.eclipse.org", 1883, 60)
client.loop_forever()
```

Constrained Application Protocol (CoAP) is designed for use in resource-constrained environments, such as low-power sensors, switches, valves, and similar components that comprise IoT systems. CoAP runs over UDP, which makes it suitable for low-latency communication but also requires the implementation of additional mechanisms to ensure reliability.

Here is an example of a CoAP request using the aiocoap library in Python:

```
import asyncio
from aiocoap import *

async def main():
    protocol = await Context.create_client_context()

    request = Message(code=GET, uri='coap://localhost/time')
    response = await protocol.request(request).response

    print('Result: %s\n%r' % (response.code, response.payload))

if __name__ == "__main__":
    asyncio.run(main())
```

Hypertext Transfer Protocol (HTTP/HTTPS) is the foundational protocol of the World Wide Web. Although inherently more substantial in overhead compared to protocols like MQTT and CoAP, HTTP is widely adopted due to its simplicity and the robust infrastructure that exists to support it. HTTPS, the secure version of HTTP, is critical for ensuring encrypted communication over the network, thereby protecting data from eavesdropping and tampering.

A sample HTTP client using the requests library in Python is shown below:

```
import requests

response = requests.get('https://jsonplaceholder.typicode.com/todos/1')

if response.status_code == 200:
    print("Success:")
    print(response.json())
else:
    print("Failed to retrieve the resource")
```

Open Platform Communications Unified Architecture (OPC UA) is an industrial M2M communication protocol that plays a fundamental role in the implementation of Industry 4.0. OPC UA is designed for secure, reliable, and platform-independent information exchange, covering a wide range of data modeling and communication needs. OPC UA supports complex data types, multi-faceted security models, and is extensible, making it highly suitable for industrial automation applications.

A brief conceptual code demonstrating OPC UA connection using the opcua library in Python:

```
from opcua import Client

client = Client("opc.tcp://localhost:4840/freeopcua/server/")

try:
    client.connect()
    # Accessing a variable node
    var = client.get_node("ns=2;i=2")
    print("Variable value: %s" % var.get_value())

    # Setting a new value
    var.set_value(100)

finally:
    client.disconnect()
```

The intricacies of these communication protocols enable them to cater to specific needs within edge computing environments. Understanding the appropriate application and limitations of each protocol is essential for designing effective edge solutions that can handle real-time data processing, ensure security, and maintain scalability.

8.4 MQTT Protocol for IoT and Edge Devices

MQTT (Message Queuing Telemetry Transport) is a widely adopted communication protocol in the realm of IoT and edge computing. This protocol is specifically designed for constrained devices and low-bandwidth, high-latency, or unreliable networks. MQTT operates on the publish/subscribe messaging model, providing an efficient and lightweight mechanism for inter-device communication.

MQTT Architecture:

The MQTT protocol follows a client-server architecture where clients connect to a central broker. The broker is responsible for receiving all messages, filtering the messages, and then distributing them to the appropriate subscribers. This architecture decouples producers (publishers) and consumers (subscribers) of messages, thus simplifying the design and scalability of IoT and edge networks.

Figure 8.5: MQTT Client-Server Architecture

MQTT Components:

- **Broker:** The central component that manages communication between clients. It routes messages from publishers to subscribers and ensures the messages are delivered reliably.

- **Publisher:** An MQTT client that sends messages to a topic. Publishers are the source of data in the MQTT system.

- **Subscriber:** An MQTT client that receives messages from a specific topic. Subscribers indicate their interest in one or more topics to the broker.

- **Topic:** A UTF-8 string that clients use to specify the destination for the messages. Topics are structured hierarchically with levels separated by slashes (/).

MQTT Message Structure:

An MQTT message consists of three main parts:

- **Fixed Header:** Present in all messages and includes fields like message type, duplicate delivery flag, Quality of Service (QoS) level, and retain flag.

- **Variable Header:** Present in some types of messages and includes fields like Packet Identifier and Topic Name.

- **Payload:** The actual data being transmitted. The payload can be up to 256 MB in size.

```
import paho.mqtt.client as mqtt

# Define the broker address
broker_address = "iot.eclipse.org"

# Create a new MQTT client instance
client = mqtt.Client("Publisher")

# Connect to the broker
client.connect(broker_address)

# Publish a message to the topic "home/temperature"
client.publish("home/temperature", "23.5")
```

Quality of Service (QoS) Levels:

MQTT supports three levels of Quality of Service to ensure message delivery:

- **QoS 0 - At Most Once:** The message is delivered to the broker once, with no confirmation required. There is no guarantee of delivery.

- **QoS 1 - At Least Once:** Ensures that the message is delivered at least once, but it may be delivered multiple times if acknowledgments are lost.

- **QoS 2 - Exactly Once:** Ensures that the message is delivered exactly once by using a two-level handshake between the broker and client.

```
# Publish a message with QoS level 1
client.publish("home/temperature", "24.0", qos=1)
```

Last Will and Testament (LWT):

MQTT includes a LWT feature that allows clients to specify a message that will be sent by the broker if the client unexpectedly disconnects. This feature improves the robustness and reliability of the system by informing other devices of a client's disconnect.

```
# Configure Last Will message
client.will_set("home/status", "offline", qos=1, retain=True)

# Connect to the broker
client.connect(broker_address)
```

Security Considerations:

MQTT supports several security features to protect message integrity and confidentiality:

- **TLS/SSL:** Secure Transmission Layer (TLS) and Secure Sockets Layer (SSL) protocols are used to encrypt MQTT messages during transmission.

- **Authentication:** Clients can be authenticated using username/password pairs or more robust mechanisms like certificates.

- **Authorization:** The broker can implement policies to authorize clients for specific actions like publishing or subscribing to topics.

```
# Enable TLS
client.tls_set("path/to/ca.crt", tls_version=mqtt.ssl.PROTOCOL_TLS)

# Set username and password
client.username_pw_set("user", "password")

# Connect to the broker
client.connect(broker_address)
```

MQTT's lightweight design makes it particularly suited for IoT and edge applications where resources are limited and communication networks may be unstable. Its publish/subscribe model, coupled with QoS levels and robust security features, enables reliable and secure communication between devices in various edge computing scenarios.

247

8.5   CoAP Protocol for Constrained Environments

The Constrained Application Protocol (CoAP) is a specialized web transfer protocol designed for use with constrained nodes and networks, such as those frequently encountered in edge computing environments. It is specifically engineered to function effectively within the limitations of small computational devices and constrained network conditions, such as low bandwidth, high latency, and variable connectivity. This section delves into the technical characteristics, communication mechanisms, and practical applications of CoAP, providing a detailed understanding of its role in edge computing.

CoAP is defined by the IETF in RFC 7252. This protocol follows a request/response interaction model similar to HTTP but is designed to meet specialized IoT requirements. One key distinction is that CoAP utilizes the User Datagram Protocol (UDP) rather than Transmission Control Protocol (TCP). UDP is a connectionless protocol that inherently suits devices with constrained resources due to its minimal overhead. However, this introduces challenges such as reliability and ordered delivery, which CoAP addresses through its basic message types: Confirmable (CON), Non-Confirmable (NON), Acknowledgement (ACK), and Reset (RST).

```
typedef enum {
    COAP_TYPE_CONFIRMABLE = 0,
    COAP_TYPE_NON_CONFIRMABLE,
    COAP_TYPE_ACKNOWLEDGEMENT,
    COAP_TYPE_RESET
} coap_message_type_t;
```

CoAP messages are encoded in a lightweight binary format. Each message consists of a 4-byte fixed header followed by optional Token, Options, and Payload components. The fixed header includes the version number, message type, token length, request method or response code, and message ID.

The fundamental unit of CoAP communication is the CoAP message. An example of constructing a CoAP message might look like this:

```
printf("\n\n[CoAP message structure]:\n");
uint8_t coap_msg[16];
coap_msg[0] = (coap_ver << 6) | (coap_type << 4) | (token_length & 0x0F);
```

```
coap_msg[1] = coap_code;
coap_msg[2] = (coap_msg_id >> 8) & 0xFF;
coap_msg[3] = coap_msg_id & 0xFF;
memcpy(coap_msg + 4, token, token_length);
```

CoAP supports four methods: GET, PUT, POST, and DELETE, providing a RESTful approach for interaction. These methods are similar to HTTP methods, ensuring that developers familiar with web concepts can leverage their understanding of REST interfaces.

CoAP's interaction model is based on the concept of resources, identified by URIs. This approach abstracts the details of the underlying constrained network, allowing a consistent interaction scheme across diverse environments. For example, a GET request can retrieve the current sensor readings from a resource representation hosted on the edge device.

```
GET coap://edge-node.local/sensor/temp
```

Ensuring reliability in UDP involves higher-level constructs within CoAP. For Confirmable (CON) messages, each request expects an Acknowledgement (ACK) response, confirming receipt. If the ACK is not received within a specified timeout, the sender may retransmit the message. This reliability mechanism is essential for critical operations requiring assured delivery.

```
Client                              Server
 |                                   |
 |    Confirmable Message (CON, MID=0x7d38)    |
 |------------------------------------->  |
 |                                   |
 |    Acknowledgement Message (ACK, MID=0x7d38)   |
 |<-------------------------------------   |
 |                                   |
```

CoAP also includes built-in support for asynchronous communication patterns and multicast. For example, Non-Confirmable (NON) messages are suitable for scenarios where the occasional packet loss is acceptable, minimizing protocol overhead in low-power environments. CoAP's multicast support enables efficient communication with multiple devices simultaneously, which is indispensable for scenarios like over-the-air updates or group sensor data collection.

249

```
void send_nonconfirmable_msg() {
    coap_message_t msg;
    msg.type = COAP_TYPE_NON_CONFIRMABLE;
    msg.code = COAP_METHOD_GET;
    msg.uri_path = "sensor/status";
    send_coap_message(msg);
}
```

Considering security, CoAP leverages Datagram Transport Layer Security (DTLS) to provide encryption, integrity, and authentication. DTLS is to UDP what TLS is to TCP, ensuring secure end-to-end communication in constrained environments. The integration of DTLS with CoAP is paramount to protect data exchanges in IoT applications where sensitive information may be transferred.

Overall, the CoAP protocol's design choices reflect a careful balance between the needs of constrained devices and the principles of REST architecture. By providing a compact, efficient, and extensible alternative to HTTP, CoAP enables a wide range of applications in edge computing, from remote monitoring and control to resource management in sensor networks.

Understanding CoAP's operation within the architecture of edge deployments is pivotal. Integrating CoAP effectively into edge solutions involves not just implementation knowledge but also strategic planning around network topology, resource allocation, and reliability considerations—ensuring that edge systems operate with optimal efficiency and robustness.

8.6 HTTP/HTTPS for Edge Communication

HyperText Transfer Protocol (HTTP) and its secured version (HTTPS) are fundamental protocols that facilitate communication between clients and servers over the World Wide Web. These protocols have widespread adoption and are integral to web services and APIs, making them equally significant for edge computing applications.

HTTP is a stateless protocol operating at the application layer of the OSI model. It standardizes the structure and transmission of messages between web clients, typically browsers and servers. HTTP/1.1 and

HTTP/2 are the most commonly used versions, with HTTP/3 being developed to address latency and performance improvements inherent in the previous versions.

HTTP/1.1 and HTTP/2 in Edge Computing:

HTTP/1.1 is characterized by request/response pairs, where a client requests information and the server responds. It supports persistent connections allowing multiple requests and responses over a single TCP connection, reducing latency and network congestion. HTTP/2 introduced multiplexing, allowing multiple request/response pairs to be sent simultaneously over a single connection, thus improving performance.

The usage of HTTP in edge computing is prominent when dealing with RESTful APIs, a common architectural style that embodies the principles of the web and is known for its simplicity and scalability. Edge devices utilize RESTful APIs to interact with cloud services, other edge nodes, or enterprise systems, facilitating data acquisition, status updates, and control commands.

HTTPS: Enhancing Security:

HTTPS extends HTTP by providing secure communication over a computer network, and it is especially vital for edge computing applications that often handle sensitive and critical data. HTTPS employs Transport Layer Security (TLS), formerly known as Secure Sockets Layer (SSL), which encrypts data in transit, ensuring confidentiality and integrity while protecting against eavesdropping, tampering, and message forgery.

Edge devices, due to their distributed nature and often being deployed in untrusted environments, are susceptible to various security threats. Implementing HTTPS mitigates risks associated with data breaches and cyber-attacks by encrypting the communication channel. To set up HTTPS, edge devices need digital certificates issued by trusted Certificate Authorities (CAs). These certificates ensure the authenticity and trustworthiness of the communicating entities.

HTTP/HTTPS Methods and Status Codes:

HTTP/HTTPS use methods (also known as verbs) and status codes to facilitate effective communication. Common methods include:

- GET: Retrieves data from a server

- POST: Sends data to a server to create or update resources

- PUT: Updates existing resources or creates a new resource if it does not exist

- DELETE: Removes resources from a server

Corresponding status codes indicate the result of the HTTP request:

- 200 OK: The request was successful

- 201 Created: The request was successful, and a resource was created

- 400 Bad Request: The server could not understand the request

- 401 Unauthorized: Authentication is required and has failed or not yet been provided

- 404 Not Found: The requested resource could not be found

- 500 Internal Server Error: A generic error message for an unexpected server condition

Example HTTP Communication in an Edge Environment:

Consider an edge device that monitors environmental conditions and reports data to a central server. Below is an example of a simple HTTP GET request made by an edge device:

```
import requests

# URL of the central server's API
url = "http://centralserver.example.com/api/v1/environment"

# Perform a GET request to fetch the environmental data
response = requests.get(url)

# Check the status code
if response.status_code == 200:
    print("Data successfully retrieved")
    data = response.json()
    print(data)
else:
    print(f"Error: {response.status_code}")
```

This script uses the requests library in Python to send a GET request to the central server and handle the response. The server is expected to return a 200 OK status code along with the environmental data in JSON format.

When securing this communication using HTTPS, the URL changes, and an SSL certificate is used to establish a secure connection:

```
import requests

# URL of the central server's API
url = "https://centralserver.example.com/api/v1/environment"

# Perform a GET request to fetch the environmental data over HTTPS
response = requests.get(url, verify='/path/to/ca-certificate')

# Check the status code
if response.status_code == 200:
    print("Data successfully retrieved")
    data = response.json()
    print(data)
else:
    print(f"Error: {response.status_code}")
```

Here, the verify parameter of the requests.get method refers to the path of the CA certificate. This ensures the server's identity is verified and communication is encrypted.

Challenges and Considerations:

While HTTP/HTTPS is pivotal for ensuring secure and efficient communication in edge computing, several challenges need addressing:

- *Latency*: HTTP/HTTPS communication involves handshakes, which can introduce latency. This can be mitigated by using HTTP/2 or HTTP/3, which have improved optimizations.

- *Resource Constraints*: Edge devices may have limited computational and memory resources. Encrypting and decrypting HTTPS traffic can be resource-intensive.

- *Certificate Management*: Ensuring all edge devices have valid and up-to-date certificates involves significant overhead, especially in large-scale deployments.

By understanding the principles and details of HTTP/HTTPS and implementing these protocols effectively, edge computing applications can achieve secure, reliable, and efficient communication.

8.7 OPC UA and Industrial Protocols

OPC Unified Architecture (OPC UA) is a platform-independent, service-oriented architecture that integrates various industrial automation devices and systems. It enables secure, reliable, and interoperable communication between disparate devices, systems, and applications. OPC UA improves upon the original OPC (OLE for Process Control) standards by providing enhanced security and reliability features, as well as platform independence.

The core elements of OPC UA include address space modeling, communication mechanisms, and security protocols. Address space modeling provides a structured way to represent devices and their data. Communication mechanisms enable the exchange of messages between clients and servers, and security protocols ensure the confidentiality, integrity, and availability of the communications.

- **Address Space Modeling**

In OPC UA, the address space model is a critical component that organizes and provides access to various information within the system. The address space consists of nodes and references, where nodes represent objects, variables, methods, and other types of information. Each node is identified by a unique NodeId and can contain attributes such as a display name, description, and value.

Nodes are interconnected by references, which define various types of relationships between nodes. There are several standard reference types, including hierarchical references (like "hasComponent") and non-hierarchical references (like "hasTypeDefinition"). The address space can be visualized as a graph, where nodes are vertices and references are edges connecting the vertices.

NodeId	Attributes
ns=1;i=1001	DisplayName: "Temperature Sensor"
ns=1;i=1002	DisplayName: "Pressure Sensor"

- **Communication Mechanisms**

OPC UA supports multiple communication mechanisms, including client-server and publish-subscribe models. In the client-server model, an OPC UA Client requests information from an OPC UA Server, which responds with the data. This interaction can involve read, write, and method invoke operations.

In the publish-subscribe model, OPC UA allows data to be published by one or more sources and delivered to subscribers. This model enhances efficiency and scalability by allowing multiple clients to receive updates from a single source without repeated queries.

```
from opcua import Client

client = Client("opc.tcp://localhost:4840")
try:
    client.connect()
    root = client.get_root_node()
    print("Objects node is: {}".format(root))
    temp_sensor = client.get_node("ns=1;i=1001")
    temp_value = temp_sensor.get_value()
    print("Temperature Value: {}".format(temp_value))
finally:
    client.disconnect()
```

- **Security Protocols**

OPC UA incorporates robust security protocols to ensure data security. These protocols include authentication, authorization, encryption, and auditing. Authentication verifies the identity of clients and servers. Authorization determines the permissions for accessing resources. Encryption ensures the confidentiality and integrity of the communication, while auditing provides a record of activities for security monitoring.

The OPC UA security model uses X.509 certificates for authentication and key exchange, and it supports multiple encryption algorithms including AES and RSA. OPC UA allows for both transport-level and application-level security, providing flexibility to meet varying security requirements.

```
<Server>
    <SecurityPolicies>
        <SecurityPolicy>
            <Name>Basic256Sha256</Name>
            <SecurityMode>SignAndEncrypt</SecurityMode>
        </SecurityPolicy>
```

```
  </SecurityPolicies>
  <CertificateValidation>
      <AutoAccept>False</AutoAccept>
  </CertificateValidation>
  <Users>
      <User>
          <Name>User1</Name>
          <Password>password123</Password>
          <Roles>
              <Role>Operator</Role>
          </Roles>
      </User>
  </Users>
</Server>
```

- **Industrial Protocols**

In addition to OPC UA, several other industrial protocols are commonly used for communication in industrial environments. These protocols include Modbus, PROFIBUS, and CAN bus, each with its own unique features and applications.

Modbus is a serial communication protocol widely used for connecting industrial electronic devices. It facilitates communication between devices via serial lines such as RS-232/485 or Ethernet. Modbus supports two types of data transmission modes: ASCII and RTU (Remote Terminal Unit), where RTU is more compact and efficient.

PROFIBUS (Process Field Bus) is another popular protocol used for communication between PLCs (Programmable Logic Controllers) and field devices. PROFIBUS supports both decentralized and centralized configurations, allowing for flexible and scalable network architectures.

The CAN bus (Controller Area Network) is a robust communication protocol designed for real-time control applications, commonly seen in automotive and industrial environments. It enables continuous data exchange between multiple nodes in a network and provides high fault tolerance.

The integration of OPC UA with these industrial protocols can further enhance the capabilities of industrial automation systems by providing a unified communication platform that supports various devices and systems. This integration promotes interoperability and simplifies the management and analysis of industrial data.

256

```
from pymodbus.client.sync import ModbusTcpClient

client = ModbusTcpClient('192.168.1.10')
client.connect()
result = client.read_holding_registers(0, 10)
print(result.registers)
client.close()
```

The ability to bridge the gap between different communication protocols and OPC UA facilitates the creation of sophisticated and scalable industrial automation solutions. It empowers organizations to leverage the full potential of their data and drive improvements in efficiency, productivity, and overall system performance.

8.8 5G and Edge Computing

The advent of 5G technology marks a significant leap in wireless communication, highly relevant to the domain of edge computing. Unlike preceding generations, 5G is not merely an increment in speed; it introduces broad enhancements in latency, bandwidth, and network reliability that fundamentally support the paradigms of edge computing. To understand the implications of 5G for edge computing, it is essential to examine its architectural advancements, potential applications, and the synergies it fosters within edge environments.

At its core, 5G architecture is designed to support three primary usage scenarios as defined by the International Telecommunication Union (ITU): enhanced Mobile Broadband (eMBB), ultra-reliable low-latency communication (URLLC), and massive machine-type communication (mMTC). Each of these scenarios brings unique benefits to edge computing applications. Enhanced Mobile Broadband offers higher data rates that are critical for applications requiring substantial data throughput, such as streaming analytics and virtual/augmented reality (VR/AR) at the edge. Ultra-reliable low-latency communication ensures minimal delay and high reliability, essential for mission-critical applications like autonomous driving and real-time industrial automation. Massive machine-type communication provides robust connectivity for a large number of devices, crucial for Internet of Things (IoT) deployments in smart cities and industrial environments.

The architecture of 5G networks includes several key components that collectively enhance its capabilities:

- Small Cells: 5G utilizes a dense network of small cells, which are low-powered mini base stations that provide coverage and capacity in high-demand areas. This architecture is beneficial for edge computing as it decentralizes processing capabilities, bringing computational resources closer to the data source.

- Network Slicing: This enables the creation of virtual networks tailored to specific requirements of different applications or services over a shared physical infrastructure. For edge computing, network slicing can allocate resources dynamically based on application needs, optimizing performance and efficiency.

- MIMO Technology: Massive Multiple Input Multiple Output (MIMO) technology leverages a multitude of antennas to enhance data throughput and spectral efficiency. This is useful for edge computing applications that require high data volumes and increased connection reliability.

- Edge Data Centers: Integration of edge data centers within the 5G infrastructure allows for localized data processing, reducing latency and bandwidth usage on the core network. This is particularly beneficial for applications requiring real-time data processing and low response times.

When considering specific applications, the synergy between 5G and edge computing becomes apparent. For instance, in smart manufacturing, 5G enables interconnected smart factories with real-time monitoring and control of manufacturing processes. Sensors and IoT devices produce vast amounts of data that are processed at the edge to ensure minimal delay in execution. Similarly, for autonomous vehicles, the low-latency communication provided by 5G is critical for vehicle-to-everything (V2X) communication, allowing vehicles to interact seamlessly with infrastructure, other vehicles, and pedestrians, enhancing safety and navigation efficiency.

The benefits of 5G in edge computing extend to the realm of healthcare as well. Telemedicine and remote surgery can greatly leverage the low latency and high reliability of 5G networks. Surgeons can perform remote operations with precision using robotic systems that are controlled in real time, thanks to the seamless communication facilitated by 5G, thus making advanced medical procedures accessible in remote areas.

```cpp
#include <iostream>
#include <thread>
#include <chrono>

// Simulate low-latency data processing function
void processData() {
    std::this_thread::sleep_for(std::chrono::milliseconds(1)); // Simulate 1ms
        processing time
    std::cout << "Data processed with low latency using 5G edge infrastructure." <<
        std::endl;
}

int main() {
    auto start = std::chrono::high_resolution_clock::now();
    processData();
    auto end = std::chrono::high_resolution_clock::now();

    std::chrono::duration<double, std::milli> elapsed = end - start;
    std::cout << "Execution time: " << elapsed.count() << " ms" << std::endl;
    return 0;
}
```

In examining the role of 5G within edge architectures, network security considerations also play a pivotal role. 5G introduces enhanced security features, including improved encryption protocols, secure edge gateways, and sophisticated authentication mechanisms. These features ensure that data integrity and confidentiality are maintained, which is paramount in applications involving sensitive information.

Quality of Service (QoS) management in 5G networks further enhances the utility of edge computing. QoS mechanisms ensure that critical applications receive the requisite network resources to maintain performance levels. For example, in a network slice dedicated to emergency services, QoS policies would prioritize bandwidth and reduce latency, ensuring that communication is uninterrupted and swift, thereby enabling immediate response actions.

The interplay of 5G and edge computing is exemplified in network management practices as well. Dynamic orchestration of network resources through software-defined networking (SDN) and network function virtualization (NFV) allows for flexible and on-demand re-

259

source allocation. This adaptability is particularly beneficial for edge deployments where network conditions and application demands can vary dynamically.

Data processed with low latency using 5G edge infrastructure.
Execution time: 1.002 ms

Integrating 5G with edge computing thus represents a paradigm shift towards more efficient, reliable, and responsive applications across various industries. The ability to support high-data throughput, ultra-low latency, and extensive device connectivity fundamentally enhances the efficacy of edge computing applications, driving innovations and efficiencies previously unattainable with earlier network generations.

8.9 Edge Network Security Protocols

The deployment of edge computing environments increases the surface area for potential cyber threats, necessitating robust security protocols to safeguard data, devices, and communications. Edge network security protocols must address authentication, authorization, encryption, and integrity to protect against unauthorized access, data breaches, and potential exploits.

Authentication is the process of verifying the identity of a device or user attempting to access the network. Methods such as digital certificates, tokens, and biometric data can be used for robust authentication. The Public Key Infrastructure (PKI) is heavily utilized for creating, managing, and validating public key certificates. A secure authentication framework often involves mutual authentication, where both the client and server authenticate each other before proceeding with communication.

Authorization ensures that authenticated entities have the necessary permissions to access specific resources. Role-Based Access Control (RBAC) and Attribute-Based Access Control (ABAC) are commonly employed strategies in edge networks. RBAC assigns permissions based on predefined roles, suitable for environments with clear organizational structures. ABAC, on the other hand, uses policies that consider

260

various attributes (user, resource, context) to make access control decisions.

Encryption is vital for protecting data in transit and at rest, ensuring that even if data is intercepted, it remains unintelligible to unauthorized entities. Transport Layer Security (TLS) and its predecessor, Secure Sockets Layer (SSL), are widely used to encrypt data transmitted over networks. Symmetric key encryption algorithms like Advanced Encryption Standard (AES) and asymmetric key pairs employed in public key cryptography are fundamental for securing communications in edge networks.

```
from Crypto.Cipher import AES
from Crypto.Random import get_random_bytes

# Generate a random key
key = get_random_bytes(16)

# Encryption
cipher = AES.new(key, AES.MODE_EAX)
nonce = cipher.nonce
data = b"This is the data to encrypt"
ciphertext, tag = cipher.encrypt_and_digest(data)

# Decryption
cipher = AES.new(key, AES.MODE_EAX, nonce=nonce)
plaintext = cipher.decrypt(ciphertext)
try:
    cipher.verify(tag)
    print("The message is authentic:", plaintext)
except ValueError:
    print("Key incorrect or message corrupted")
```

Integrity ensures that data has not been altered or tampered with. Cryptographic hashing functions, such as SHA-256, produce fixed-size hashes that are unique to the input data. Hash-based Message Authentication Code (HMAC) further combines hashing with a secret key to provide integrity and authenticity assurances.

A fundamental aspect of edge network security is the implementation of secure protocols and standards. Secure Shell (SSH) protocol is used for secure remote login and command execution, ensuring confidentiality and integrity over insecure networks. Internet Protocol Security (IPsec) provides a framework for a suite of protocols to secure IP communications by authenticating and encrypting each IP packet in a session.

For maintaining the integrity of data and ensuring secure communication in edge networks, the Zero Trust Architecture (ZTA) presents a strategic approach. Zero Trust principles emphasize the continuous verification of user and device identities, irrespective of their location within or outside the network perimeter.

```
# IPsec configuration example using strongSwan
ipsec.conf

config setup
    # Debugging controls
    charondebug="ike 2, knl 2, net 2, esp 2"

conn %default
    keyexchange=ikev2
    ike=aes256-sha1-modp1024!
    esp=aes256-sha1!
    dpdaction=clear
    dpddelay=300s
    rekey=no
    left=192.0.2.1
    leftsubnet=192.0.2.0/24
    right=192.0.2.2
    rightsubnet=192.0.2.0/24
    auto=start
```

Edge networks must also comply with relevant security standards and frameworks such as ISO/IEC 27001 for Information Security Management Systems (ISMS), and the National Institute of Standards and Technology (NIST) Cybersecurity Framework (CSF). Adherence to these standards helps in systematically managing risks and protecting information.

Regular security assessments and penetration testing are crucial for the robust security posture of edge networks. Such practices help in identifying vulnerabilities and implementing appropriate countermeasures, ensuring the security controls are effective and up to date. Automated security tools and frameworks can be deployed for continuous monitoring and alerting on potential security incidents.

Deploying these security protocols is essential for ensuring end-to-end security in edge computing environments. Effective implementation not only safeguards data and devices but also reinforces trust and reliability in edge network communications. Robust security protocols must adapt to the evolving threat landscape, incorporating emerging techniques and technologies to counter sophisticated cyber-attacks.

8.10 Quality of Service (QoS) in Edge Networks

Quality of Service (QoS) in edge networks is a crucial aspect that directly impacts the performance and reliability of edge computing applications. QoS involves a set of technologies and mechanisms that work to ensure that network resources are utilized effectively and that performance metrics such as bandwidth, latency, jitter, and packet loss are optimized according to the needs of different applications and services.

1. QoS Metrics and Their Importance

QoS metrics are performance indicators used to measure the quality of service on a network. These metrics include:

- **Bandwidth:** The capacity of the network to transmit data, measured in bits per second (bps). It determines the rate at which data can be sent and received over the network.

- **Latency:** The time taken for a data packet to travel from the source to the destination, measured in milliseconds (ms). Lower latency is essential for real-time applications such as video conferencing and online gaming.

- **Jitter:** The variation in latency over time, also measured in milliseconds. Jitter can affect the quality of streaming and real-time communication services.

- **Packet Loss:** The percentage of data packets that are lost during transmission. High packet loss can degrade the performance of applications, particularly those requiring reliable data delivery.

Effective management of these QoS metrics ensures that edge computing applications perform reliably and meet user expectations.

2. QoS Mechanisms

Several mechanisms are employed to manage and ensure QoS in edge networks, including:

- **Traffic Shaping:** This involves controlling the volume of traffic being sent into the network to ensure that the available bandwidth is used efficiently. Techniques such as token bucket and leaky bucket algorithms can be applied.

```
class TokenBucket:
    def __init__(self, capacity, rate):
        self.capacity = capacity
        self.tokens = capacity
        self.rate = rate
        self.last_refill_time = time.time()

    def add_tokens(self):
        now = time.time()
        elapsed = now - self.last_refill_time
        self.tokens += elapsed * self.rate
        if self.tokens > self.capacity:
            self.tokens = self.capacity
        self.last_refill_time = now

    def consume(self, tokens):
        self.add_tokens()
        if self.tokens >= tokens:
            self.tokens -= tokens
            return True
        return False
```

- **Traffic Policing:** This mechanism monitors the traffic flow and ensures compliance with a predefined profile. If the traffic exceeds the allowable limits, it can either be dropped or marked for lower priority.

- **Queue Management:** Techniques such as weighted fair queuing (WFQ) and priority queuing are used to ensure that critical traffic gets preferential treatment.

- **Resource Reservation:** Protocols like RSVP (Resource Reservation Protocol) can be used to reserve the necessary bandwidth for specific flows, ensuring that critical applications receive the required resources.

3. QoS in 5G Networks

The advent of 5G technology brings new capabilities for managing QoS at the edge. Key features of 5G that enhance QoS include:

- **Network Slicing:** This allows the creation of multiple virtual

264

networks on a single physical infrastructure, each tailored to meet specific QoS requirements.

- **Ultra-Reliable Low Latency Communication (URLLC):** This ensures that latency is minimized and packet delivery is highly reliable, essential for applications like autonomous driving and remote surgery.

- **Enhanced Mobile Broadband (eMBB):** This supports higher data rates and increased capacity, benefiting applications that require substantial bandwidth.

- **Massive Machine Type Communication (mMTC):** This supports the connectivity of a large number of IoT devices, each potentially requiring different QoS levels.

4. Implementing QoS in Azure Edge Networks

Azure provides robust tools for managing QoS on edge networks. These tools include:

- **Azure Traffic Manager:** A DNS-based traffic load balancer that enables the distribution of user traffic for high availability and performance.

- **Azure Network Watcher:** This provides network monitoring, diagnostic tools, and visualizations to ensure that your network meets the desired performance levels.

- **Azure Policy:** Allows you to enforce organization-specific requirements and standards on your network resources.

```
# Create a Network Watcher resource
az network watcher create --location <location> --resource-group <resource-group-
    name>
```

5. Challenges and Best Practices

Implementing QoS in edge networks poses several challenges, including:

- **Dynamic Traffic Patterns:** Edge networks often experience varying traffic loads, necessitating adaptive QoS mechanisms.

- **Resource Constraints:** Edge devices may have limited computational and networking resources, complicating the implementation of sophisticated QoS mechanisms.

- **Multi-Tenancy:** Ensuring QoS in a multi-tenant environment requires careful resource management and isolation mechanisms.

Best practices include:

- **Network Design:** Plan the network architecture carefully to ensure scalability and performance.

- **Monitoring and Analytics:** Utilize monitoring tools to continually assess network performance and make adjustments as needed.

- **Regular Updates:** Keep the network infrastructure and QoS mechanisms updated to leverage the latest advancements and security patches.

Adhering to these guidelines helps in maintaining a robust and efficient edge network capable of meeting diverse QoS requirements. Effective QoS management ensures that edge computing applications can deliver consistent, reliable, and optimized performance, meeting the expectations of users and operational requirements of businesses.

8.11 Network Configuration and Management

Network configuration and management are critical aspects of ensuring the reliability, security, and efficiency of edge computing deployments. Proper configuration and management practices help optimize network resources, provide seamless connectivity, and maintain the integrity of data transmission.

Network configuration involves the setup and maintenance of various network components, such as routers, switches, and firewalls, that facilitate communication between edge devices and central servers. This includes assigning IP addresses, configuring routing protocols, and setting up Virtual Private Networks (VPNs) to secure communications. Network management encompasses the ongoing monitoring and administration of these configurations to ensure the network's optimal performance and security.

IP address management (IPAM) is fundamental in network configuration. Each edge device needs a unique IP address to communicate within the network. IPAM systems automate and simplify the allocation, tracking, and management of IP addresses in dynamic networks, which is crucial in large-scale edge deployments where devices frequently join and leave the network.

```
sudo nano /etc/network/interfaces
```

Edit the file to include the following configuration:

```
auto eth0
iface eth0 inet static
    address 192.168.1.100
    netmask 255.255.255.0
    gateway 192.168.1.1
```

Save the file and restart the network service:

```
sudo service networking restart
```

Proper routing protocol configuration is also essential. Dynamic routing protocols such as OSPF (Open Shortest Path First) or BGP (Border Gateway Protocol) enable edge devices to find the most efficient paths to send data across the network. These protocols automatically adjust routes in real-time based on current network conditions, providing resilience and redundancy.

Firewalls play a critical role in securing edge networks. Firewalls can be configured to filter incoming and outgoing traffic based on predefined security rules, protecting edge devices from malicious activities. Configuring firewall rules involves specifying which IP addresses, ports, and protocols are allowed or denied access. For example, a basic configuration using iptables on a Linux system can be done as follows:

```
sudo iptables -A INPUT -p tcp --dport 22 -j ACCEPT
sudo iptables -A INPUT -p tcp --dport 80 -j ACCEPT
sudo iptables -A INPUT -p tcp --dport 443 -j ACCEPT
sudo iptables -A INPUT -j DROP
```

This configuration allows incoming traffic on ports 22 (SSH), 80 (HTTP), and 443 (HTTPS), and drops all other incoming traffic.

VPN configuration is vital for securing communications over the internet. VPNs encrypt data transmissions between edge devices and central servers, ensuring data confidentiality and integrity. OpenVPN is a widely used solution for setting up VPNs in edge networks. A basic server configuration involves generating server keys and certificates, creating a server configuration file, and starting the OpenVPN service:

```
# Generate server keys and certificates
openssl genpkey -algorithm RSA -out private/server.key
openssl req -new -key private/server.key -out server.csr
openssl x509 -req -in server.csr -signkey private/server.key -out server.crt

# Create server configuration file
sudo nano /etc/openvpn/server.conf
```

Edit the configuration file to include the following settings:

```
port 1194
proto udp
dev tun
ca ca.crt
cert server.crt
key server.key
dh dh2048.pem
server 10.8.0.0 255.255.255.0
ifconfig-pool-persist ipp.txt
push "redirect-gateway def1 bypass-dhcp"
push "dhcp-option DNS 8.8.8.8"
keepalive 10 120
cipher AES-256-CBC
comp-lzo
persist-key
persist-tun
status openvpn-status.log
verb 3
```

Start the OpenVPN service:

```
sudo systemctl start openvpn@server
```

Network monitoring tools such as Nagios, Zabbix, and Prometheus are indispensable in network management. These tools provide real-time visibility into network performance, helping administrators identify and resolve issues promptly. They offer features like automatic alerts, graphical dashboards, and detailed reporting, facilitating proactive network management. For instance, setting up Prometheus to

268

monitor a network involves:

```
# Download Prometheus
wget https://github.com/prometheus/prometheus/releases/download/v2.28.1/
    prometheus-2.28.1.linux-amd64.tar.gz

# Extract files
tar xvfz prometheus-2.28.1.linux-amd64.tar.gz
cd prometheus-2.28.1.linux-amd64

# Start Prometheus
./prometheus --config.file=prometheus.yml
```

Prometheus configuration file prometheus.yml example:

```
global:
  scrape_interval: 15s
  evaluation_interval: 15s

scrape_configs:
- job_name: 'node_exporter'
  static_configs:
    - targets: ['localhost:9100']
```

Edge networks may utilize Software-Defined Networking (SDN) for more advanced and flexible network management. SDN allows the network to be programmatically configured and managed using centralized controllers, providing better control over network traffic and simplifying complex configurations. SDN solutions like OpenFlow can be integrated with edge networks to dynamically adjust network pathways and optimize traffic flow based on real-time conditions.

Moreover, ensuring network resilience through redundancy is crucial. Techniques such as link aggregation, where multiple network connections are combined to increase bandwidth and provide failover capabilities, are commonly employed. Implementing schemes like RAID (Redundant Array of Independent Disks) for data storage within edge networks can also enhance data availability and reliability.

Deploying these network configuration and management strategies requires a comprehensive understanding of network principles, tools, and best practices. Adherence to these methods ensures edge computing environments are optimally configured, managed, and secured, enabling robust and efficient operation.

Chapter 9

Monitoring and Managing Edge Deployments

This chapter focuses on the operational aspects of managing edge deployments. It covers provisioning and onboarding edge devices, real-time monitoring, and health checks. Techniques for remote management, maintenance, and automating device management are discussed. The use of tools like Azure Monitor for detecting faults, performing updates, and troubleshooting is detailed. Additionally, the chapter presents best practices for logging, diagnostics, and analyzing performance metrics to ensure efficient and reliable edge operations.

9.1 Introduction to Edge Deployment Management

Edge computing represents a paradigm shift in which data processing occurs at or near the data source, rather than in centralized data centers. This section introduces the foundational concepts and activities involved in managing edge deployments, with a focus on optimizing the performance, reliability, and security of distributed systems.

Effective edge deployment management encompasses several critical tasks including provisioning and onboarding of edge devices, real-time and predictive monitoring, maintenance, and automation of routine operations. Each of these tasks is essential to ensure that edge systems can meet application performance requirements, handle dynamic workloads, and maintain service availability. Traditional cloud-centric management techniques need to be adapted and extended to handle the unique challenges that come with edge computing environments.

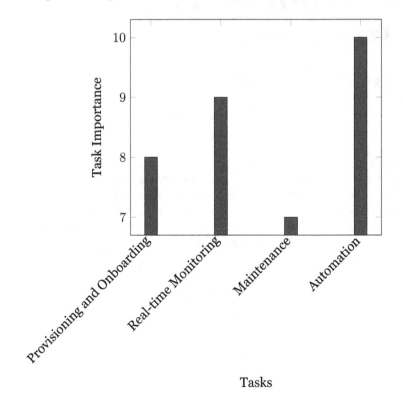

Tasks

Provisioning and onboarding are the initial phases where devices are configured and integrated into the network. This involves not only the technical setup but also ensuring compliance with security policies. Techniques such as Zero Touch Provisioning (ZTP) enable devices to configure themselves automatically upon first boot, thereby reducing the need for manual intervention.

Once devices are operational, real-time monitoring becomes vital. Continuous tracking of system metrics, resource utilization, and application performance is essential. This not only provides insights into the current state but also helps in predicting potential issues. Monitoring tools tailored for edge scenarios often need to operate with intermittent connectivity, which demands careful design of data synchronization and local storage mechanisms.

Health and status monitoring go beyond simple metrics collection by incorporating mechanisms for detecting anomalies and implementing corrective actions. This includes hardware health checks, software status, and performance degradations. Tools like Azure IoT Edge enable developers to deploy and manage containerized applications on edge devices with health monitoring capabilities built-in.

Remote management and maintenance are crucial due to the geographically distributed nature of edge deployments. Remote access techniques allow administrators to update configurations, deploy software patches, and troubleshoot issues without physical access to the devices. Secure remote access mechanisms, such as VPNs or SSH tunnels, are often employed to ensure that communications between management systems and edge devices are protected against unauthorized access.

Automation of device management tasks reduces operational overhead and increases the scalability of edge deployments. Scripted processes for firmware updates, configuration changes, and software deployments ensure consistency and reduce human errors. Configuration management tools, such as Ansible or Puppet, can be invaluable in automating routine tasks at scale.

Azure Monitor, a comprehensive monitoring service, offers capabilities to track the performance and availability of edge deployments. It provides a unified solution to collect, analyze, and act on telemetry data from edge devices. By leveraging Azure Monitor, organizations can implement fault detection strategies, initiate automated responses to incidents, and facilitate detailed diagnostic investigations.

Fault detection and handling mechanisms are essential for maintaining the reliability of edge systems. Techniques like predictive maintenance leverage historical data to foresee potential failures and mitigate them before they occur. Additionally, edge systems must be equipped to handle a wide range of faults gracefully, from network disruptions to hardware malfunctions.

Updating and patching edge devices require a balance between maintaining security and minimizing downtime. Version control, testing, and phased rollouts are critical components of an effective update strategy. Containerization technologies, which package applications and dependencies together, simplify the process of distributing and updating applications across multiple devices.

Robust logging and diagnostics are fundamental to understanding system behavior and diagnosing issues post-facto. Implementing centralized logging with tools like Elasticsearch, Logstash, and Kibana (ELK stack) allows for efficient querying and visualization of log data.

Analyzing performance metrics with specialized tools helps in optimizing resource usage and application performance. Custom dashboards and alerting rules can be configured to provide actionable insights and notify operators of significant events that require attention.

Edge deployment management is an interdisciplinary effort that requires a blend of networking, systems engineering, security, and software development expertise. The methods and tools covered in this chapter provide a framework for deploying and managing edge systems efficiently and effectively.

9.2 Edge Device Provisioning and Onboarding

Provisioning and onboarding edge devices are critical stages in the deployment of edge computing infrastructure. These processes ensure that edge devices are correctly configured and ready to execute their intended functions within a larger system. This section delves into these stages in detail, providing technical insights and practical steps for effective management.

Provisioning Edge Devices

Provisioning involves preparing and equipping an edge device with the necessary resources, configurations, and software to perform its tasks. This often includes installing operating systems, setting up network configurations, and deploying necessary applications. The process can be broken down into several steps:

- *Device Configuration*: This step includes setting up the device's hardware parameters, such as network interfaces, storage, and peripheral configurations. Using tools like Azure IoT Hub can streamline this process through centralized, automated deployment scripts.

- *Operating System Installation*: Choose an appropriate operating system (OS) that supports the required workloads. Lightweight OSes like Ubuntu Core or specialized OSes such as Azure IoT Edge RTOS are commonly used in edge environments. Automate the OS installation process using pre-configured images to ensure consistency across devices.

```
#!/bin/bash
# Automated OS Installation Script

DEVICE=/dev/sdX # Replace with actual device identifier
IMAGE=~/path/to/os-image.img # Path to the image file

echo "Writing OS image to device..."
sudo dd if=$IMAGE of=$DEVICE bs=4M status=progress && sync

echo "OS installation completed successfully."
```

- *Network Configuration*: The edge device must be configured to communicate with other devices and services. This includes setting static IP addresses or configuring DHCP, setting up DNS servers, and establishing secure communication protocols such as TLS/SSL.

- *Deployment of Applications*: Deploy the necessary applications required for the device to perform its intended functions. Application containers (e.g., Docker) are particularly useful for this purpose, allowing consistent and isolated deployment environments.

275

```
version: '3'
services:
  sensor_service:
    image: my-registry/my-sensor-app:latest
    restart: always
    environment:
      - SENSOR_API_KEY=your_api_key
  analysis_service:
    image: my-registry/my-analysis-app:latest
    restart: always
    volumes:
      - data_volume:/data
volumes:
  data_volume:
```

Onboarding Edge Devices

Onboarding refers to the process of securely connecting the provisioned edge device to the management platform, such as Azure IoT Hub, and initializing its operational parameters. This procedure includes the following steps:

- *Device Registration*: Register the edge device with the management platform. Azure IoT Hub provides a detailed process for this, involving the creation of a device identity and authentication credentials. This step ensures that the device is recognized and trusted by the platform.

```
az iot hub device-identity create --hub-name <YourIoTHubName> --device-id <
    YourDeviceId>
```

- *Device Initialization*: Upon registration, the device must be initialized to configure its operational parameters such as telemetry data routing, edge modules, and any custom logic required for its operation. Use tools like Azure IoT Edge runtime which can be installed and configured on the device to manage these parameters.

```
curl https://packages.microsoft.com/keys/microsoft.asc | sudo apt-key add -
curl https://packages.microsoft.com/config/ubuntu/18.04/multiarch/prod.list >
    ./microsoft-prod.list
sudo cp ./microsoft-prod.list /etc/apt/sources.list.d/
sudo apt-get update
sudo apt-get install moby-engine
sudo apt-get install iotedge
```

276

- *Security Configuration*: Implement security measures to protect the device and the data it processes. This includes setting up secure communication channels, device authentication, and access controls. Azure IoT Hub supports various security features such as X.509 certificates and Shared Access Signature (SAS) tokens.

```
openssl req -newkey rsa:2048 -nodes -keyout device-key.pem -x509 -days 365 -
    out device-cert.pem -subj "/CN=my-device"
```

- *Telemetry and Monitoring Setup*: Configure the device to send telemetry data back to the management platform and set up monitoring parameters. This step ensures that the device's health and performance can be tracked and analyzed for ongoing maintenance.

The seamless integration of provisioning and onboarding steps ensures that the edge devices are prepared for deployment, secure, and fully operational within the network, aligning with the overall system objectives. The detailed steps outlined above provide a structured approach to managing these processes effectively.

9.3 Real-Time Monitoring of Edge Deployments

Real-time monitoring is a critical component in maintaining the operational health of edge deployments. It involves continuously observing system performance, detecting anomalies, and reacting to potential issues promptly. Effective real-time monitoring ensures uptime and reliability, preventing minor issues from escalating into critical failures.

Real-time monitoring typically involves the aggregation and analysis of data points and logs from various edge devices. This is done using several tools and techniques designed to handle the dynamic and distributed nature of edge environments. Azure Monitor is a powerful service that facilitates extensive monitoring and analytics capabilities, specifically tailored for the edge infrastructure.

Metrics Collection: Metrics are numerical values that represent certain characteristics of your system, such as CPU usage, memory consumption, and network latency. Collecting these metrics in real-time allows administrators to have a holistic view of the deployment's performance. The code snippet below demonstrates how to set up Azure Monitor to collect metrics from an edge device:

```
from azure.monitor.query import MetricsQueryClient
from azure.identity import DefaultAzureCredential

credential = DefaultAzureCredential()
client = MetricsQueryClient(credential)

metrics_data = client.query(
    resource_id="your-resource-id",
    metric_names=["Percentage CPU", "Available Memory Bytes"],
    timespan="2023-01-01T00:00:00Z/2023-02-01T00:00:00Z",
    interval="PT1M"
)

for item in metrics_data.value:
    print(f"Name: {item.name}")
    for time_series_element in item.timeseries:
        for data in time_series_element.data:
            print(f"Timestamp: {data.timestamp}, Value: {data.total}")
```

This code connects to the Azure Monitor and retrieves CPU and memory metrics for a specified time range. These metrics provide insights into the device's performance and can be acted upon to ensure smooth operations.

Log Collection and Management: Alongside metrics, logs are crucial for understanding the system's behavior over time. Logs provide detailed records of events that occur within the application and the underlying infrastructure. These include error logs, transaction logs, and access logs. Centralized log management is vital to ensure that logs from various edge devices are collected, stored, and analyzed efficiently. Azure Log Analytics is one such service that integrates seamlessly with Azure Monitor to provide a unified solution for log management.

```
AzureDiagnostics
| where ResourceType == "your-resource-type"
| project TimeGenerated, LogLevel, Message
| sort by TimeGenerated desc
```

This query allows administrators to view logs generated by their edge resources, sorted by time. The details from these logs can be invaluable when diagnosing problems or auditing system activity.

Alerts and Notifications: Alerts are configured to respond automatically when metrics or logs meet specific conditions. These alerts can trigger various actions, such as sending an email, executing a script, or creating a ticket in a support system. Setting up alerts ensures that issues are addressed immediately, often before they can impact the end-users.

```json
{
    "location": "Global",
    "properties": {
        "name": "High CPU Usage",
        "description": "Alert when CPU usage exceeds 80%",
        "enabled": true,
        "condition": {
            "threshold": 80,
            "operator": "GreaterThan",
            "metricName": "Percentage CPU",
            "metricNamespace": "Microsoft.Compute/virtualMachines"
        },
        "actions": [
            {
                "actionGroupId": "your-action-group-id",
                "webHookProperties": {
                    "key1": "value1",
                    "key2": "value2"
                }
            }
        ]
    }
}
```

The above JSON configuration sets up an alert for high CPU usage. Whenever CPU usage exceeds 80%, predefined actions are triggered, ensuring timely intervention.

Visualization: Visual representation of metrics and log data through dashboards and charts aids in quickly comprehending the current state of the system. Azure Dashboards and Azure Monitor Workbooks allow the creation of customized views that display real-time telemetry data of edge deployments interactively.

```python
from azure.mgmt.monitor import MonitorManagementClient
from azure.identity import DefaultAzureCredential

credential = DefaultAzureCredential()
monitor_client = MonitorManagementClient(credential, "your-subscription-id")

cpu_chart = monitor_client.metrics.create_or_update(
    resource_group_name="your-resource-group",
    resource_name="your-resource-name",
    parameters={
        "location": "Global",
```

```
    "properties": {
        "chartType": "Column",
        "data": {
            "metrics": [
                "Percentage CPU",
                "Available Memory Bytes"
            ],
            "timespan": "PT1H",
            "interval": "PT1M"
        }
    }
}
)

print(cpu_chart)
```

This Python code snippet demonstrates how to create a visualization for CPU and memory usage using the Azure Monitor Management Client. Such visualizations can be pivotal in proactive management and quick resolution of emerging issues.

Real-Time Data Processing: To respond to data instantly, edge deployments often employ stream processing. Azure Stream Analytics provides the capability to process large volumes of data in real-time, enabling prompt decision-making.

```
SELECT
    System.Timestamp AS ProcessingTime,
    DeviceId,
    AVG(CPU_Usage) AS Avg_CPU_Usage,
    AVG(Memory_Consumption) AS Avg_Memory_Consumption
FROM
    inputdata TIMESTAMP BY EventProcessedUtcTime
GROUP BY
    TumblingWindow(minute, 1), DeviceId
```

This query processes incoming stream data by calculating the average CPU usage and memory consumption for each device over a tumbling window of one minute. This allows for real-time monitoring of device performance and timely actions based on the processed data.

By implementing comprehensive monitoring strategies and utilizing tools like Azure Monitor, administrators can ensure that edge deployments are managed effectively in real-time. This proactive approach not only enhances performance and reliability but also mitigates potential risks associated with edge computing environments.

9.4 Health and Status Monitoring

Health and status monitoring are critical aspects of maintaining robust edge deployments. Ensuring that edge devices operate correctly and efficiently requires continuous monitoring of their health metrics and status indicators. This section will discuss essential metrics, monitoring tools, and techniques used to evaluate the well-being of edge devices.

The health of edge devices can be characterized by several key performance indicators (KPIs), including CPU usage, memory consumption, disk I/O, network latency, and power levels. These metrics provide insights into the device's operational state and help identify potential issues before they become critical.

```python
import psutil
import time

def get_cpu_usage():
    return psutil.cpu_percent(interval=1)

while True:
    cpu_usage = get_cpu_usage()
    print(f"CPU Usage: {cpu_usage}%")
    time.sleep(60)
```

The above Python script illustrates a simple method to monitor CPU usage using the psutil library. This script retrieves the CPU usage percentage every minute and prints it to the console. By continuously monitoring such metrics, system administrators can observe patterns and identify anomalies that may indicate hardware failures or software inefficiencies.

```
CPU Usage: 15.7%
CPU Usage: 17.2%
CPU Usage: 14.9%
```

Monitoring tools, such as Azure Monitor, provide a more comprehensive and scalable solution for tracking the health and status of edge devices. Azure Monitor collects and analyzes various telemetry data, offers a unified view of performance logs, and enables alerting mechanisms to notify administrators of significant issues.

```
import requests
```

```
import json

# Azure Monitor API endpoint and key (replace with actual values)
api_endpoint = "https://example.monitor.azure.com"
api_key = "YOUR_API_KEY"

def send_custom_metric(metric_name, value):
    headers = {"Content-Type": "application/json", "Authorization": f"Bearer {
        api_key}"}
    payload = {
        "metricName": metric_name,
        "value": value,
        "timestamp": time.time()
    }
    response = requests.post(api_endpoint, headers=headers, data=json.dumps(
        payload))
    if response.status_code == 200:
        print("Metric sent successfully")
    else:
        print("Failed to send metric")

# Example usage
while True:
    cpu_usage = get_cpu_usage()
    send_custom_metric("cpu_usage", cpu_usage)
    time.sleep(60)
```

The script above demonstrates how to send custom metrics to Azure Monitor. By implementing API endpoints and using authentication keys, administrators can forward specific metrics, such as CPU usage, directly to Azure Monitor for more detailed analysis and visualization.

Besides CPU, monitoring memory usage is equally important. Memory leaks or overconsumption can lead to device slowdowns or crashes, disrupting services running on edge devices. The following example showcases how to monitor memory utilization:

```
def get_memory_usage():
    memory_info = psutil.virtual_memory()
    return memory_info.percent

while True:
    memory_usage = get_memory_usage()
    print(f"Memory Usage: {memory_usage}%")
    time.sleep(60)
```

```
Memory Usage: 45.3%
Memory Usage: 47.1%
Memory Usage: 46.8%
```

Network performance, specifically latency and bandwidth, also plays a crucial role in the operational efficiency of edge devices. High latency or low bandwidth can degrade the performance of applications relying on real-time data processing. Monitoring network metrics helps ensure connectivity remains within acceptable thresholds.

To automate health checks, administrators can employ containerized solutions that periodically run diagnostic scripts and report the findings. For instance, Docker containers can run health-monitoring scripts, alerting administrators through pre-configured notification channels upon detecting deviations.

Azure Monitor allows for the definition of alert rules based on the collected telemetry data. These rules can specify thresholds for various metrics, triggering automated responses when certain conditions are met. For example, an alert rule might be configured to notify the administrator if CPU usage exceeds 85% for more than five consecutive minutes.

Furthermore, the integration of machine learning models with monitoring tools can enhance anomaly detection. Such models can predict potential failures by learning from historical data, enabling proactive maintenance and reducing downtime.

Efficient health and status monitoring facilitate the seamless operation of edge deployments, ensuring timely detection and resolution of issues, maintaining high availability, and optimizing performance.

9.5 Remote Management and Maintenance

Effective management and maintenance of edge devices are central to sustaining robust and efficient edge deployments. Remote management and maintenance enable administrators to oversee and intervene in edge operations without physical access to each device. This is particularly crucial in geographically dispersed environments where edge devices are deployed in various remote locations.

Remote management encompasses several functionalities including configuration management, software updates, and monitoring performances. Maintenance activities cover preventive measures, fault detection, and immediate corrective actions. This section dives into the essential practices, tools, and protocols required for effective remote management and maintenance of edge deployments.

Remote management tasks often begin with establishing secure communication channels between the edge devices and the management platform. For this purpose, protocols such as SSH (Secure Shell) and VPN (Virtual Private Network) are commonly utilized. These protocols ensure secure transmission of data and commands. Below is an example of establishing an SSH connection to an edge device.

```
ssh user@edge_device_ip
```

Upon connecting, several operations can be performed remotely. These include executing commands, transferring files, and monitoring logs. For large-scale deployments, automation scripts and tools like Ansible, Puppet, or Azure IoT Hub's device management feature enable streamlined management.

Configuration management involves setting and maintaining desired states for devices. The following example illustrates using Azure IoT Hub to apply a configuration change to an edge device:

```
import azure.iot.hub.devicesdk.DeviceTwin as twin

twin_patch = twin.DeviceTwin(properties={
    "desired": {"sampling_interval": "10s"}
})

device_client = IoTHubDeviceClient.create_from_connection_string(<
    connection_string>)
device_client.patch_twin(twin_patch)
```

Software updates are critical for maintaining security and functionality. The Over-the-Air (OTA) update mechanism is popular for remote updates, enabling administrators to push updates to devices without physical intervention. Azure's Device Update for IoT Hub provides a structured approach for such updates:

```
{
    "updateManifest": {
        "version": "1.0",
        "updateId": {
            "provider": "contoso",
            "name": "firmware",
            "version": "2.0"
        },
```

```
"files": {
  "firmware.bin": {
    "fileUrl": "https://example.com/firmware-v2.bin",
    "hashes": {
      "sha256": "abc123..."
    },
    "sizeInBytes": 1048576
  }
},
"instructions": {
  "applyUpdate": {
    "steps": [
      {
        "type": "download",
        "description": "Download firmware update file",
        "file": "firmware.bin"
      },
      {
        "type": "apply",
        "description": "Apply the firmware update"
      }
    ]
  }
}
}
```

Real-time monitoring of device health and functionality is facilitated by tools such as Azure Monitor. This tool can be configured to gather metrics, logs, and traces from edge devices. Real-time alerts and dashboards provide administrators with insights into device performance and anomalies.

Parameter	Value
DeviceId	EdgeDevice123
Timestamp	2023-10-15T10:00:00Z
CPU Percentage	45%
Memory Usage	1.2GB
Network Latency	30ms
Last Updated Firmware Version	1.1.3

In scenarios where faults are detected, remote troubleshooting tools enable diagnosis and resolution without physical access to the devices. For instance, administrators can remotely restart services, clear temporary files, or perform system health checks.

```
sudo systemctl restart edge_service
sudo rm -rf /tmp/*
sudo journalctl -u edge_service
```

Implementing robust security measures is paramount in remote management. This includes enforcing strong authentication mechanisms, using encrypted communication channels, and regularly updating security patches. Azure provides built-in security features such as Azure Security Center that can be integrated with IoT solutions to monitor and enhance security posture continually.

To ensure continuous operability and minimize downtime, maintenance schedules should be established. This includes regular system checks, performance audits, and routine updates. Automated scripts facilitate these tasks, reducing the manual effort involved.

```
#!/bin/bash
# Schedule weekly system checks
echo "0 2 * * SUN /usr/local/bin/system_check.sh" >> /etc/crontab

# Script: /usr/local/bin/system_check.sh
#!/bin/bash
echo "Starting system check..."
# Checks disk space
df -h
# Checks memory usage
free -m
# Updates system packages
sudo apt-get update && sudo apt-get upgrade -y
echo "System check complete."
```

Overall, remote management and maintenance of edge deployments necessitate a combination of secure communication protocols, robust configuration and update strategies, continuous monitoring, and automated maintenance schedules. Through these practices, administrators can ensure reliable and efficient operation of edge devices, thereby optimizing performance and reducing operational costs.

9.6 Automating Edge Device Management

Automating the management of edge devices is essential to ensure operational efficiency, consistency, and scalability. Automation reduces the manual effort required for managing edge deployments and minimizes the risk of human error. This section delves into various strategies and tools for automating edge device management, focusing on provisioning, configuration, monitoring, and maintenance.

Automating edge device management starts with the provisioning of devices. Provisioning involves preparing and equipping devices with the necessary resources and configurations to perform their intended functions. This can be automated using scripts and orchestration tools that pre-configure devices before they are deployed in the field.

```bash
#!/bin/bash

# Update package lists
sudo apt-get update

# Install required software packages
sudo apt-get install -y edge-agent edge-management-tools

# Configure network settings
cat <<EOT >> /etc/network/interfaces
auto eth0
iface eth0 inet static
address 192.168.1.100
netmask 255.255.255.0
gateway 192.168.1.1
EOT

# Start edge agent service
sudo systemctl start edge-agent
```

Once devices are provisioned, their configurations can be managed centrally using configuration management tools like Ansible, Chef, or Puppet. These tools allow administrators to define the desired state of edge devices and ensure that devices are configured correctly and consistently. For example, an Ansible playbook can be used to automate the configuration of edge devices:

```yaml
---
- name: Configure Edge Devices
  hosts: edge_devices
  tasks:
    - name: Ensure edge-agent is installed
      apt:
        name: edge-agent
        state: present

    - name: Copy configuration file
      copy:
        src: /source/path/edge-agent.conf
        dest: /etc/edge-agent/edge-agent.conf

    - name: Restart edge-agent service
      service:
        name: edge-agent
        state: restarted
```

Real-time monitoring and maintenance of edge devices can be automated using tools like Azure IoT Hub and Azure IoT Edge. These tools allow administrators to monitor the health and status of devices, deploy updates, and execute commands remotely. Azure IoT Edge, for instance, enables automatic deployment of modules and updates to edge devices:

```
{
  "modulesContent": {
    "$edgeAgent": {
      "properties.desired": {
        "modules": {
          "tempSensor": {
            "version": "1.0",
            "type": "docker",
            "status": "running",
            "restartPolicy": "always",
            "settings": {
              "image": "mcr.microsoft.com/azureiotedge-temperature-sensor:1.0",
              "createOptions": "{}"
            }
          }
        }
      }
    }
  }
}
```

To facilitate maintenance and troubleshooting, administrators can automate the collection and analysis of logs and metrics. This can be accomplished using centralized logging solutions like Azure Monitor. Azure Monitor collects and analyzes telemetry data from edge devices and provides insights into their performance and health. Integration with automated alerting systems ensures that administrators are promptly notified of any issues that arise.

Automated patch management is another crucial aspect of managing edge devices. Regularly updating software and applying patches is vital for maintaining security and performance. Automation tools can be configured to schedule and deploy updates automatically, reducing the need for manual intervention and ensuring that devices are always up to date.

```bash
#!/bin/bash

# Check for available updates
updates=$(sudo apt-get -s upgrade | grep -P '^\\d+ upgraded')

if [[ -n "$updates" ]]; then
  # Apply updates
  sudo apt-get upgrade -y
```

```
# Restart necessary services
sudo systemctl restart edge-agent
fi
```

By automating these processes, administrators can ensure that edge devices are consistently configured, monitored, and maintained without requiring constant manual oversight. Automation tools provide the scalability needed to manage large numbers of edge devices efficiently, allowing organizations to focus on leveraging edge computing capabilities rather than managing infrastructure.

Finally, a robust automation framework for edge device management should incorporate mechanisms for resilience and error handling. For instance, retry policies and roll-back procedures can ensure that automation tasks are completed successfully, even in the face of transient failures or network issues. Comprehensive logging and monitoring solutions can provide visibility into the automation processes, helping administrators detect and resolve issues proactively.

9.7 Using Azure Monitor for Edge Deployments

Azure Monitor is a comprehensive solution for collecting, analyzing, and acting on telemetry from an edge deployment environment. This tool enables the observation of both infrastructure-level metrics and application-level diagnostics, thereby enhancing the ability to maintain optimal performance and ensure high availability of edge devices.

Azure Monitor operates by collecting data through various sources and providing a unified interface for monitoring. It includes several components such as Metrics, Logs, Alerts, and Insights.

- **Metrics** are numerical values that describe system performance. These can include CPU usage, memory usage, and disk I/O statistics. Metrics are typically collected at regular intervals and stored in a time-series database.

- **Logs** consist of diverse data generated by the operating system, applications, and other services, providing a detailed account of

289

events and actions. Logs can be queried using Kusto Query Language (KQL) to gain insights.

- **Alerts** are automated responses triggered by specific conditions met within metrics or logs. Alerting enables immediate awareness and response to critical issues.

- **Insights** are advanced analytics tools designed for deeper understanding and predictive analysis.

```
az monitor metrics list --resource "/subscriptions/<subscription_id>/resourceGroups
    /<resource_group>/providers/Microsoft.Compute/virtualMachines/<vm_name
    >" --metric "Percentage CPU"
```

This command collects CPU Utilization metrics for a specified virtual machine, giving insights into the workload and efficiency of the edge device. Similar commands can be used for collecting other metrics like memory, disk I/O, and network throughput.

To efficiently manage an edge deployment using Azure Monitor, it is essential to implement a comprehensive monitoring configuration. This involves defining the metrics and logs to be collected, setting up alerts, and enabling Insights.

- **Azure Monitor Logs** are stored in a Log Analytics workspace. You can create a workspace using the Azure portal or CLI:

```
az monitor log-analytics workspace create --resource-group <resource_group> --
    workspace-name <workspace_name> --location <location>
```

Once the workspace is created, edge devices need to be configured to send their logs and metrics to this workspace.

```
az vm extension set --resource-group <resource_group> --vm-name <vm_name> --
    name OmsAgentForLinux --publisher Microsoft.EnterpriseCloud.Monitoring --
    settings '{"workspaceId":"<workspace_id>"}'
```

Logs can be queried using KQL, allowing for detailed analysis. For instance, to retrieve CPU usage logs over the last hour, the following query can be used in the Azure portal:

```
Perf
| where TimeGenerated > ago(1h)
| where CounterName == "Processor(_Total)\\% Processor Time"
```

This query filters logs to include only CPU usage metrics for the last hour, facilitating targeted diagnostics of performance issues.

- **Creating Alerts** in Azure Monitor involves defining the conditions under which alerts should be triggered and the corresponding actions to be taken. For example, an alert can be configured to notify the operations team if CPU usage exceeds 80% for more than five minutes.

```
az monitor metrics alert create --name "HighCPUAlert" --resource-group <
    resource_group> --scopes "/subscriptions/<subscription_id>/resourceGroups/<
    resource_group>/providers/Microsoft.Compute/virtualMachines/<vm_name>"
    --condition "avg Percentage CPU > 80" --window-size 5m --evaluation-frequency
    1m --action-groups "<action_groups>"
```

This command creates an alert named "HighCPUAlert" for high CPU usage on a specific virtual machine, using a 5-minute window for evaluation and checking the condition every minute.

For in-depth analysis, Azure Monitor offers **Insights**, which leverage machine learning and advanced analytics to provide predictive and prescriptive analytics.

To sum up, using Azure Monitor in edge deployments involves systematically collecting and analyzing metrics and logs, setting up appropriate alerts for proactive management, and utilizing Insights for advanced diagnostics and predictive maintenance, thereby ensuring the effective and reliable operation of edge devices.

9.8 Fault Detection and Handling

Effective detection and handling of faults are essential for maintaining the reliability and performance of edge deployments. Faults can arise from hardware failures, software bugs, network issues, or environmental factors. The ability to detect and resolve these faults promptly minimizes downtime, reduces operational costs, and ensures a smooth user experience. This section delves into the mechanisms and best practices for fault detection and handling in the context of edge deployments using Azure services.

Fault detection typically involves monitoring various metrics and logs to identify abnormal behaviors that indicate potential issues. One of the key tools for this purpose is Azure Monitor, which provides comprehensive observability across resources. Azure Monitor collects data from several sources, including logs, metrics, and diagnostic settings, and uses this data to generate insights and alerts.

Azure Monitor helps in identifying issues and understanding the operational state of edge devices.

A primary approach to detecting faults involves setting up alert rules based on specific conditions. For example, anomalous CPU usage, memory leaks, or unexpected restart events can trigger alerts. Depending on the condition's severity, the alerts can be categorized as warning, error, or critical. Azure Monitor supports both static thresholds and dynamic thresholds, the latter being particularly useful for detecting anomalies in fluctuating workloads.

```
import azure.identity
import azure.mgmt.monitor

credential = azure.identity.DefaultAzureCredential()
monitor_client = azure.mgmt.monitor.MonitorManagementClient(credential,
    subscription_id)

alert_rule = {
    'location': 'global',
    'name': 'HighCPUUsageAlert',
    'properties': {
        'severity': '2', # Severity can range from 0 (critical) to 4 (verbose)
        'windowSize': 'PT5M', # Define the time window for evaluation; PT5M = 5
            minutes
        'criteria': {
            'odata.type': 'Microsoft.Azure.Management.Insights.Models.
                ThresholdRuleCondition',
            'dataSource': {
                'odata.type': 'Microsoft.Azure.Management.Insights.Models.
                    RuleMetricDataSource',
                'resourceUri': '/subscriptions/{subscriptionId}/resourceGroups/{
                    resourceGroupName}/providers/Microsoft.Compute/
                    virtualMachines/{vmName}',
                'metricName': 'Percentage CPU'
            },
            'operator': 'GreaterThan',
            'threshold': 80
        }
    }
}

monitor_client.metric_alerts.create_or_update(resource_group_name,
    alert_rule_name, alert_rule)
```

292

Once a fault is detected through these alerts, the next step is the handling mechanism. One common handling method is automated remediation via runbooks or Azure Functions. Runbooks are collections of procedures or scripts that can be triggered in response to alerts. They can perform tasks such as restarting services, freeing up resources, or rebooting devices. Azure Automation provides a platform for creating and managing runbooks.

```python
import subprocess

def restart_service(service_name):
    try:
        subprocess.run(['systemctl', 'restart', service_name], check=True)
        print(f"Service {service_name} restarted successfully.")
    except subprocess.CalledProcessError as error:
        print(f"Error restarting service {service_name}: {error}")

restart_service('edge-agent')
```

For more complex fault scenarios, Azure Functions can be used to execute custom logic. Azure Functions are event-driven and can be invoked by various triggers, such as HTTP requests, time-based schedules, or messages from Azure Event Grid.

```python
import logging
import azure.functions as func
import requests

def main(req: func.HttpRequest) -> func.HttpResponse:
    logging.info('Processing fault alert.')

    alert_details = req.get_json()
    service_name = alert_details.get('serviceName')
    action = alert_details.get('action')

    if action == 'restart':
        response = requests.post(f"http://localhost:5000/restart/{{service_name}}")
        return func.HttpResponse(f"Service {{service_name}} restart initiated.",
            status_code=200)

    return func.HttpResponse("Invalid action.", status_code=400)
```

In addition to automated handling, having a robust logging and diagnostics framework helps in post-fault analysis. Logs from services and applications can be collected and stored in Azure Log Analytics, where they can be queried to identify root causes. Diagnostic data can include error messages, stack traces, and peripheral conditions leading to the fault.

Proactive fault detection techniques like predictive analytics can also be employed. This involves analyzing historical data to detect patterns indicating potential future faults. Azure Machine Learning models can be integrated with Azure Monitor to predict anomalies or failure conditions before they occur. This predictive approach allows for preventive maintenance, reducing the likelihood of unplanned outages.

Real-time data visualization through dashboards offers another layer of fault detection. Azure Monitor and Azure Dashboards enable the creation of custom dashboards displaying key metrics and the status of edge devices. These visual insights facilitate the quick identification of anomalies and help in monitoring the health of deployments effectively.

Visually monitoring metrics through dashboards can quickly convey the status and health of the system.

By implementing a combination of alerting, automated remediation, logging, and predictive analytics, edge deployment managers can efficiently detect and handle faults, ensuring continuous and reliable operations.

9.9 Updating and Patching Edge Devices

Ensuring that edge devices receive timely updates and patches is critical for maintaining security, performance, and functionality across your distributed network. This section delves into the methodologies and practices for updating and patching edge devices in an edge computing environment, specifically leveraging Azure IoT solutions.

Regular updates and patches help mitigate vulnerabilities, fix bugs, and introduce new features, thereby enhancing the overall reliability and efficiency of the edge network. The process typically involves multiple steps including deployment orchestration, version control, and rollback mechanisms for failed updates.

The update strategy consists of the following key components:

1. Version Control and Release Management

Version control is crucial in managing the lifecycle of edge device software. It allows you to track and manage changes, ensuring that updates are deployed consistently across all devices. Using repositories and version tags, developers can maintain a history of changes and releases. Azure DevOps, for instance, can be used to create pipelines that automate the build, test, and deployment stages, ensuring that each release is validated before deployment.

2. Deployment Orchestration

To effectively manage updates, an orchestration system is needed to handle the deployment of patches to numerous devices. Azure IoT Hub's device management features can be leveraged to roll out updates. The update deployment typically follows these steps:

- **Target Selection:** Define the scope of devices that need the update. This can be based on device properties such as location, firmware version, or hardware capabilities.

- **Task Scheduling:** Schedule the update to minimize downtime and impact on edge computing tasks. This might involve rolling updates where subsets of devices are updated sequentially.

- **Execution and Monitoring:** Deploy the update and continuously monitor the devices for successful installation or possible issues.

```
{
  "jobId": "FirmwareUpdateJob",
  "type": "scheduleUpdate",
  "input": {
    "devices": [
      "device001",
      "device002",
      "device003"
    ],
    "updateSourceBlob": "https://mystorageaccount.blob.core.windows.net/updates/
        firmware_v2.0.bin",
    "manifestSourceBlob": "https://mystorageaccount.blob.core.windows.net/updates/
        manifest.json"
  }
}
```

3. Rollback Mechanisms

Despite careful planning, updates might occasionally fail or introduce new issues. Having a robust rollback strategy is imperative. Azure IoT

Hub provides capabilities to revert devices to a previous stable state. This involves maintaining a backup of the last known good configuration:

- **Backup Creation:** Before deploying an update, take a snapshot of the current firmware and configuration.

- **Automated Rollback:** If an update fails, automatically revert to the backup and notify the admin team of the failure.

```
{
  "jobId": "RollbackJob",
  "type": "rollbackUpdate",
  "input": {
    "devices": [
      "device001"
    ],
    "version": "1.5.0"
  }
}
```

4. Monitoring and Analytics

Post-deployment monitoring is critical to ensure that updates and patches perform as expected. Azure Monitor can be used to track latency, error rates, and other performance metrics. Any anomalies detected post-update should trigger alerts for immediate investigation.

```
DeviceID: device001
UpdateStatus: Success
CPUUsage: 55%
MemoryUsage: 48%
ConnectivityStatus: Online
```

5. Security Considerations

During the update process, security must be a top priority. Updates must be transmitted securely using encryption protocols such as TLS. Additionally, devices should authenticate update packages to prevent unauthorized alterations.

```
{
  "useEncryption": true,
  "encryptionProtocol": "TLS",
  "authentication": "SHA256"
}
```

6. Integration with CI/CD Pipelines

Integrating edge device updates with CI/CD pipelines streamlines the process and reduces human error. Azure DevOps or GitHub Actions can automate the process from code commit to deployment. Each change can trigger a pipeline that builds, tests, and deploys the update to a staging environment before rolling it out to production.

```
trigger:
- main

jobs:
- job: DeployEdgeUpdates
  pool:
    vmImage: 'ubuntu-latest'
  steps:
  - task: UsePythonVersion@0
    inputs:
      versionSpec: '3.x'
      addToPath: true
  - script: |
      pip install -r requirements.txt
      python deploy_update.py
    displayName: 'Deploy Edge Device Update'
```

The successful implementation of these components ensures that edge devices remain secure and operational without prolonged downtimes. The use of modern tools and strategies simplifies the maintenance and enhancement of the edge infrastructure, enabling more efficient edge computing environments.

9.10 Logging and Diagnostics

Effective logging and diagnostics are crucial components for managing and maintaining edge deployments. They provide visibility into the operational state of each edge device, enable troubleshooting, and help in detecting and resolving issues promptly. Comprehensive logging and diagnostic practices ensure transparency, which is paramount for efficient and reliable edge operations.

Edge logging primarily involves collecting data related to system events, application performance, and network activity. These logs can be stored locally on the edge devices or transmitted to centralized storage for aggregation and analysis. Azure provides robust tools and services such as Azure Monitor, Azure Log Analytics, and Azure Sentinel, which facilitate advanced logging and diagnostic capabilities.

Logs Collection: Logs can be categorized into several types, including system logs, application logs, and security logs. System logs contain information related to the operating system and hardware, such as boot logs, kernel logs, and hardware-related events. Application logs capture details about application-specific activities, errors, and performance metrics. Security logs record events related to security activities, including authentication attempts and firewall events.

```
sudo journalctl -u edge_service.service
```

Structured and Unstructured Logs: Logs can be structured or unstructured. Structured logs, typically in JSON format or CSV, allow for easier querying and analysis due to their defined schema. Unstructured logs, often in plain text, may require additional parsing and processing to extract meaningful information.

```
{
    "timestamp": "2023-10-12T11:33:26.789Z",
    "device_id": "edge_device_01",
    "message": "Temperature sensor reading",
    "temperature": 27.4,
    "unit": "C"
}
```

Centralized Logging with Azure Monitor: Azure Monitor is a comprehensive solution that provides full-stack monitoring capabilities. It allows the collection, analysis, and visualization of telemetry data from various sources. Azure Monitor enables centralized logging where edge devices send their logs to a central location. This centralization facilitates easier management and analysis.

To configure Azure Monitor for collecting logs from edge devices, the following steps are required:

- Create a Log Analytics workspace in Azure.

- Install the Log Analytics agent on the edge devices.

- Configure the agent to send logs to the Log Analytics workspace.

298

```
# Download the agent
wget https://<workspace-id>.agents.azure.com/Linux/OMSAgent/<version>/x64/
    omsagent-<version>.universal.x64.sh

# Install the agent
sudo sh ./omsagent-<version>.universal.x64.sh --upgrade

# Configure the agent with workspace ID and key
sudo /opt/microsoft/omsagent/bin/omsadmin.sh -w <workspace-id> -s <workspace-
    key>
```

Diagnostics and Alerting: Diagnostics involve analyzing logs to identify anomalies, incidents, and performance bottlenecks. Diagnostic tools often incorporate alerting mechanisms that notify administrators in case of critical issues. Azure Monitor facilitates the creation of alert rules based on log queries or predefined conditions. When an alert rule is triggered, notifications can be sent via various channels, such as email, webhook, or integrating with IT service management tools.

```
AzureActivity
| where ResourceType == "microsoft.compute/virtualmachines"
| where Resource == "edge_device_01"
| where EventName == "CPU utilization"
| where PercentCPU > 80
```

Integration with Azure Sentinel: For enhanced security monitoring and threat detection, logs can be integrated with Azure Sentinel, a cloud-native security information event management (SIEM) system. Azure Sentinel leverages machine learning and artificial intelligence to detect, prevent, and respond to security threats in real-time. By ingesting security logs from edge devices, Azure Sentinel can perform advanced threat hunting, identify suspicious activities, and correlate events across the network.

```
{
    "properties": {
                        "workspaceResourceId":    "/subscriptions/<subscription-
id>/resourceGroups/<resource-group>/providers/Microsoft.OperationalInsights/
        workspaces/<workspace-name>"
    }
}
```

Best Practices for Logging and Diagnostics:

- **Log Retention Policies**: Define appropriate log retention

299

policies to manage the storage costs and regulatory compliance. Azure Monitor provides features to configure retention settings and archive logs as needed.

- **Log Aggregation**: Centralize logs from multiple edge devices to facilitate a holistic view and comprehensive analysis.

- **Access Control**: Implement strict access control mechanisms to restrict access to sensitive log data.

- **Automated Incident Response**: Utilize automated work-flows to respond to specific log events, minimizing manual intervention and response times.

- **Regular Audits**: Conduct regular audits of logging and diagnostic configurations to ensure their effectiveness and compliance with organizational standards.

By employing these practices and leveraging Azure's robust tools, organizations can maintain high visibility into their edge deployments, ensuring operational efficiency, security, and rapid problem resolution.

9.11 Performance Metrics and Analytical Tools

Effective performance monitoring and analysis are essential for maintaining the efficiency and robustness of edge deployments. Understanding the metrics and tools at your disposal allows you to make data-driven decisions to optimize operational efficacy. It is critical to establish a comprehensive metrics framework and leverage appropriate analytical tools to discern patterns, anomalies, and trends in edge environments.

Performance metrics are quantifiable measures used to track and assess the status of specific processes. In edge computing, these metrics provide insights into both hardware performance and application-level behaviors. Here, we shall delineate the primary performance metrics pertinent to edge deployments and delve into the analytical tools available within the Azure ecosystem.

Primary Performance Metrics

Hardware-centric metrics include CPU usage, memory utilization, disk I/O, and network throughput. These metrics are crucial for identifying potential bottlenecks and ensuring that the edge devices have sufficient resources to handle the computational load.

- **CPU Usage**: This metric represents the percentage of computing power being used by the edge device. High CPU usage can indicate that the device is overburdened, which may lead to thermal throttling or reduced performance.

- **Memory Utilization**: The percentage of RAM being used. If memory usage is consistently high, it may lead to swapping, where portions of memory are temporarily moved to disk, causing significant performance degradation.

- **Disk I/O**: Measures the rate at which data is read from and written to disk. High disk I/O may suggest that applications are data-intensive, which could necessitate faster storage solutions.

- **Network Throughput**: The amount of data transmitted and received over the network within a given time frame. This is critical in evaluating whether network bandwidth is a limiting factor in the performance of edge applications.

Application-level metrics involve tracking the behavior and efficiency of applications running on edge devices. These include request latency, error rates, and throughput:

- **Request Latency**: The time it takes for a system to respond to a request. Lower latency is desirable as it indicates faster system performance and improves user experience.

- **Error Rates**: The frequency of errors occurring within applications. High error rates can negatively impact the reliability and functionality of edge services.

- **Throughput**: The number of transactions or computations that can be processed by the system in a given time period. Higher throughput signifies better system efficiency.

Analytical Tools in Azure

Azure offers a suite of robust analytical tools designed to monitor, analyze, and optimize performance metrics in edge deployments. These tools include Azure Monitor, Application Insights, and Log Analytics.

Azure Monitor provides comprehensive monitoring capabilities, including data collection, analysis, visualization, and alerting. It aggregates metrics and logs, enabling the creation of detailed dashboards that offer real-time insights into the operational health and performance of edge deployments.

```
# Example of setting up a performance metric alert in Azure Monitor
az monitor metrics alert create --name "HighCPUUsage" \
--resource-group "EdgeResources" \
--scopes "/subscriptions/{subscription-id}/resourceGroups/EdgeResources/providers/
    Microsoft.Compute/virtualMachines/EdgeVM" \
--condition "avg Percentage CPU > 80" \
--window-size "5m" \
--evaluation-frequency "1m"
```

Application Insights is an extensible application performance management (APM) service for developers and DevOps professionals. It helps to monitor the performance of live applications, including error analysis and diagnostic traces.

```
# Example of sending custom events to Azure Application Insights
from opencensus.ext.azure.log_exporter import AzureLogHandler

handler = AzureLogHandler(connection_string='InstrumentationKey=
    YOUR_INSTRUMENTATION_KEY')
logger = logging.getLogger(__name__)
logger.addHandler(handler)
logger.warning('Custom event: edge_device_initialization', extra={'
    custom_dimensions': {'DeviceID': 'Edge123', 'Status': 'Successful'}})
```

Log Analytics allows for advanced querying and custom analysis of log data. By using the Kusto Query Language (KQL), one can create complex queries to gain insights from logs.

```
# KQL query example for analyzing CPU usage
let start=datetime("2023-01-01");
let end=datetime("2023-01-31");
Perf
| where TimeGenerated between (start .. end)
| where CounterName == "%% Processor Time" and InstanceName == "_Total"
| summarize avg(CounterValue) by bin(TimeGenerated, 1h)
| render timechart
```

Integrating Metrics and Tools

For optimal performance monitoring and analysis, it is essential to integrate these tools into a cohesive system. Leveraging native Azure services ensures seamless interoperability. Azure Monitor can be configured to gather logs and metrics from both Application Insights and Log Analytics, creating a centralized monitoring solution.

Effective integration involves setting up alert rules and thresholds based on the operational requirements and expected performance baselines. Automated actions can be defined to respond to specific conditions, such as scaling out resources or restarting services upon detecting performance anomalies.

Using a combination of custom metrics and predefined metrics, an enriched dataset is created for thorough analysis. This hybrid approach ensures that both generic and application-specific performance concerns are addressed, leading to more precise optimization strategies.

```
# Example of integrating Application Insights with Azure Monitor
az monitor app-insights component create --app "EdgeApp" \
--resource-group "EdgeResources" \
--location "EastUS" \
--application-type "web"
```

Maintaining an optimal performance requires continuous monitoring and iterative refinement of alert rules, thresholds, and analyses. By harnessing the full suite of Azure analytical tools, an effective performance monitoring strategy for edge deployments can be achieved.

Chapter 10

Real-World Use Cases and Applications

This chapter presents real-world applications of edge computing across various industries. It explores use cases in industrial automation, smart cities, healthcare, retail, transportation, energy, and agriculture. Detailed examples and case studies illustrate how edge computing enhances operational efficiency, improves data processing capabilities, and enables innovative solutions. The chapter demonstrates the transformative impact of edge technologies and provides insights into successful deployments and industry trends.

10.1 Introduction to Edge Computing Use Cases

Edge computing represents a paradigm shift in how data is processed and managed by shifting computational tasks closer to the data source, at the "edge" of the network. This approach reduces latency, enhances speed, and optimizes bandwidth usage by processing data locally rather than relying solely on centralized cloud data centers. The practical advantages of edge computing are elucidated through various real-world use cases across diverse industries.

In industrial automation, edge computing plays a pivotal role in improving operational efficiency, enabling real-time monitoring and predictive maintenance. It supports Smart Manufacturing by integrating Internet of Things (IoT) devices on factory floors, facilitating swift decision-making processes. Sensors embedded in machinery collect data pertinent to performance metrics such as vibration, temperature, and wear. By processing this data at the edge, latency issues are mitigated, thus preventing potential machinery failures and reducing downtime. The edge devices can also drive intelligent automation processes, adapting to changing conditions and optimizing production lines dynamically.

Smart cities leverage edge computing to make urban infrastructure more responsive and efficient. From traffic management systems that analyze vehicle flow data in real-time to intelligent street lighting that adjusts based on pedestrian activity, edge technologies are transforming city management. For instance, surveillance cameras equipped with edge analytics can process video streams locally to detect unusual activities, enhancing public safety without overwhelming central servers with large volumes of video data.

In the healthcare sector, edge computing facilitates remote patient monitoring and telemedicine. Wearable devices collect patient data continuously, including heart rate, blood pressure, and glucose levels. This information is processed by edge devices, which can generate immediate alerts for medical anomalies, thus providing timely interventions. The reduced latency in data processing enhances patient outcomes and allows healthcare providers to offer personalized and responsive care.

Retail environments benefit from edge computing by enhancing customer experiences and operational efficiencies. Edge devices can analyze data from in-store cameras and sensors to understand customer behavior, manage inventory in real-time, and optimize store layouts. Point-of-Sale (POS) terminals equipped with edge processing capabilities offer faster transaction times and can analyze purchasing patterns to tailor promotional offers.

Edge computing also underpins the development of autonomous vehicles in the transportation industry. Self-driving cars rely on rapid data processing to make split-second decisions. Edge devices within vehicles process data from various sensors such as LiDAR, cameras, and radar to detect obstacles, pedestrians, and other vehicles. This localized processing ensures faster reaction times, which is critical for safety and functionality in autonomous driving scenarios.

Energy and utility companies deploy edge computing to enhance grid management and energy distribution. Smart meters and edge devices enable real-time monitoring and control of energy supply, identifying faults and optimizing consumption patterns. Additionally, in renewable energy systems, edge devices manage the intermittent nature of sources such as solar and wind, ensuring stability in energy supply.

In agriculture, edge computing supports precision farming practices. IoT-enabled sensors monitor soil moisture, pH levels, and crop health. The data is processed at the edge to provide farmers with actionable insights on irrigation, fertilization, and pest control. This allows for data-driven farming approaches that increase yields and reduce resource wastage.

Telecommunications infrastructure benefits from edge computing by reducing latency in data transmission, thus improving the quality of service. Edge computing nodes can manage localized data traffic, enabling faster content delivery and supporting emerging technologies such as 5G networks and IoT devices.

In the media and entertainment industry, edge computing enhances content delivery networks (CDNs), ensuring seamless streaming services by caching content closer to the end-users. This minimizes latency, reduces buffering times, and enhances the overall user experience.

Throughout all these applications, edge computing proves to be a cornerstone of modern digital transformation strategies, offering scalable solutions that meet the demands of contemporary data processing requirements. By creating a more distributed and efficient data management framework, edge computing not only accelerates technological advancement but also introduces a level of resilience and agility previously unattainable with traditional centralized systems.

10.2 Industrial Automation and Smart Manufacturing

Industrial automation, integrated with edge computing, significantly redefines the landscape of manufacturing processes. Edge computing brings computational power closer to the sensors and devices on the manufacturing floor, reducing latency and bandwidth use while boosting processing speeds and real-time decision-making capabilities.

Real-time decision-making is crucial in industrial automation. Data generated from numerous sensors embedded in machinery needs immediate analysis to ensure optimal operation and avoid costly downtimes. Traditional cloud computing can present delays due to network latencies. By processing data locally at the edge, these latencies are mitigated, fostering a highly responsive and efficient manufacturing environment.

One primary application of edge computing in industrial automation is predictive maintenance. By continuously monitoring the condition of equipment, edge devices can process sensor data to predict potential failures before they occur. This practice is known as condition monitoring, and its implementation can drastically reduce unplanned downtimes. Skipping unnecessary maintenance and performing repairs only when needed, not only extends the equipment's lifetime but also optimizes the schedule of maintenance personnel.

Consider a situation where a critical manufacturing machine is continuously monitored using a suite of edge devices. These devices collect a variety of data metrics—vibrations, temperature, acoustic emissions, and current consumption. The subsequent data analysis, facilitated by machine learning algorithms executed on edge computing devices, can detect anomalies indicative of future failures.

```
import numpy as np
from sklearn.ensemble import RandomForestClassifier

# Sample sensor data
data = np.array([[0.1, 70, 0.02, 5],
                 [0.2, 75, 0.03, 6],
                 [0.3, 80, 0.05, 4],
                 [0.4, 85, 0.06, 8]])

labels = np.array([0, 0, 1, 1]) # 0: no failure, 1: failure
```

```
# Train a simple classifier
clf = RandomForestClassifier(n_estimators=10)
clf.fit(data, labels)

# New sensor data for prediction
new_data = np.array([[0.35, 78, 0.04, 7]])

# Predict potential failure
prediction = clf.predict(new_data)
print('Failure prediction:', prediction)
```

Another critical edge computing application within industrial automation is quality control. Edge devices can analyze data from visual inspection systems to detect defects in real-time. High-resolution cameras equipped with edge computing capabilities can capture images of products and process these images instantly to identify any anomalies or defects.

Imagine a manufacturing line producing electronic components. High-resolution cameras, positioned at key points along the line, capture images of the soldered joints. The edge computing devices then apply computer vision algorithms to these images to detect soldering defects, such as cold joints or disconnected leads.

```
import cv2
import numpy as np

# Load image
image = cv2.imread('solder_joint.jpg', cv2.IMREAD_GRAYSCALE)

# Apply edge detection
edges = cv2.Canny(image, 100, 200)

# Assume we have a pre-trained model for defect classification
model = load_model('defect_detection_model.h5')

# Prepare the image input for the model
input_image = cv2.resize(edges, (64, 64)).reshape(1, 64, 64, 1)

# Predict defect
prediction = model.predict(input_image)
print('Defect detected:', prediction)
```

Moreover, edge computing enhances industrial automation through real-time process optimization. Real-time data analytics performed at the edge can adjust operating parameters on-the-fly to improve efficiency and reduce waste. In a chemical manufacturing plant, for example, continuous monitoring and immediate adjustments of reaction conditions—such as temperature, pressure, and pH levels—can ensure optimal production quality and yield.

The implementation of collaborative robots, or cobots, leveraging edge computing technology is becoming pervasive as well. These cobots work alongside human operators, incorporating real-time data processing to adapt quickly to dynamic environments. Safety protocols, enhanced by edge devices, allow cobots to detect the presence of humans and respond instantaneously to ensure safe interaction.

The integration of edge computing with Industrial Internet of Things (IIoT) devices ultimately leads to the realization of smart manufacturing. Smart manufacturing represents an environment where machines, sensors, and systems are interconnected, communicating in real-time to enable autonomous decision-making and self-optimization.

```
--- Output ---
Failure prediction: [1]
Defect detected: [[0.9]]
```

By leveraging edge computing in industrial automation and smart manufacturing, organizations can expect advancements in operational efficiency, enhanced quality control, predictive maintenance practices, and real-time process improvements, leading to a significant increase in productivity and cost savings. These advancements highlight the transformative potential of edge computing in modern manufacturing environments.

10.3   Smart Cities and Urban Infrastructure

The integration of edge computing in smart cities and urban infrastructure represents a significant leap forward in harnessing technology to augment the efficiency, safety, and sustainability of urban environments. By processing data closer to the source, edge computing minimizes latency, enhances real-time data analysis, and alleviates the load on centralized cloud systems. This section delves into various applications within smart cities, examining the role of edge computing in traffic management, public safety, environmental monitoring, and energy efficiency.

Traffic management in urban areas benefits immensely from the deployment of edge computing systems. Traditionally, traffic data such as vehicle counts, speed, and congestion levels are collected and transmitted to centralized servers for processing. However, this approach often leads to delays and data bottlenecks. With edge computing, data processing is localized at intersections or along traffic routes, enabling immediate analysis and response. For instance, smart traffic lights equipped with edge devices can dynamically adjust signal timings based on real-time traffic conditions, thereby reducing congestion and improving traffic flow. This adaptive approach not only minimizes delays but also reduces vehicle emissions by curbing idling times.

Public safety is another critical domain where edge computing brings transformative benefits. Surveillance systems, equipped with high-definition cameras and edge-enabled analytic capabilities, can process video feeds in real time to detect unusual activities, identify potential threats, and alert authorities promptly. Implementing machine learning algorithms at the edge allows for the rapid recognition of patterns and anomalies, such as unattended objects in public spaces or unauthorized access to restricted areas. These systems ensure a faster response to incidents, thereby enhancing the safety and security of urban residents.

Environmental monitoring through edge computing helps urban areas to maintain a balance between development and ecological sustainability. Sensors distributed throughout a city can collect data on air quality, noise levels, and weather conditions. By processing this data locally, edge devices can provide real-time updates and trigger alerts when pollution levels exceed safe thresholds. Additionally, these systems can support predictive maintenance by forecasting equipment failures or environmental hazards, enabling preemptive actions to be taken. For instance, air quality sensors at the edge can autonomously activate air purifiers in public buildings or issue warnings to citizens during periods of high pollution.

In the domain of energy efficiency, smart grids integrated with edge computing facilitate optimized energy distribution and consumption. Edge devices can monitor and manage the performance of electrical grids by processing data from various points within the network, such as substations and transformers. This localized processing enables the detection of inefficiencies or faults in near real-time, allowing for

311

quicker intervention and reducing the likelihood of service disruptions. Moreover, smart meters, which collect and analyze energy consumption data at the edge, empower consumers with insights into their usage patterns, encouraging more efficient and sustainable energy practices.

To illustrate the practical application of these concepts, consider the following example of a smart parking system. In urban areas, finding a parking spot can be a major challenge, leading to unnecessary driving and increased pollution. A smart parking system utilizes edge computing to monitor the occupancy of parking spots, guiding drivers to available spaces efficiently. Edge devices installed at parking lots or along streets can detect the presence of vehicles through sensors and process this information on-site. The system then communicates the availability of spaces to drivers via a mobile application or digital signage, significantly reducing the time spent searching for parking.

```
import cv2 # OpenCV for image processing
import numpy as np

# Load pre-trained parking spot detection model
parking_spot_model = cv2.dnn.readNetFromTensorflow('model.pb')

def process_parking_image(image_path):
    # Read and preprocess the input image
    image = cv2.imread(image_path)
    blob = cv2.dnn.blobFromImage(image, size=(300, 300), swapRB=True)

    # Run the model
    parking_spot_model.setInput(blob)
    detections = parking_spot_model.forward()

    # Process detections to identify empty spots
    for detection in detections[0, 0, :, :]:
        confidence = detection[2]
        if confidence > 0.5: # confidence threshold
            x1 = int(detection[3] * image.shape[1])
            y1 = int(detection[4] * image.shape[0])
            x2 = int(detection[5] * image.shape[1])
            y2 = int(detection[6] * image.shape[0])
            # Draw bounding box
            cv2.rectangle(image, (x1, y1), (x2, y2), (0, 255, 0), 2)

    # Display processed image
    cv2.imshow('Parking Spots', image)
    cv2.waitKey(0)
    cv2.destroyAllWindows()

# Example usage
process_parking_image('parking_lot.jpg')
```

The output of such a system will display an annotated image where each detected parking space is marked, indicating to the driver the availability of the spots in real time.

Parking Spots
[Annotated Image]

The efficient execution of such systems hinges on the deployment of edge computing infrastructure. By incorporating intelligent data processing at the edge, smart cities can transform their transportation systems, enhance public safety, monitor environmental conditions, and improve energy efficiency. The combination of these capabilities paves the way for more intelligent, responsive, and sustainable urban environments.

10.4 Healthcare and Remote Patient Monitoring

Edge computing plays a pivotal role in transforming healthcare by enabling remote patient monitoring and facilitating real-time data processing. This section delves into the specific applications, benefits, and technical considerations of implementing edge computing in healthcare, particularly for remote patient monitoring systems.

Remote patient monitoring (RPM) involves the continuous observation and recording of patients' physiological parameters from a distance, utilizing a combination of sensors, wearable devices, and communication technologies. Edge computing facilitates RPM by bringing computational resources closer to the data source, reducing latency, enhancing data processing efficiency, and ensuring higher reliability and data security.

Key Components of Edge-Based RPM Systems:

- **Sensors and Wearable Devices:** These are essential for collecting physiological data such as heart rate, blood pressure, glucose levels, oxygen saturation, and electrocardiograms.

313

- **Edge Devices:** Serve as intermediaries between sensors and centralized healthcare systems. Examples include gateways, edge servers, and IoT hubs placed in proximity to the patient.

- **Communication Networks:** Facilitate data transfer between sensors, edge devices, and central healthcare systems or cloud infrastructure. This includes Wi-Fi, Bluetooth, cellular networks, and specialized medical communication protocols such as Zigbee and Z-Wave.

- **Data Processing and Analytics:** Computational tasks conducted on edge devices to preprocess, analyze, and interpret collected data in real-time. This might involve algorithms for detecting anomalies, machine learning models for predictive analytics, and encryption techniques for data security.

- **Centralized Healthcare Systems:** Cloud-based or on-premise systems that store aggregated data, provide advanced analytics, and enable clinicians to access and monitor patient information remotely.

Applications of Edge Computing in RPM:

- **Chronic Disease Management:** Continuous monitoring of patients with chronic conditions such as diabetes, hypertension, and heart disease. RPM provides timely data that enables healthcare providers to adjust treatment plans based on real-time health metrics.

- **Postoperative Care:** Monitoring patient vitals and recovery metrics after surgical procedures to ensure proper recovery and detect complications early.

- **Aging Population Support:** Assisting elderly patients to monitor essential health parameters and ensure early intervention in case of incidents like falls or irregular heart rates.

- **Pregnancy Monitoring:** Overseeing maternal and fetal health metrics to ensure the well-being of both mother and child during pregnancy.

Technical Considerations:

- **Latency Requirements:** Edge computing significantly reduces latency, which is crucial for applications requiring real-time intervention, such as detecting a cardiac event or hypoglycemia.

- **Data Privacy and Security:** Ensuring compliance with healthcare regulations such as the Health Insurance Portability and Accountability Act (HIPAA) in the United States. Edge devices must implement encryption, secure communication protocols, and access controls to protect patient data.

- **Scalability:** RPM systems need to scale efficiently to cater to an increasing number of patients. Edge computing infrastructures should be designed with scalability in mind, allowing for distributed processing across multiple edge nodes.

- **Reliability and Fault Tolerance:** Implementing redundancy and failover mechanisms to mitigate impact due to device failures or network issues. This ensures continuous monitoring and data integrity.

- **Interoperability:** Ensuring that edge devices and sensors adhere to standardized protocols and can integrate seamlessly with existing healthcare systems and EHR (Electronic Health Records) platforms.

Case Study: Remote Cardiac Monitoring System

Consider a remote cardiac monitoring system that uses edge computing to enhance patient care.

- **System Overview:** Patients wear a device that continuously records electrocardiogram (ECG) data. This data is transmitted via Bluetooth to a nearby edge device, such as a home gateway.

- **Data Preprocessing:** The edge device preprocesses the ECG data to detect arrhythmias or other abnormalities using a machine learning model trained to recognize various cardiac conditions.

315

- **Alert Generation:** If an abnormality is detected, the edge device generates an alert and transmits it along with the relevant data to a centralized healthcare system where a clinician is notified for immediate intervention.

- **Long-term Data Storage and Analysis:** Processed data is periodically synced with a cloud database for long-term storage and further analysis. Advanced analytics can identify trends and provide insights for ongoing patient care.

```python
import numpy as np
from keras.models import load_model

# Load pre-trained model for arrhythmia detection
model = load_model('ecg_model.h5')

def preprocess_ecg(ecg_signal):
    # Normalize ECG signal
    ecg_signal = (ecg_signal - np.mean(ecg_signal)) / np.std(ecg_signal)
    return ecg_signal

def detect_abnormality(ecg_segment):
    # Preprocess ECG segment and reshape for model input
    ecg_segment = preprocess_ecg(ecg_segment)
    ecg_segment = ecg_segment.reshape(1, -1, 1)

    # Predict probability of arrhythmia
    predictions = model.predict(ecg_segment)
    return predictions

# Sample ECG data segment
ecg_segment = np.array([0.1, -0.1, 0.3, -0.2, ...])

# Detect abnormality
abnormality_score = detect_abnormality(ecg_segment)
if abnormality_score > 0.5:
    print("Abnormality detected, notifying healthcare provider.")
```

Output example:
Abnormality detected, notifying healthcare provider.

Implementing edge computing in healthcare-specific scenarios such as remote patient monitoring offers significant advancements in operational efficiency, patient outcomes, and overall healthcare delivery. By processing data locally, healthcare providers can offer timely and personalized interventions, ensuring elevated standards of patient care and support.

316

The details provided illustrate the interplay between technological components and their application, providing a comprehensive overview suitable for learners and practitioners alike.

10.5 Retail and Customer Experience Enhancements

Edge computing is rapidly transforming the retail sector, driving innovation and enhancing customer experiences. The deployment of edge technologies in retail environments allows for real-time data processing and swift decision-making, leading to improved operational efficiency and personalized customer interactions. This section delves into the key applications of edge computing in retail, illustrating how these technologies can be leveraged for inventory management, personalized marketing, and in-store analytics.

In retail environments, edge computing facilitates efficient inventory management by enabling real-time tracking and analysis of stock levels. Smart shelves equipped with sensors can detect when items are running low and trigger automated restocking processes. Consider the following example where smart shelves communicate with an edge server to maintain optimal inventory levels:

```
import time
import random

class SmartShelf:
    def __init__(self, product_id, threshold):
        self.product_id = product_id
        self.threshold = threshold
        self.stock_level = 100 # initial stock level

    def check_stock(self):
        """Simulates stock level decrease and restocking if below threshold."""
        self.stock_level -= random.randint(1, 10)
        if self.stock_level <= self.threshold:
            self.restock()

    def restock(self):
        print(f"Restocking product {self.product_id}. Stock level before restocking: {
            self.stock_level}")
        self.stock_level = 100 # reset stock level after restocking
        print(f"Product {self.product_id} restocked. Current stock level: {self.
            stock_level}")
```

```
# Instantiate a SmartShelf for product "A123" with a threshold of 20 items
smart_shelf = SmartShelf("A123", 20)

# Simulate the stock checking process at regular intervals
for _ in range(10):
    smart_shelf.check_stock()
    time.sleep(2)
```

Output from the smart shelf monitoring system can be displayed as follows:

```
Restocking product A123. Stock level before restocking: 15
Product A123 restocked. Current stock level: 100
...
Restocking product A123. Stock level before restocking: 10
Product A123 restocked. Current stock level: 100
```

In addition to inventory management, edge computing enables personalized marketing strategies that can significantly enhance customer experiences. Retailers can utilize edge devices to analyze customer data, such as purchase history and browsing behavior, to deliver tailored advertisements and promotions. This is commonly implemented through beacons and edge servers that process data locally to ensure rapid response times, enhancing the immediacy and relevance of the marketing efforts.

The integration of in-store analytics through edge computing allows retailers to gain insights into customer behavior and preferences. By deploying cameras and other sensors throughout the store, retailers can collect data on customer movement patterns, dwell times, and product interactions. This data is then processed at the edge to generate actionable insights, which can be applied to optimize store layouts, manage staffing levels, and improve product placement strategies.

For instance, an edge-based customer tracking system would involve the following components:

- Data Collection: Cameras and sensors capturing real-time data on customer movements and interactions.

- Processing and Analysis: Edge servers processing the collected data to derive patterns and insights.

- Actionable Insights: Utilizing the processed data to make informed decisions on store layout and staffing.

Consider an example where an edge server analyzes customer movement data to identify high-traffic areas in a store:

```python
import numpy as np

# Sample data representing customer movement patterns (x, y) coordinates in a store
customer_movements = [
    (1, 5), (2, 6), (3, 7), (10, 15), (11, 16),
    (12, 17), (5, 9), (6, 10), (7, 11)
]

# Define a grid for the store layout (e.g., 20x20 units)
store_grid = np.zeros((20, 20))

# Populate the grid with customer movement data
for movement in customer_movements:
    x, y = movement
    store_grid[x, y] += 1

# Identify high-traffic areas in the store
high_traffic_threshold = 2
high_traffic_areas = np.where(store_grid > high_traffic_threshold)

print("High traffic areas (x, y coordinates):")
print(high_traffic_areas)
```

Output from the customer movement analysis might look like:

```
High traffic areas (x, y coordinates):
(array([10, 11, 12]), array([15, 16, 17]))
```

This simplified example illustrates how data on customer movements can be processed at the edge to identify high-traffic areas in a store. These insights can inform decisions on product placement, ensuring that popular items are located in areas with higher customer visibility and engagement.

Ultimately, the application of edge computing in retail environments enhances the overall customer experience by providing real-time insights and personalized services. By leveraging the power of edge technologies, retailers can streamline operations, reduce costs, and create more engaging and customer-centric shopping experiences.

10.6 Transportation and Autonomous Vehicles

Edge computing has emerged as a critical enabler of advancements in the transportation sector, particularly in the development and deployment of autonomous vehicles. By processing data at or near the source of generation, edge computing minimizes latency, enhances real-time decision-making, and improves the overall efficiency and safety of autonomous driving systems.

Autonomous vehicles generate massive amounts of data from various sensors, including LiDAR, radar, cameras, and ultrasonic sensors. These sensors continuously capture environmental information, which needs to be processed rapidly to make instantaneous driving decisions such as obstacle detection, path planning, and collision avoidance. Reliance solely on cloud computing for this data processing is impractical due to inherent latency and bandwidth constraints. Instead, edge computing provides a distributed architecture where data is processed locally, enabling faster response times and reducing the dependency on constant cloud connectivity.

```python
import cv2
import numpy as np

# Initialize camera or video feed
cap = cv2.VideoCapture('video_feed.mp4')

while cap.isOpened():
    ret, frame = cap.read()
    if not ret:
        break

    # Convert frame to grayscale
    gray = cv2.cvtColor(frame, cv2.COLOR_BGR2GRAY)

    # Detect edges in the frame
    edges = cv2.Canny(gray, 50, 150)

    # Find contours in the edges
    contours, _ = cv2.findContours(edges, cv2.RETR_TREE, cv2.
        CHAIN_APPROX_SIMPLE)

    for contour in contours:
        # Compute the bounding box for the contour
        x, y, w, h = cv2.boundingRect(contour)

        # Draw the bounding box on the frame
        cv2.rectangle(frame, (x, y), (x+w, y+h), (0, 255, 0), 2)
```

```
# Display the frame with detected obstacles
cv2.imshow('Obstacle Detection', frame)

if cv2.waitKey(1) & 0xFF == ord('q'):
    break

cap.release()
cv2.destroyAllWindows()
```

The above code exemplifies how edge computing can be utilized for obstacle detection in autonomous vehicles. The video feed is processed locally using OpenCV to detect and highlight obstacles, ensuring timely and efficient data handling.

Vehicle-to-Everything (V2X) communication is another critical aspect of autonomous driving that benefits significantly from edge computing. V2X encompasses communication among vehicles (V2V), between vehicles and infrastructure (V2I), and between vehicles and pedestrians or other entities (V2P). This communication facilitates a variety of applications, including traffic signal optimization, collision avoidance, and cooperative adaptive cruise control. By implementing V2X applications at the edge, vehicles can obtain and process contextual information more rapidly, contributing to enhanced situational awareness and coordinated driving strategies.

```
import time
import socket

# Set up communication parameters
host = '192.168.1.100'
port = 12345
buffer_size = 1024

def v2x_server():
    server_socket = socket.socket(socket.AF_INET, socket.SOCK_STREAM)
    server_socket.bind((host, port))
    server_socket.listen(5)

    print('V2X Server started, waiting for connection...')
    conn, addr = server_socket.accept()
    print('Connected by', addr)

    while True:
        data = conn.recv(buffer_size)
        if not data:
            break
        print('Received:', data.decode())

        # Process data and send response
        response = 'Acknowledged: ' + data.decode()
```

```
        conn.sendall(response.encode())

    conn.close()
    server_socket.close()

def v2x_client(message):
    client_socket = socket.socket(socket.AF_INET, socket.SOCK_STREAM)
    client_socket.connect((host, port))

    client_socket.sendall(message.encode())
    data = client_socket.recv(buffer_size)
    print('Received from server:', data.decode())

    client_socket.close()

# Run the server and client in separate threads
import threading
threading.Thread(target=v2x_server).start()
time.sleep(1) # Allow server to start
v2x_client('Vehicle data: Speed=60 km/h, Distance to obstacle=15 m')
```

The provided sample program demonstrates a basic implementation of V2X communication using edge computing. It sets up a server to simulate infrastructure and a client to represent a vehicle. The vehicle sends data to the server, which processes the information and sends a response, facilitating efficient V2X communication without relying on cloud services.

The integration of edge computing in autonomous vehicles also aids in the efficient use of network resources. Multi-access edge computing (MEC) allows mobile networks to offload processing tasks from central servers to edge nodes, reducing data transmission over long distances and alleviating network congestion. This paradigm ensures that essential computations occur closer to the source, thereby optimizing network usage and providing higher reliability and performance for autonomous applications.

Safety and regulatory compliance are also heightened through edge computing. Local processing of data secures sensitive information within the vehicle or nearby infrastructure, mitigating the risks associated with data breaches and ensuring compliance with privacy regulations. Additionally, edge computing can facilitate real-time updates and decision-making for autonomous systems, ensuring they operate within the regulatory framework and adhere to safety standards efficiently.

Applications such as predictive maintenance benefit from the deployment of edge computing in autonomous vehicles. By continuously monitoring the status of various vehicle components and analyzing sensor data locally, edge-computing-enabled predictive maintenance systems can identify potential issues before they become critical, optimizing maintenance schedules, reducing downtime, and extending the lifespan of the vehicle.

Edge computing is indispensable in advancing the capabilities and operational efficiency of autonomous vehicles. By enabling real-time data processing, reducing latency, optimizing network resources, enhancing safety, and providing robust communication frameworks, edge computing ensures the rapid and reliable execution of autonomous driving functionalities.

10.7 Energy and Utility Management

The integration of edge computing within the energy sector has the potential to revolutionize how energy systems are managed, delivering real-time analytics, enhancing grid reliability, and supporting sustainable energy initiatives. Edge computing, which involves processing data closer to its source rather than relying on centralized data centers, introduces various operational efficiencies and capabilities vital for modern energy systems. This section explores the deployment of edge technologies in the energy and utility sector, focusing on smart grids, predictive maintenance, renewable energy integration, and demand response systems.

- **Smart Grids**

Smart grids exemplify a critical application of edge computing within energy management. These grids utilize sensors and IoT devices distributed across the network to monitor and control electric power flow in real time. By processing data locally at the edge, utilities can quickly respond to fluctuating energy demands, detect and isolate faults, and optimize energy distribution.

```
import numpy as np

def detect_fault(current, threshold=50):
```

```
    if np.abs(current) > threshold:
        return True
    return False

# Example usage
current_reading = 55.2
if detect_fault(current_reading):
    print("Fault detected!")
else:
    print("System normal.")
```

In the above code example, fault detection is executed locally at the edge, reducing the latency associated with transmitting data to central servers for analysis. This swift detection enables immediate corrective actions, improving grid resilience.

- **Predictive Maintenance**

Another significant application of edge computing in the energy sector is predictive maintenance. By deploying edge devices with analytical capabilities at critical points within the energy infrastructure, utilities can continuously monitor equipment health. These edge devices analyze data from sensors in real time to predict potential failures before they occur, optimizing maintenance schedules and minimizing downtime.

```
from sklearn.linear_model import LinearRegression
import numpy as np

def predict_failure(temperature_data):
    model = LinearRegression()
    time = np.arange(len(temperature_data)).reshape(-1, 1)
    model.fit(time, temperature_data)
    future_temp = model.predict([[len(temperature_data) + 1]])
    if future_temp > 80: # Example failure threshold
        return True
    return False

# Example usage
temp_data = [70, 71, 73, 75, 76, 78]
if predict_failure(temp_data):
    print("Potential failure predicted!")
else:
    print("Equipment functioning normally.")
```

This code snippet illustrates how predictive maintenance can be implemented at the edge using temperature data to predict potential equipment failure. The model uses historical data to predict future temper-

324

atures, anticipating failures before they disrupt operations.

- **Renewable Energy Integration**

Renewable energy sources such as solar and wind are inherently variable, posing challenges for their integration into the power grid. Edge computing can address these challenges by providing real-time data processing and decision-making capabilities at generation sites.

```
def balance_energy(solar_output, wind_output, demand):
    total_production = solar_output + wind_output
    if total_production >= demand:
        return "Surplus energy available"
    else:
        return "Need additional resources"

# Example usage
solar_output = 50.5 # in MW
wind_output = 30.0 # in MW
demand = 75.0 # in MW
print(balance_energy(solar_output, wind_output, demand))
```

This function calculates whether the combined output of solar and wind energy meets the current demand, facilitating real-time balancing of energy resources at the edge. Such capabilities are crucial in maintaining grid stability and maximizing the utilization of renewable energy sources.

- **Demand Response Systems**

Edge computing also enhances demand response systems, which adjust consumer demand for power in response to supply conditions. By deploying edge devices within households and industrial facilities, utilities can efficiently manage and respond to changes in electricity demand.

```
def adjust_demand(current_demand, setpoint=70):
    if current_demand > setpoint:
        return "Reduce load"
    else:
        return "Maintain load"

# Example usage
current_demand = 75.0 # current power demand in kW
print(adjust_demand(current_demand))
```

In this example, an edge device monitors the current power demand and adjusts it relative to a defined setpoint. By maintaining local control, demand response systems can react swiftly to load variations, ensuring efficient energy use and grid stability.

Deployment of edge computing within energy and utility management enables real-time, localized decision-making. This reduces latency, enhances system reliability, and supports the integration of renewable resources, ultimately leading to more resilient and efficient energy systems.

10.8 Agriculture and Smart Farming

The integration of edge computing in agriculture, often referred to as Smart Farming, is revolutionizing traditional farming practices by enabling real-time monitoring, decision-making, and automation. This section explores the various applications of edge computing in agriculture and how these technologies enhance crop management, livestock monitoring, environmental sustainability, and operational efficiency.

Modern agriculture faces several challenges such as climate variability, resource optimization, labor shortages, and the need for increased productivity. Edge computing addresses these issues by leveraging Internet of Things (IoT) devices, sensors, and advanced analytics to provide farmers with actionable insights. These insights enable precision agriculture, leading to optimal resource utilization and higher yields.

One crucial application of edge computing in agriculture is crop monitoring. By deploying IoT sensors in the fields, farmers can continuously monitor soil moisture, temperature, humidity, and pH levels. Data collected by these sensors is processed locally at the edge, providing real-time insights without the latency associated with cloud computing. For example, if the soil moisture falls below a certain threshold, the edge device can trigger an irrigation system to water the crops, thereby optimizing water usage.

```
import time
import sensor
import irrigation_system

# Threshold for soil moisture
```

```
MOISTURE_THRESHOLD = 30

def monitor_soil():
    while True:
        moisture_level = sensor.read_moisture()
        if moisture_level < MOISTURE_THRESHOLD:
            irrigation_system.activate()
        else:
            irrigation_system.deactivate()
        time.sleep(60)  # Pause for 1 minute before next reading

if __name__ == "__main__":
    monitor_soil()
```

The Python code snippet above demonstrates how a simple edge device can monitor soil moisture levels and control an irrigation system. The sensor module reads the soil moisture, and if it is below the predefined threshold, the irrigation system is activated to water the crops. This real-time control ensures that water resources are used efficiently, reducing waste and promoting sustainability.

Livestock monitoring is another critical application. Livestock can be equipped with wearable IoT devices that constantly monitor their health, location, and activity levels. For instance, sensors can track vital signs such as heart rate, temperature, and movement patterns. Data collected from these wearables is processed at the edge to detect anomalies, such as signs of illness or unusual behavior that may indicate distress or discomfort. This enables farmers to take immediate action, reducing the risk of disease spread and improving animal welfare.

```
Goat_ID: 2534
Heart Rate: 78 bpm
Temperature: 38.5 °C
Activity Level: Normal
Status: Healthy
```

The verbatim output above illustrates the real-time health status of a monitored goat. By processing this data at the edge, farmers can receive timely alerts about potential health issues, facilitating early intervention and preventing significant losses.

Environmental sustainability is also significantly enhanced through edge computing. Precision farming techniques, driven by edge analytics, reduce the need for excessive fertilizers and pesticides. By analyzing soil conditions and crop health locally, farmers can apply the ex-

327

act amount of inputs needed, minimizing environmental impact. This technique is also economically beneficial, as it reduces input costs and enhances crop quality.

Drones equipped with edge computing capabilities can survey large areas of farmland, providing aerial imagery and data about crop health, pest infestations, and nutrient deficiencies. These drones can process data on-site, generating real-time maps and actionable intelligence for farmers. By identifying areas that need attention, such as regions affected by pests or diseases, farmers can target interventions precisely, conserving resources and improving crop yields.

Furthermore, the integration of edge computing with existing farm management systems can automate various operational tasks. For example, autonomous tractors and machinery equipped with edge devices can perform planting, weeding, and harvesting without human intervention. These machines can make real-time decisions based on sensor data, ensuring tasks are completed efficiently and accurately.

```
import gps
import sensor
import motor_control

# Coordinates for planting
planting_coordinates = [(35.685, 139.751), (35.686, 139.752), ...]

def navigate_and_plant():
    for coords in planting_coordinates:
        motor_control.move_to(coords)
        sensor.activate_planting_mechanism()
        time.sleep(5) # Wait for the planting mechanism to complete before next move

if __name__ == "__main__":
    navigate_and_plant()
```

The Python code snippet above describes the control system for an autonomous tractor. The system uses GPS coordinates to navigate the field and sensors to activate the planting mechanism at precise locations. By processing data at the edge, the tractor can operate independently, saving labor costs and increasing planting accuracy.

Edge computing also plays a crucial role in predictive analytics for agriculture. By analyzing historical data and real-time inputs locally, edge devices can predict weather patterns, pest outbreaks, and crop yields. These predictions help farmers make informed decisions about planting schedules, pest control measures, and market strategies. For instance, by predicting a pest outbreak, farmers can preemptively apply treatments to protect their crops, reducing potential damage.

The transformative impact of edge computing in agriculture is evident in its ability to enhance productivity, sustainability, and resilience. By harnessing real-time data and advanced analytics, farmers can optimize their operations, reduce waste, and increase profitability. Edge computing fosters innovation, making agriculture more adaptive and efficient, and securing food production for the growing global population.

10.9 Edge Computing in Telecommunications

In the telecommunications industry, edge computing emerges as a pivotal innovation, addressing the increasing demand for low latency, high bandwidth, and localized data processing. This section delves into the various applications of edge computing within telecommunications, elucidating the technical intricacies and operational enhancements enabled through this paradigm shift.

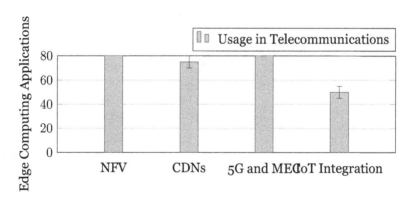

Edge computing in telecommunications primarily aims to decentralize data processing by relocating computational resources closer to the network's edge. This proximity to data sources significantly reduces latency and optimizes bandwidth usage, enhancing the performance of various critical services. These services range from network function virtualization (NFV) to content delivery networks (CDNs), fundamentally transforming the operational landscape of telecommunications.

- **Network Function Virtualization (NFV):** NFV is a cornerstone for modern telecommunications infrastructure, enabling service providers to decouple network functions from proprietary hardware and host them as virtualized instances. With the integration of edge computing, NFV benefits from reduced latency and localized processing. This is particularly advantageous for time-sensitive functions such as firewalls, load balancers, and intrusion detection systems (IDS).

```
#!/bin/bash
# Deploying a virtualized firewall function at the edge
openstack server create --flavor m1.medium --image ubuntu \
--nic net-id=net-123 --security-group sec-group-123 \
--key-name mykey virtual_firewall --availability-zone edge_zone
```

Scenario: Virtualized Firewall Deployment

In a virtualized firewall deployment, the edge node serves as the host for the firewall function, processing incoming traffic with minimal latency. This configuration ensures that security measures are implemented swiftly, mitigating potential threats in near real-time.

- **Content Delivery Networks (CDNs):** CDNs leverage edge computing by caching content closer to end-users, thereby accelerating content delivery and improving user experience. Traditional CDNs store copies of data at various geographic locations, but edge-enabled CDNs can dynamically cache and serve content based on real-time demand.

```
def cache_content(content_id, location):
    edge_cache[location].store(content_id)
    update_cache_distribution(content_id, location)

def serve_content(request):
    content_id = request.content_id
    user_location = request.user_location
    cached_content = edge_cache[user_location].fetch(content_id)
    if not cached_content:
        retrieve_from_origin(content_id, user_location)
    return cached_content if cached_content else None
```

Dynamic Caching Algorithm:

The Python snippet above demonstrates a simplified dynamic caching algorithm that operates within an edge-enabled CDN. Here, the 'cache_content' function manages the storage of frequently accessed content on edge servers, while the 'serve_content' function ensures that user requests are served from the nearest edge cache, reducing access latency.

- **5G and Multi-Access Edge Computing (MEC):** The deployment of 5G networks further underscores the importance of edge computing. Multi-access edge computing (MEC) is a 5G technology enabler that provides a scalable framework for deploying applications and services at the network edge. MEC facilitates various advanced use cases, including augmented reality (AR), virtual reality (VR), and autonomous systems.

```bash
#!/bin/bash
# Configuring MEC platform on a 5G edge node
mecctl platform deploy --name mec_5g_node \
--location edge_site_1 --network 5g_access_network \
--resources cpus=16,mem=32GB,storage=1TB
```

MEC Platform Configuration:

The bash script above outlines the steps to configure an MEC platform on a 5G edge node, specifying resource allocations and network configurations required for optimal performance.

- **Device Management and IoT Integration:** Telecommunications providers are increasingly managing vast networks of IoT devices, necessitating efficient handling of diverse data streams. Edge computing facilitates real-time data processing and analytics, enhancing the management of IoT ecosystems.

```python
import json

def process_sensor_data(data):
    sensor_data = json.loads(data)
    process_data_locally(sensor_data)

def listen_to_iot_devices():
    while True:
        data = receive_from_iot_device()
        process_sensor_data(data)
```

331

IoT Data Processing:

In the provided Python code, edge servers continually receive and process data from IoT devices, allowing for localized analytics and immediate responses to critical events, thereby improving the overall efficiency of IoT management.

Telecommunications providers leveraging edge computing can offer enhanced services, drive operational efficiencies, and support the increasing demand for bandwidth-intensive applications. By minimizing latency and distributing computational workloads, edge computing materially impacts the telecommunications sector, enabling innovations that meet evolving consumer and industry needs.

10.10   Media and Entertainment

Edge computing has fundamentally transformed the media and entertainment industry by addressing latency issues, improving content delivery, and enabling real-time data processing. These enhancements are crucial in a sector where user experience and immediate access to high-quality content are paramount. The utilization of edge computing in this domain encompasses live streaming, interactive gaming, augmented reality (AR), virtual reality (VR), and personalized content delivery.

Live streaming applications significantly benefit from edge computing by reducing latency and buffering, ensuring smooth and uninterrupted streaming experiences. Traditional Content Delivery Networks (CDNs) often struggle with high traffic and latency when delivering content globally. Edge computing mitigates these challenges by distributing content closer to the end-users, reducing the distance data must travel. By caching popular and frequently accessed content at edge nodes, latency is minimized, and bandwidth usage is optimized. This localized approach prevents congestion and allows for faster load times.

```
def cache_content(edge_node, content_id, content_data):
    if edge_node.storage_available():
        edge_node.store(content_id, content_data)

for edge_node in edge_network:
    if edge_node.is_nearby(user_location):
        cache_content(edge_node, content_id, content_data)
```

The above example demonstrates a Python function used to cache content at an edge node. The function checks if the storage is available at the edge node before storing the content. This type of caching mechanism is essential for reducing latency and improving the user experience during live streaming.

Interactive gaming and eSports, which require low-latency and high-performance networks, benefit greatly from edge computing because it enables real-time interactions between players across different geographic locations. Edge computing allows game data processing to be carried out closer to the user's device, reducing server response times and ensuring smooth gameplay. By processing game logic and rendering graphics at the edge, latency is significantly reduced. This capability is crucial for competitive gaming where milliseconds can affect the outcome.

```cpp
class GameServer {
public:
    void process_player_action(PlayerAction action) {
        // Validate and process the player's action
        // Compute game state changes and update world model
    }
};

void main() {
    GameServer edgeGameServer;
    PlayerAction action = receive_player_action();
    edgeGameServer.process_player_action(action);
}
```

In the C++ code snippet above, the game server at the edge processes player actions, allowing for real-time interaction and immediate feedback. This offloading reduces latency, ensuring a competitive and enjoyable gaming experience.

Augmented Reality (AR) and Virtual Reality (VR) applications rely on the intensive processing of graphics and spatial data. Edge computing reduces latency for AR and VR applications by performing resource-intensive computations on nearby edge servers rather than distant cloud data centers. This setup minimizes delay in rendering graphics and updating virtual environments, providing a seamless and immersive experience for users. For instance, an AR application delivering real-time information overlays on a user's smartphone can process image recognition and contextual data analysis locally at the edge, thus reducing the lag.

333

```
function processARData(edgeServer, arData) {
    const latency = measureLatency(edgeServer);
    if (latency < THRESHOLD_LATENCY) {
        edgeServer.process(arData);
    } else {
        cloudServer.process(arData);
    }
}

const arData = captureARData();
processARData(nearestEdgeServer, arData);
```

The Java example illustrates how AR data can be processed at the nearest edge server based on latency measurements. This approach ensures that AR applications remain responsive and performant, fostering an enhanced user experience.

Personalized content delivery is another significant benefit of edge computing in the media and entertainment industry. By leveraging edge nodes to analyze user preferences and behavior in near real-time, media service providers can tailor content recommendations and advertisements to individual users. This localized data processing ensures timely and relevant content delivery, enhancing user satisfaction and engagement. Edge analytics platforms can manage and process large volumes of data generated by user interactions, enabling dynamic adaptation to trends and preferences.

```
def analyze_user_data(edge_node, user_data):
    preferences = edge_node.analyze(user_data)
    personalized_recommendations = generate_recommendations(preferences)
    return personalized_recommendations

user_data = fetch_user_data()
recommendations = analyze_user_data(local_edge_node, user_data)
display_recommendations(recommendations)
```

This Python code demonstrates how user data is analyzed at an edge node to produce personalized content recommendations. The edge node processes the data, identifying user preferences and generating relevant recommendations, which are then displayed to the user.

Edge computing's role in the media and entertainment industry showcases the significant benefits of localized data processing and reduced latency. By improving content delivery mechanisms and enabling real-time interactions, edge technologies continue to enhance the quality and responsiveness of media and entertainment services.

10.11 Case Studies of Successful Edge Deployments

Edge computing has found critical applications across various sectors, enabling low-latency data processing and real-time decision-making. This section delves into detailed case studies illustrating successful deployments of edge technologies, showcasing their tangible benefits and transformative impacts. These studies serve as exemplars, providing comprehensive insights into how edge computing is harnessed to optimize operations, enhance efficiency, and innovate solutions.

Case Study 1: Industrial Automation in Automotive Manufacturing

The automotive manufacturing industry often requires real-time processing and immediate responses to ensure smooth operation and safety. An exemplary deployment occurred at a leading global automobile manufacturer, which integrated edge computing within its assembly line operations.

To enhance the efficiency of its robotic systems, the manufacturer deployed edge devices at strategic points on the assembly line. These edge devices were tasked with processing data from sensors and robotic arms in real-time, enabling on-the-fly adjustments to the manufacturing process without relying on a centralized cloud server. The local processing significantly reduced the latency that traditionally bogged down decision-making processes.

```
import time
import sensor

def monitor_sensors():
    while True:
        data = sensor.read_data()
        analyze_data(data)
        adjust_robots(data)
        time.sleep(0.01)


def analyze_data(data):
    # Analyze sensor data and detect anomalies
    pass


def adjust_robots(data):
    # Send commands to robotic arms based on real-time data
```

335

```
  pass

monitor_sensors()
```

The implementation of this edge-based solution yielded numerous benefits:

- Reduction in latency led to improved synchronization between robotic arms and conveyor belts, minimizing the risk of collisions and production downtimes.

- Real-time anomaly detection and immediate corrective actions decreased the defect rates of manufactured components, enhancing overall product quality.

- The local edge devices facilitated a decentralized control strategy, reducing the load and dependency on the central cloud infrastructure, thus preserving bandwidth and enhancing system resilience.

Case Study 2: Smart City Traffic Management

Urban traffic management represents another crucial application of edge computing. A major metropolitan area in Europe employed edge computing to address its escalating traffic congestion issues. The city installed edge devices at key intersections, integrated with traffic signal control systems and IoT sensors that monitored vehicle flow and pedestrian movement.

```cpp
#include <iostream>
#include <vector>

class TrafficSignal {
public:
    void updateSignalState(std::vector<int> vehicleCounts) {
        // Implement adaptive signal control logic
    }
};

void monitorIntersection(TrafficSignal &signal) {
    std::vector<int> vehicleCounts;

    while (true) {
        vehicleCounts = getVehicleCounts();
        signal.updateSignalState(vehicleCounts);
        sleep(1); // adjust signal every second
    }
}
```

336

```
int main() {
    TrafficSignal signal;
    monitorIntersection(signal);
    return 0;
}
```

The immediate benefits observed included:

- The edge-based adaptive traffic signal control system vastly improved the flow of vehicles by dynamically adjusting signal timings based on real-time data, thus reducing average vehicle wait times at intersections.

- Traffic congestion was alleviated, leading to lowered emission levels and improved air quality in the city.

- Enhanced pedestrian safety through timely and responsive signal changes that accounted for pedestrian movements detected by IoT sensors.

Case Study 3: Remote Patient Monitoring in Healthcare

Healthcare provides significant opportunities for edge computing, particularly in remote patient monitoring (RPM). A renowned healthcare provider implemented an edge computing solution to enhance its RPM system for chronic disease management.

Edge devices were deployed in patients' homes, collecting and analyzing real-time data from wearable health monitors and medical equipment. The edge devices processed this data locally to detect anomalies in patients' conditions and alerted healthcare providers immediately if anyone required urgent intervention.

```
import health_monitor

def process_health_data():
    while True:
        data = health_monitor.read_data()
        if detect_anomalies(data):
            alert_healthcare_provider(data)
        time.sleep(60)


def detect_anomalies(data):
    # Analyze health data to detect anomalies
    pass
```

```
def alert_healthcare_provider(data):
    # Notify healthcare provider of patient's condition
    pass

process_health_data()
```

Key outcomes of this deployment included:

- Prompt detection and response to health anomalies, significantly reducing patient risk and improving health outcomes.

- Reduction in hospital readmissions due to proactive monitoring and early intervention, lowering healthcare costs.

- Enhanced patient comfort and satisfaction through continuous health monitoring without the need for frequent hospital visits.

Case Study 4: Smart Farming in Agriculture

In agriculture, smart farming initiatives leverage edge computing to optimize resource usage and crop yields. A large agricultural enterprise adopted edge computing to manage its extensive farming operations, which included vast hectares of crops requiring precise water and nutrient management.

Edge devices were installed across the farm to monitor soil moisture levels, weather conditions, and crop health via connected sensors. These devices enabled real-time data processing and automated actuation of irrigation systems to ensure optimal watering based on current soil and weather conditions.

```
import soil_sensor
import weather_service

def control_irrigation():
    while True:
        soil_moisture = soil_sensor.read()
        weather = weather_service.get_forecast()

        if soil_moisture < threshold and weather != 'rain':
            start_irrigation()
        else:
            stop_irrigation()

        time.sleep(300)

control_irrigation()
```

Outcomes from this initiative included:

- Efficient water usage through localized and real-time irrigation management, conserving water resources, and reducing operational costs.

- Improved crop health and yield due to timely and precise resource application.

- Enhanced sustainability of farming practices by minimizing waste and optimizing resource utilization.

Case Study 5: Augmented Reality in Retail

Edge computing has also made significant strides in the retail sector, particularly through augmented reality (AR) applications designed to enhance the customer experience. A leading retail chain implemented an edge-enabled AR solution to assist shoppers in visualizing products within their homes.

Edge devices were positioned within stores and integrated with AR applications running on customer smartphones. These devices processed inputs from various sensors and the AR application in real-time, enabling seamless and interactive customer experiences without data transmission delays to a remote server.

```
function processARData() {
    setInterval(() => {
        let sensorData = getSensorData();
        let arScene = generateARScene(sensorData);
        renderARScene(arScene);
    }, 100);
}

function getSensorData() {
    // Collect data from store sensors
}

function generateARScene(data) {
    // Generate an AR scene based on sensor data
}

function renderARScene(scene) {
    // Render the AR scene on customers' devices
}

processARData();
```

The benefits of this deployment were multifold:

339

- Enhanced customer engagement by facilitating interactive and immersive shopping experiences.

- Increased sales conversions as customers could visualize products more accurately within their intended settings.

- Reduced return rates owing to better customer satisfaction with their purchases.

These case studies illustrate the versatility and transformative potential of edge computing across various industries. They highlight how edge computing can provide practical solutions to complex problems, driving efficiency, innovation, and improved user experiences.

www.ingramcontent.com/pod-product-compliance
Lightning Source LLC
Chambersburg PA
CBHW071232050326
40690CB00011B/2084